CW01508438

Queried Sick

DALLAS SMITH

This book is a work of fiction. Names, characters, businesses, organizations, places, events and incidents either are the product of the author's imagination or are used fictitiously. Any resemblance to actual persons, living or dead, events, or locales is entirely coincidental.

Queried Sick
Copyright © 2023 by Dallas Smith

All rights reserved. Printed in the United States of America. No part of this book may be used or reproduced in any manner whatsoever without written permission, except in the case of brief quotations embodied in critical articles or reviews.

Contact Info: authordallassmith.com

Cover Design: mitxeran
Editor: Kathy Bosman, Indie Editing Chick
Author Photo: Owen Paterline

First Edition: May 2023
Paperback ISBN: 979-8-9881766-0-2

Dedicated to my husband, Will: the man who, when I jokingly asked who I should dedicate this book to, said "the cats," and inspired Oliver's love of baking

The very essence of romance is uncertainty.
— Oscar Wilde, *The Importance of Being Earnest*

Content Notes

Queried Sick is a contemporary, queer adult romance that contains strong language, sexual themes, and content that may be troubling to some readers, including but not limited to, the COVID-19 pandemic, quarantine, toxic family dynamics, disownment, biphobia, references to past death, grief, off-page parental death, panic attacks, chronic illness, hospitalization, and coming out. Reader discretion is advised.

Representation: bisexuality, anxiety disorder, ADHD, chronic illness.

Tropes and tags: workplace romance; epistolary; very-brief-enemies to friends to lovers; mutual pining; slow burn; found family; foul-mouthed cinnamon roll; grumpy/sunshine adjacent; the literary quotes are bad on purpose; gratuitous references to *The Importance of Being Earnest*; beware of potential *Game of Thrones* spoilers; they're both bisexual disasters, are you still in forced proximity if you're socially distanced?

1

Ezra

Sunday Night, February 23, 2020

Ryan Coleman
February 23, 2020, 8:53 PM

Ezra Beaumont

Caroline found me.

Well, actually the private detective she hired did.

Either way, I'm officially being dis-owned.

Ezra's leg bounced as he sat on a rickety folding chair on Alessi's tiny balcony that overlooked the city, waiting for Ryan to respond to his text. Rome was six hours ahead of New York, which meant that it was mid-afternoon for Ryan in New York and he was still at work. It rarely prevented him from messaging Ezra back, seeing as Ryan did half of his marketing job from his cell phone anyway. Ezra unlocked his phone to check the read-receipt again, then blew out a sigh. He was not usually so impatient, but after the evening he'd had, he couldn't help it.

He'd gotten off the video call where his mother had informed him over an hour ago that he was being completely disinherited, but then he had to do some damage control. He'd been staying at his friend Alessi's apartment during this trip to Rome, which meant he was there to witness the drama. His mother had sent a private detective to find him. An actual PI—one that was likely on his family's payroll already. When the man knocked on the door and realized Ezra's relationship with Alessi, he'd video-called Caroline Beaumont. Thankfully, Alessi was only fluent in Italian and bare-bones English, so he hadn't understood a majority of what Caroline had screamed. Nevertheless, Alessi had questions and was understandably shaken, and Ezra's conversational Italian was mediocre at best, so trying to calm him down was…a challenge.

Although he wasn't sure if it would have been any easier if he and Alessi spoke the same language. It would likely take him years of therapy to understand the tumultuous history he had with his family, much less explain it to someone else. But he had never been in one place long enough to find a therapist, and even if he did, the concept of being that vulnerable wasn't something he was ready for. So instead, he sat, staring out at the view of Rome, hoping it would somehow calm his nerves as it usually did. There was something about the twinkling night sky and the antiquity of the cityscape that brought him a sense of peace; it was the main reason he'd stayed in Europe after his university graduation. But tonight, it brought him no comfort. The city was too quiet after the stay-at-home order had gone into effect, making the scene more unsettling than peaceful.

Ezra glanced down at his phone again and breathed

out a sigh of relief at the bubbles on WhatsApp that meant Ryan was typing.

Ryan Coleman

February 23, 2020, 9:03 PM

Ryan Coleman

Shit

Sorry I was in a meeting

Where are you?

Are you ok?

What time is it where you are?

Can I call you?

Fuck it, I'm calling anyway

He couldn't help his faint smile at the barrage of messages, which were immediately replaced with a notification of an incoming call.

He accepted and held the phone up to see his best friend's face fill the screen. On a normal day, he would comment on the pile of haphazard curls on Ryan's head that he'd never been able to tame in the 10 years he'd known him, but all he could do was let out another sigh of relief. "Hey—"

"What happened?" Ryan demanded, skipping right over the pleasantries. "Actually, scratch that. First, are you okay?"

"Depends on your definition of okay," Ezra answered honestly. "Physically, I'm both exhausted and amped up—like I feel I could sleep for three days, but also, I can't seem to sit still."

"And emotionally?" Ryan prompted.

Ezra shrugged. "I've been worse," he said, then sighed, taking in the look on Ryan's face, clearly unamused with his false positivity, "but I've also been a hell of a lot better."

"Sounds about right. So, what happened?"

Ezra ran a hand through his brown hair, which he'd grown past his shoulders in the seven years since his mother was no longer around to force him to keep it cropped short. "I guess Caroline got tired of me ignoring her calls, so she hired a PI to track me down. Not that it's that difficult to find me. My Instagram is public, and Rome is pretty recognizable."

"You didn't tell me she's been trying to call you," Ryan said, frowning.

"You've been busy with wedding stuff, and I know how you get when my mother is involved. I didn't want to stress you out because she and my uncle have been trying to get me to come home and—and these are their words, not mine—stop running away from my birthright."

"I haven't been that busy with wedding stuff. Anna and Juliet have most of it covered," Ryan insisted. "I mean, I still go to all the vendor meetings, but I mostly tune out. Side note: Do you know how many shades of white there are? Too many."

Ezra let out a much-needed laugh.

"My point is, you could have told me," Ryan continued.

"I had it handled," Ezra protested. "After the first few calls, I blocked the entire family except for my cousin Josie, which is probably why Caroline hired the PI. I should have just gone completely off the grid, but I didn't think she'd go through the trouble."

"Why do you think she did?" Ryan asked.

"Hell if I know. And whatever she was looking for, she won't get it now."

"So you're really—"

"Completely cut off," Ezra finished for him. "She

called for an emergency board meeting to get my name removed from any and all company records right there in the middle of our video call. You should have seen the look on her poor assistant's face when she walked into the room. I thought she was going to faint."

"How bad was it?" Ryan asked.

"Remember when we got caught smoking weed our junior year? Worse than that."

Ryan grimaced. "Fuck."

"It was also in French—because God forbid anyone in the office overhear her and understand the bigoted nonsense she was spouting—so that was fun to keep up with," Ezra deadpanned.

"What did she say?"

"The specifics aren't important. But you know what she's like, and you know who I stay with when I'm in Rome, so…" Ezra trailed off, letting Ryan fill in the blanks.

Ryan's golden-brown skin went pale, and he gave Ezra a sympathetic look. "Oh."

Ezra looked down at his feet. "Yeah."

"I'm sorry."

Ezra shrugged but didn't look up. "She had to find out some time. It's not like I didn't expect this reaction, either."

"Still, it's not right," Ryan insisted.

"No, but it is what it is." Ezra glanced up to see Ryan opening his mouth to protest, so he cut him off. "I'm fine, really. I'm more concerned with the fact that I'm now stuck in Europe without a safety net. My family bank accounts have been collecting dust since graduation, but they were always there in case of emergency, and now they're not. Also, being able to stay in Europe is going to be more complicated. I've been able to skate around getting a visa because of my UK passport and not staying in one place for too long, but now with

Brexit and coronavirus…I'm stuck in Italy."

"You aren't going to be stuck in Italy," Ryan insisted as he sat down at his desk and propped the phone up, freeing his hands to use his computer.

"I don't have anywhere to stay if I were to try to go back to the UK now that I've been disowned, and I wouldn't want to go back to the family home anyway. And I can't travel like I have been doing with a plague making its way through Europe. Which leaves Italy." Ezra sank down into the chair and scrubbed his hand over his face again. "Except, getting a work visa is going to be difficult during said plague, and Alessi has been okay with me staying for the past few weeks, but I can't stay here indefinitely, especially if I can't offer him anything in return. But I don't have enough saved to get my own place, either. Ryan, I think I'm fucked."

"You aren't fucked. But I think that maybe it's time you finally come home."

Ezra let out a bitter laugh. "What home? Caroline made it clear I don't have one anymore."

"She's not the only family you have in New York, remember?"

"I guess I could call Josie."

"Oh, yeah," Ryan said absentmindedly. "Not who I was talking about, though." Ezra frowned in confusion as Ryan pulled his gaze away from his computer to stare at his phone. "I was talking about Anna and me. We have a spare bedroom, and I just looked up flights from Rome, and there's one on the 28th, flying into JFK, that still has seats. So if you send me your passport number, I'll—"

"I can't let you do that," Ezra interjected.

"Why not?" Ryan asked, but he didn't wait for him to respond before continuing. "Look, you've been abroad for seven years now, and I haven't seen you in person for nearly four of those years."

"Don't you have a wedding to pay for, though?"

"You know perfectly well my parents are taking care of that."

"But—"

"Just let me do this," Ryan said, exasperated. Then he softened. "It's time for you to come home. I miss my best friend."

Ezra blew out a breath and looked up at the balcony ceiling above him, willing away the tears forming behind his eyes. "Okay."

"Thank you," Ryan said. "Just send me a picture of your passport, and I'll forward you the flight details."

"Okay," Ezra repeated.

"Hey." When Ezra looked back at his phone, Ryan was face-level with the camera again. "It's going to be alright. We will figure everything out, I promise."

He simply nodded, because the exhaustion of the past few hours was starting to hit him all at once, and he was no longer able to find any words, much less the right ones, to express his gratitude to Ryan. But Ryan offered him a small smile, and Ezra realized that after over a decade of friendship, sometimes words weren't necessary.

"Get some sleep," Ryan said.

Ezra nodded again and took a deep breath. "Thanks."

"Don't worry about it," Ryan said. "I'll see you in a week."

"I'll see you in a week," he echoed. When they hung up, he dropped his phone on the small café table and bent over, resting his elbows on his knees and his head in his hands.

He wasn't sure how long he sat there, but it couldn't have been more than a few minutes when the screen door opened and a hand touched the middle of his back. He lifted his head as the hand slid up to his neck.

"Hey, handsome. Is everything alright?" Alessi asked in Italian, speaking slowly so Ezra could understand.

He couldn't help the soft sigh that escaped as Alessi threaded his fingers through his curls and started scratching his scalp. He nodded as some of the tension left his body.

"You called your friend?" he asked.

Ezra nodded again. "I'll be—uh—leaving in a few days."

"Where?"

"*Casa*—" Ezra started, but he knew that wasn't quite the right word, so he said in English, "Back to New York."

Alessi smiled and nodded in understanding. "*Paese natio*," he supplied.

His fingers stopped their light massaging of Ezra's scalp, but he barely had time to miss the feeling before Alessi extended a hand out to him. Ezra swiped his phone off the table and pocketed it before letting Alessi pull him to stand. He sighed and allowed himself to lean into him.

"*Vieni*. Time for bed," Alessi murmured in English, then continued in Italian, "It's been a long night." He leaned forward to press their lips together.

The kiss didn't last for long before Alessi pulled him back inside, and as they passed through the living area, Ezra's heart panged. Alessi was being a lot kinder than he probably deserved, and he was going to miss him. Ryan was right, though, and on some level, he knew it. It was time to go home.

Friday Afternoon, February 28, 2020

Josie Miller
February 28, 2020, 2:15 PM

Ezra Beaumont

> I just landed. Waiting at baggage claim now.

Ezra sent a duplicate message to Ryan, then shoved his phone in his pocket and leaned against a pillar to stare at the empty, non-moving luggage belt. He'd gotten off the plane as fast as possible, desperate to get away from people who could or could not be sick. He hated flying on a normal day, which was why he'd opted to take the train over flying whenever possible on his three-year post-graduation backpacking-across-Europe adventure, and the rapid spread of the coronavirus did not make him feel better about the method of transportation. Standing in a crowded atrium probably wasn't any better at preventing virus transmission, but at least it was less cramped.

His phone buzzed in his pocket, and since the conveyor belt hadn't started yet, he pulled it out to check without fear that he'd miss his baggage.

Ryan Coleman
February 28, 2020, 2:15 PM

Ryan Coleman

How was the flight?

Ezra Beaumont

> Cramped, long, and there was a kid behind me that kept kicking my seat.
>
> But I got pretzels.

Ryan Coleman

Oof, that's rough. Well I'm glad you landed safely. Have you heard from Josie?

Ezra Beaumont

I texted her when I landed but I assume she's still driving.

Ryan Coleman

And you're sure you don't want to come stay here with Anna and me?

There was a loud clanking sound, and Ezra glanced up to see the conveyor belt kicking in.

Ezra Beaumont

I'm sure. I really appreciate the offer.

But it's been so long since I've seen Josie and I've only ever met Willow via FaceTime since she I moved to Ireland for school before she was born.

Besides I have no idea how long I'll need a place to stay and I'm sure that once you two get married you'll want your private space.

Ryan Coleman

Okay. We really wouldn't mind, but only if you're sure. Anna just wanted me to ask again. She says she misses you, by the way.

Ezra smiled, then out of the corner of his eye, he saw the first of the bags arrive on the belt.

Ezra Beaumont

Tell Anna-Banana I miss her too.

Hopefully this whole plague thing will only last a few weeks so we can see each other soon.

A few weeks sounded unlikely based on how the virus seemed to be spreading in China and Europe, but the news sounded optimistic, so he could hope. He pocketed his phone and searched the conveyer belt for his luggage. After about a minute, his beat-up guitar case, covered in stickers and wrapped in twine to keep it shut, came around the curve, followed closely by his massive duffel backpack. Careful not to get too close to the other people waiting for their bags, he grabbed them off the belt. He slung the duffel bag on his back, then made a beeline toward customs.

By the time he'd made it through customs, Ezra was nearly dead on his feet. It was technically only early afternoon, but for him, it felt closer to nighttime, and he hadn't gotten a moment of sleep on the nine-hour flight thanks to the kid behind him. But he kept trudging along until he made it outside. He winced slightly at the rush of cold air that hit him. He'd meant to get his coat out of his duffel before leaving the building, but after the extended line of questioning he'd gotten from the customs agents, he'd forgotten. Thankfully, he didn't have to be outside for long.

Ezra's phone vibrated in his pocket, and he quickly fished it out and answered it. He glimpsed his cousin's name on the WhatsApp call before holding the phone up to his ear. "Hey, Josie, are you here?"

"When did your hair get so long?" his cousin asked without greeting.

Ezra laughed to himself. "I'll take that as a yes.

Which car is yours?"

"Sorry, yes, I'm here. Blue Kia Soul."

He saw a navy-blue SUV a few feet down the curb, hung up the phone, and started walking toward it as a blonde got out.

"Long time no see, Archie," Josie said with a smile.

Ezra rolled his eyes at the childhood nickname. He'd started going by his middle name as soon as he left for boarding school upstate, but his family had never made the switch. He hated most of his relatives using the name he shared with his father and grandfather, but he'd learned not to bother fighting a twenty-year nickname. Archie was at least better than Archibald, and the "childish moniker" had always mildly annoyed his parents, so there were some positive memories from it.

It had been eight years since Ezra had last seen Josie in person, and before then, he hadn't seen her very often because of her living in London. He'd looked forward to her moving to the US with her new husband, Ted, but shortly after, he'd left for college in Ireland, desperate to get as far away from their family as he could. Josie had understood that though, seeing as her move to New York with Ted was for the same reason. She was running from the Carmichael side of the family rather than the Beaumont's since Josie was his cousin on his mother's side. But the Beaumonts and Carmichaels likened themselves to a dynasty, so it was basically the same.

"God, how is it that you look even more different in person?" she asked.

"How do you look exactly the same?" Ezra replied. She was tall, only a few inches shorter than him, and her face—all cheekbones and severe bone structure, like his own—had barely aged. Her light blond hair was shorter than the last time he'd seen her post a photo on Instagram, but that was about it.

"I don't know—I'm not as big as a house anymore. I'd say that's pretty different." Josie laughed. "Speaking of, Willow has been practically jumping out of her skin in her excitement to meet you."

"I'm excited to meet her, too," he said with a smile.

"But seriously, the long hair, stubble, a rip in your jeans, and visible tattoos... How bad did Caroline faint?"

"She nearly did," Ezra said with a smile that he knew probably didn't reach his eyes. "But my unrefined appearance paled compared to the shock that I was shacking up with a guy."

He said it lightly, but Josie's smile slipped, anyway. She opened her mouth to reply, but he continued before she got anything out. "Can we catch up in the car? I left my coat in my bag."

"Of course. Give me that." She stepped forward and gestured for his guitar.

He passed it off, then followed her around to the back of the SUV. She popped the trunk and lifted his case into the car while he heaved the massive bag off his shoulder and tossed it in.

"Oh, also, I'm sure we're not supposed to hug, but we're about to be in a cramped car, and I haven't seen you in seven years, so I don't care," Josie said. Ezra laughed and held out his arms for her to step in. Since they were relatively the same height, Josie could easily hook her chin over his shoulder and whisper in his ear. "Welcome to the black-sheep club, Archie. You're gonna fit in great."

2

Oliver

Monday Morning, March 2, 2020

Oliver was going to be late for work. Not that big of a deal since the attendance policy at Coleman Press was best described as lax as long as work got done, but he liked to be in at the same time every day. He'd timed out his morning commute perfectly, figuring out the train schedule so he would always get a seat and making sure he arrived before the chatty receptionist so he wouldn't be stuck standing and talking to her for the first fifteen minutes of his day.

He didn't dislike Ms. Susan. She was a delightful woman who had been working at Coleman Press basically since its inception thirty years ago. But she was also a little long-winded, and he'd learned the hard way that if he arrived after her, he'd spend the first fifteen minutes of his day standing on the uncomfortable tiled floor while they chatted. It had happened at least a half-dozen times when he'd first started at Coleman Press fresh out of college, and every time, he was either in miserable pain the entire day or went into a flare. And if he'd had to stand on a crowded train where he couldn't get a seat—which always happened if he left later than usual—it was even worse.

And it was because of a flare that he was running late. He'd been working from bed at home for nearly three days, and he was itching to get out of his apartment. His body wasn't quite on board with that message, though. Neither was Fiona, the Himalayan rag-doll mix he inherited from a neighbor three years ago. While he hated being cooped up in his apartment, Fiona, who was a typical clingy rag-doll, loved having him home and had settled on his lap and refused to let him get up that morning. When he'd finally coaxed the cat off his lap with the promise of food, it was slow moving.

Oliver was almost ready, only needing to dig through the drawers in his dresser, which also served as the entertainment center in his glorified studio apartment, for some socks. Then his phone rang, blasting *Talk Dirty to Me*, the ringtone Ryan had picked for him when they first became roommates their sophomore year of college. He grabbed the phone, only briefly catching the time and seeing just how late he was before answering.

"Hey, have you left your apartment yet?" Ryan asked before Oliver could even greet him.

"No, I'm running a little slow today," Oliver said. "I'm about to—"

"Good. Stay home," Ryan interrupted.

"I'm fine to come in." Oliver wedged his phone between his ear and his shoulder and sat to pull on his mismatched socks. "I'm only a little stiff, and the walk might actually help."

"Well, I'm glad to hear you're feeling better, but you should still stay home. We got our first confirmed Covid case yesterday," Ryan said.

Oliver sighed. It had only been a matter of time, but

it still wasn't great news. Although one case didn't mean that he had to stay home. "It's one confirmed case."

"It's one case now, but it could easily be ten by the end of the day," Ryan pointed out.

"You're being paranoid. Look, I've got hand sanitizer, and I'll wear a scarf over my mouth on the subway if it'll make you feel better, but I can still make it to the office," Oliver said as placatingly as possible.

"I'm not being paranoid; I'm being careful. You're immunocompromised, Ollie, and the CDC is recommending—"

"I know what the CDC is recommending," Oliver snapped.

"Okay, then stay home," Ryan said. "You saw how quickly this spread in China and how it's spreading in Europe. You shouldn't risk it."

"I need to go into the office." He was losing this argument, and he knew it. He also knew Ryan was right, but it didn't mean he hated being told what to do or receiving special treatment any less. "I haven't been in for days. There are things I need to take care of. Papers to file, contracts to complete, a pile of hard-copy manuscripts to read."

"Whatever papers you need to file can wait, and I'll stop by your desk to get anything you need. I'm getting a bunch of stuff for Dad anyway because he and Mom are playing it safe and staying home, too."

"But—"

"Ollie, he's told everyone that they can work from home if they want, so it's not just you."

"Except they have a choice in the matter," Oliver said. "It seems as if I don't."

"You take public transit. It's a Petri dish for disease on a normal day." Ryan sighed, and Oliver didn't need to see him to know he was running a frustrated hand through his haphazard hair. "Look, you know I'm not generally one to tell you that you can't or shouldn't do things because of your shitty health—your words, not mine—so just this once, can you realize I'm being serious and stay home? If not for your own health, for mine, because if Anna finds out that I talked to you and you got sick from going into the office anyway…"

"If I got sick, it wouldn't be your fault," Oliver said.

"Try telling Anna that."

Oliver took a deep breath, then held it before letting it out slowly. "Fine. But only so Anna doesn't poison you in your sleep with whatever biochemical thing she's been researching lately."

"Thank you. I would hate to be murdered by my fiancée before the wedding," Ryan deadpanned.

Oliver smirked. "That would be in poor form. Are you driving into the office since, as you put it, the subway is a Petri dish?"

"Yeah, why?"

"Can you collect all the office plants and bring them here?" Oliver asked. "Because I know no one has watered them while I've been gone, and if I won't be in for what is probably going to end up being weeks, I don't want them to die."

"You are absolutely right. Everyone is too afraid to go near the plants lest they kill your babies," Ryan said, a hint of laughter in his voice.

"They aren't my babies." At his mention of babies, Fiona hopped up into his lap and curled up as if to remind him that if anything was going to be his baby, it was her.

"You named them."

"Of course I named them," Oliver said, indignant. "They're living things, and I'm not a monster." Fiona gave him a look, just as indignant, that he was disturbing her. He scratched her head to calm her.

Ryan laughed. "Of course not. I'll bring the plants, and I'll check your desk for manuscripts. Is there anything else you'll need?"

"I can't think of anything," Oliver replied.

"Okay. I'll be by before noon," Ryan said.

"Thanks."

"No problem."

Oliver hung up the phone and sighed. He scratched Fiona's head again. "Well, pretty girl, it looks like you get your wish because I'll be working from home for at least the next few weeks." And while his cat didn't lift her head, she let out a soft chirp in response.

3

Ezra

Friday Afternoon, March 13, 2020

"Got any threes?" Ezra asked, looking at Willow over his cards.

It felt good to finally be out of his room. Once he'd gotten back from Italy, he'd needed to quarantine for fourteen days, and it had driven him nuts. The first five or so days hadn't been too bad. He'd spent most of it sleeping since the jet lag had hit him harder than it usually did. It was probably the fact that it was the most time zones he'd traveled across in a while, and traveling west was always more exhausting than traveling east. Or, as Anna had suggested the other day while they were texting, his body was finally catching up on all the rest he'd skipped out on for the past three years.

Either way, after five days of sleeping, he'd started to get restless. He didn't know how to sit still anymore after three years of being almost constantly on the move—bouncing from city to city on a whim, taking in as many historical sights Europe offered as he could, and either busking or bartending under the table to get by. Willow sitting outside of his room to play twenty questions with him had helped a little, but he still felt stir-crazy from being stuck in his relatively small room. Which is why he technically hadn't even made the CDC-recommended fourteen days. After twelve days of showing no symptoms other than jet-lag-induced exhaustion, he finally texted Josie from his room asking if it would be fine with everyone for him to come out early.

"Go fish," Willow replied without looking up from her own cards.

Ezra looked down at the playing field they'd made on the living room floor and counted the number of completed sets laid out in front of Willow, then looked at the dwindling stock pile. He narrowed his eyes at her. "I feel like you're cheating."

"I am not cheating!" she exclaimed indignantly, finally looking up from her cards. "Mom, Archie is accusing me of cheating."

Josie looked up from the mass-market paperback mystery novel she was curled up on the couch reading. "Well, are you?"

"No," Willow insisted with a stubborn set of her jaw that reminded him exactly of Josie.

"Well, how else do you explain having almost three times as many completed sets as me?" Ezra gave Willow a pointed look.

"Have you considered that maybe you're just pants at Go Fish?" Josie asked him.

"You're pants at Go Fish," Ezra grumbled under his breath. He reluctantly took a card from the draw pile, and let out a triumphant "ah ha!" before playing his completed set of threes.

"Told you!" Willow exclaimed. "I don't need to cheat. I'm just better at this than you."

"Alright, fine. I suck at Go Fish," Ezra admitted. His

phone buzzed on the floor next to him, Ryan's name lighting up the screen. Ezra tossed down his cards and pushed himself off of the floor. "I surrender. But when I get back from taking this call, we're playing war because it's relatively tamper-proof."

Ezra walked out toward the back patio as he answered the call. "Hello?"

"Hey." Ryan's voice came through the phone. "You sound more well rested."

"I am," Ezra said. He slid the glass door open and stepped out. "But I also finally got out of my room. I couldn't make it the last two days of my quarantine."

"Yeah, that tracks," Ryan said with a laugh.

Ezra plopped down into a deck chair. "So is this just a check-in call, or did you have something specific? I'm currently getting my ass handed to me by a small child at card games."

"What game?"

"Most recently, Go Fish. But she also wiped the floor at Old Maid. No one should teach this kid poker," Ezra said dryly.

Ryan laughed again. "Well, I did have something specific, so I won't take too much of your time so you can get back to being a sore loser." Ezra opened his mouth to protest being a sore loser, but Ryan continued over him. "I talked to Dad. He solved your 'no money' problem."

"I'm not letting Andrew give me money," Ezra said firmly. "It was already enough that you bought me a plane ticket home. I was planning to look for a job—"

"No need," Ryan interrupted. "There's an Editorial Assistant position at Coleman Press that needs filling. It's been vacant for a while, so we've been splitting it up between several people—but it's been too long. Dad's been hesitant to hire someone, but an editor is going on maternity leave soon, so we need to make the role its own position again."

"Why has he been hesitant to hire someone?" Ezra asked.

Ryan sighed. "Well, the last guy was awful—like completely incompetent."

"But I don't know the first thing about publishing."

"Yeah, but Dad knows you as a person. Honestly, the reason the last guy ended up being such a shit show was because he just didn't fit in," Ryan said, and there was a pause before he added, "I mean, he also lied on his resume, but mostly it was that he was a complete dick. But Dad knows you. He knows you aren't a pretentious asshole, that you're a quick learner, and that you appreciate books, which are his only real criteria."

"Are we sure about that first one?" Ezra joked.

"Well, you aren't pretentious anyway, and your asshole percentage has gone way down since high school."

Ezra laughed, then Ryan's offer sank in. "So, like…a job?"

"Yeah, a job."

"With health insurance? And taxes? And vacation time?"

"Also a 401(k) if you choose to contribute to it," Ryan added.

"Shit. Like a real adult." Ezra breathed.

"Yup. It sucks. You're going to love it," Ryan said lightly.

"Ryan, I don't know how to properly adult. I've been living in hostels and on the couches of random friends in Europe for the past three years."

"Ezra, none of us know how to properly adult. We all just figure it out as we go."

"The only jobs I've had are bartending gigs under the table. I don't know how to pay taxes. I don't have a bank account since Caroline froze all of mine. Fuck, I don't even have a valid driver's license. It expired, like, two years ago."

"It's okay," Ryan assured him. "You'll figure it out. You've got me and Josie to help you out."

Ezra tried to take a deep breath, but the panic had already settled in.

Shit.

This hadn't happened in years.

It was like someone was sitting on his chest. The hand holding his phone shook. He wanted to escape. He needed to get to a place where it didn't feel like the walls were closing in on him. The last time this happened, he'd done exactly that. But he couldn't this time. He was stuck. He technically wasn't even supposed to have left his room, much less the house, and he definitely couldn't leave the country after just getting back. He tried to suck in a breath, but all he could do was gasp.

"Ezra, slow down and breathe. You're panicking," Ryan said, his voice low and soothing.

"No shit, I'm panicking," Ezra croaked. "I'm twenty-five years old, and I don't have basic life skills."

"Just breathe."

"I can't—"

"It's okay. This feeling will pass. Breathe with me. In for four, hold for seven, out for eight."

Ezra closed his eyes and followed Ryan's instructions. After a few rounds, the bands around his chest loosened.

"Okay," Ezra said on his last exhale.

"Better?" Ryan asked.

"Yeah," Ezra said. He didn't feel completely better, but he felt less like his world was collapsing around him. "Where did you learn that?"

"It's a breathing technique based on pranayama breathing," Ryan explained.

"On what?"

"It's a yoga thing."

"Since when do you do yoga?"

"I started going with Juliet. It's actually not bad. I'm not flexible at all, but it helps with work stress," Ryan said.

"Which one of your friends is Juliet, again?" Ezra hated that he had to ask. He should know more about the people in his best friend's life. But the years he'd spent in Europe were like limbo for him. He'd gone to separate himself from the bad, but in the process he'd unintentionally separated himself from the good, too. He needed to do better.

"Juliet was Anna's college roommate. They both knew Oliver, who became my roommate sophomore year, and we've all stuck together since graduation. Actually, you'll probably get to know Oliver pretty well because he works at Coleman Press. He's an editor," Ryan said. "Anyway, like I said, you don't have to figure any of this out on your own. You have Josie and me to help—Anna, too."

Ezra nodded even though he knew Ryan couldn't see him. But Ryan took his silence as a sign to continue, anyway. "A driver's license should be relatively easy to get. They just need your passport and either your social security card or your birth certificate. And you can sign up for a bank account online. You'll need an opening deposit, but usually it's not that much."

"Okay. I think my social security card and birth certificate are both in the box of stuff I mailed back to you before heading to Amsterdam before graduation." Ezra sighed and shoved a hand through his hair. "I just—I feel like such a mess."

"You're not a mess," Ryan said sternly.

"I spent three years bouncing around Europe after graduation, avoiding responsibility, and now I'm 25, trying to figure out basic skills," Ezra said. "How is that not a mess?"

"You needed to clear your head."

"For three years?"

"Based on the hand life dealt you? Yeah, I'd say three years was more than reasonable. Besides, you were getting life experience, and it's not like I'm any more of an adult than you are," Ryan reasoned.

"You have a job, a place to live, and a fiancée," Ezra deadpanned.

"You have one of those things now, too. Also, I still don't know how to do laundry without shrinking all of my T-shirts. I don't go to the doctor. I can't wash a wineglass without breaking it—just ask Anna." There was a pause, and when Ryan spoke again, his tone had softened. "You can handle this, Ezra. I know you can. Just take things one step at a time."

Ezra let out another long exhale, then let himself smile. "Okay. Thank you."

"No problem," Ryan said. "I'll email you the starting paperwork, and I stashed the box with your stuff at my parents, so I'll pick that up and drop by Josie's tomorrow."

"Sounds good," Ezra said. They said their goodbyes and hung up, then Ezra flopped back onto his bed.

He was still shaking, but now that he had a plan, he was feeling a little better. A little more solid. Just one step at a time, Ryan had said. He could handle that. Just one step at a time.

4

Oliver

Friday, March 20, 2020

Outlook (O.Wheeler@colemanpress.com)
    Franklin.C.Hoffman@gmail.com
    RE: Ashes Of Autumn

Outlook (submissions@colemanpress.com)
    350 unread emails

Subject: RE: Ashes Of Autumn

    FCH <Franklin.C.Hoffman@gmail.com>
    To: Oliver Wheeler
    3/20/2020 2:00 AM

        I don't understand. Where is Molly?
        FCH

    Oliver Wheeler <O.Wheeler@colemanpress.com>
    To: FCH
    3/20/2020 8:16 AM

Frank,

As you're probably aware, Molly was due to start her maternity leave in a few months—after the release of the final Ashes of Autumn book. Unfortunately, however, she had to start her leave early due to personal reasons. But don't worry, she has fully debriefed me on where you're at in the process, so I should be able to pick up where she left off with no problem.

On that note, I've taken a look at your draft, and I think there are some developmental changes we need to make before we can carry on with the line and copy edit. Molly told me you prefer to go over edits live, so when would you like to schedule a call to do that? This afternoon?

Oliver Wheeler
Copyeditor, Interim Developmental Editor
Coleman Press

FCH <Franklin.C.Hoffman@gmail.com>
To: Oliver Wheeler
3/20/2020 10:24 AM

Well, clearly Molly did not fill you in because if she had, she would have told you that we already did the developmental edits. You must have not gotten the correct draft.

FCH

Oliver Wheeler <O.Wheeler@colemanpress.com>
To: FCH
3/20/2020 10:32 AM

Frank,

Molly informed me that you two had gone through one round of developmental edits, and I am working from your most up-to-date draft. However, since I was not part of the editing team that handled your previous books and therefore do not have an intimate knowledge of your series, I read the first two *Ashes of Autumn* books before starting on your last installment. In doing so, I found a few things—series plot holes, world-building inconsistencies, incomplete character arcs—that need to be addressed and wrapped since this is the last book in the series. I'd be happy to go over these with you this afternoon. Would 2 p.m. EST work?

Oliver Wheeler
Copyeditor, Interim Developmental Editor
Coleman Press

Oliver closed his eyes and pressed his fingers into both temples. Ten-thirty in the morning was way too early for the beginnings of a tension headache, but here he was. Molly had warned him that Frank was a little difficult to work with, but she'd clearly undersold it. He should have known that, though. Molly was a sweet woman and often gave people the benefit of the doubt, so if she said someone was a little difficult, it basically meant that they were the devil incarnate.

He didn't have time to dwell on that, though, because his computer pinged with a message from Skype.

Ryan Coleman
ASSOCIATE DIGITAL MARKETING MANAGER, Available - Video Capable

Friday, March 20, 2020

R.Coleman (10:40 AM)

Hey, are you busy?

O.Wheeler (10:41 AM)

Yes, but what's up?

R.Coleman (10:41 AM)

Do you have a quick minute to chat?

O.Wheeler (10:42 AM)

Yeah, but I can't get on the phone. Sore throat today.

R.Coleman (10:42 AM)

Sore throat?

Have you been outside?

Have you come in contact with anyone?

O.Wheeler (10:43 AM)

No, I haven't seen anyone. Sometimes my vocal cords get inflamed which makes my throat sore and my voice hoarse. It's an RA thing, remember?

R.Coleman (10:43 AM)

Right

Sorry. I'm a little on edge with this whole thing.

O.Wheeler (10:43 AM)

Me too. So what did you want to talk about?

R.Coleman (10:44 AM)

I have some news, but I'm not sure you're going to like it.

O.Wheeler (10:44 AM)

Oh no.

R.Coleman (10:44 AM)

Okay, so you know how you're amazing and have been basically doing the job of three people?

O.Wheeler (10:44 AM)

Yes...

Ryan, unless the next words you type are "Andrew finally hired someone to fill the editorial assistant position," I don't want to hear it.

I've exchanged five emails with Frank, and I already want to pull my hair out.

R.Coleman (10:45 AM)

Yikes.

Yeah, Hoffman is pretty much the worst. He nearly made Stella cry over the cover design of his last book.

O.Wheeler (10:45 AM)

Okay, I love Stella, but she does sort of cry at the drop of a hat. But that's beside the point. Why do we still deal with this guy if he's such a miserable bastard?

R.Coleman (10:45 AM)

We contracted him for the entire series.

And he was great while we were publishing his first book, but then the series blew up, and he got a big head. And because the series is so popular, and it basically put Coleman Press on the map, we suck it up.

But anyway, my dad did, in fact, hire an editorial assistant.

O.Wheeler (10:46 AM)

Oh, thank fuck.

Wait, you said I may not like your news. What's the catch?

R.Coleman (10:46 AM)

Ezra doesn't exactly have a lot of publishing experience.

O.Wheeler (10:47 AM)

And by "not a lot of publishing experience," you mean...?

R.Coleman (10:47 AM)

Okay, he doesn't have any publishing
experience.

So we kind of need you to train him.

O.Wheeler (10:47 AM)

Ryan, WHY?

R.Coleman (10:47 AM)

Because you're the person on the team
that knows the entire process in and out
and would best be able to get him up to
speed.

O.Wheeler (10:48 AM)

Actually, wouldn't that be you, since
your dad is training you to take over
for him one day? But actually, by
"why" I meant: why did your dad hire
yet ANOTHER person who doesn't
know jack shit about publishing to be
an editorial assistant?

Wait...Ezra. That name is familiar.
Ezra, as in your best friend from that
fancy boarding school you went to upstate?

R.Coleman (10:49 AM)

My best man, yeah.

O.Wheeler (10:49 AM)

The spoiled, rich playboy who skipped
his own college graduation to traipse

around Europe for three years just because he could?

R.Coleman (10:49 AM)

Okay, I don't know where that description of him came from because I have never once called him spoiled, and I don't think I've used the word "playboy" to describe anyone ever.

But, yes, that Ezra. He's in a bit of a tight spot and needs a job now that he's back home, and you know how my dad is; if he can help someone, he will.

O.Wheeler (10:50 AM)

So we're on the same page: this is Ezra Beaumont we're talking about? What kind of tight spot could the heir to a multi-national business conglomerate be in that he would need to take a job at a publishing company that pays $35K a year? Did his parents cut him off or something?

R.Coleman (10:50 AM)

Well, his dad passed away in high school, so it's just his mom, but yeah, something like that.

Look, I know that most of what you know about Ezra from the media doesn't portray him or his family in a good light, and the stories I've told about him in high school probably don't help either.

But he's not like that.

At least not anymore. Any of the stuff he's gotten up to that makes him look bad was to piss off his parents.

O.Wheeler (10:52 AM)

That doesn't exactly make him sound better.

R.Coleman (10:52 AM)

Good point.

But he's not like that anymore. He's always been a good guy. It's why he's been my best friend for nearly 10 years. Yeah, he was a bit of a jerk in high school, but so was I. We both grew out of it.

Trust me, once you get to know him, you'll love him.

O.Wheeler (10:53 AM)

But why do I have to train him? You know just as much as I do, and he's your best friend.

R.Coleman (10:53 AM)

I wanted to, but then my dad remembered that nothing productive ever gets done when someone leaves Ezra and me to our own devices.

O.Wheeler (10:56 AM)

But I don't have time. I've got my own projects plus the ones from Molly I picked up—which are a lot more work than I thought since Frank's book needs a fuck-ton of developmental edits so readers don't get pissed with all the loose ends—and our slush pile is multiplying like rabbits, and I can't have him dwindle that down since I'm assuming he doesn't even know what a slush pile is, much less a query.

R.Coleman (10:56 AM)

He's a quick learner, so it'll only be a few weeks, I promise.

Just think. Once he's trained, you won't have to deal with the slush pile at all anymore, and there will be someone you can farm some of the nit-picky stuff out to, which will leave you more time to do the important work and might even leave some downtime for you to work on your own book?

O.Wheeler (10:58 AM)

You mean my SECRET book that Anna wasn't supposed to tell anyone about?

R.Coleman (10:59 AM)

She got excited about it and couldn't help it. You know she's like your biggest cheerleader.

O.Wheeler (11:01 AM)

...Fine.

R.Coleman (11:01 AM)

I can basically hear the heavy sigh through the computer.

O.Wheeler (11:01 AM)

Yeah, well, I just got what is probably another snippy email from Frank, and now I officially have a tension headache, so I won't bother putting up a fight.

When does he start?

R.Coleman (11:03 AM)

Monday.

O.Wheeler (11:03 AM)

Monday? That gives me almost no

time to come up with a training plan.

R.Coleman (11:03 AM)

I was only just able to get him into the
office to get set up with IT.

He was under isolation for two weeks
until he got a negative coronavirus test
after getting back from Italy.

O.Wheeler (11:04 AM)

You still could have given me some
warning.

R.Coleman (11:04 AM)

And have you sit and stew over it? Not
likely.

His email is E.Beaumont@coleman-
press.com. I told him to expect a prelim-
inary instruction email from you to get
him started.

O.Wheeler (11:07 AM)

Great.

R.Coleman (11:07 AM)

I realize that was sarcastic, but I don't
care. You're the best, Ollie.

Subject: RE: Ashes Of Autumn

FCH <Franklin.C.Hoffman@gmail.com>
To: Oliver Wheeler
3/20/2020 11:00 AM

Fine.
FCH

Monday, March 23, 2020

ACTION CENTER

Outlook (O.Wheeler@colemanpress.com)
   Franklin.C.Hoffman@gmail.com
   RE: Ashes Of Autumn

Outlook (submissions@colemanpress.com)
   376 unread emails

Subject: Training Documents

   Oliver Wheeler <O.Wheeler@colemanpress.com>
   To: Ezra Beaumont
   3/23/2020 7:45 AM

   Ezra,

   I'm sure Ryan already told you I would be in charge of training you for the editorial assistant position. He mentioned you don't have any prior experience or knowledge about the publishing process, so here are a few documents you can read to familiarize yourself with the publishing process. Since I've been doing the job in addition to my copyediting for the past seven and a half months and now developmental editing work, I won't have much time to walk you through everything myself.

   If you have questions, just shoot me an email or a message on Skype, and I should be able to help. But it may take me a while to get back to you since I'm doing the job of three people.

   Good luck,
   Oliver Wheeler
   Copyeditor, Interim Developmental Editor
   Coleman Press

ATTACHMENTS
Coleman Press Employee manual.pdf
Book Publishing 101.pdf

Ezra Beaumont <E.Beaumont@colemanpress.com>
To: Oliver Wheeler
3/23/2020 8:30 AM

Oliver,

Thank you. I'll start reading these and get back
to you with questions I have. And it's nice to meet
you! I've heard all about you from Ryan and
Anna. All good things, I promise ☺

Ezra

Thursday, March 26, 2020

ACTION CENTER

Outlook (O.Wheeler@colemanpress.com)
   Franklin.C.Hoffman@gmail.com
   RE: Ashes Of Autumn

Outlook (submissions@colemanpress.com)
   379 unread emails

Skype
   E.Beaumont
   Good morning!

Ezra Beaumont
EDITORIAL ASSISTANT, Available - Video Capable

Thursday, March 26, 2020

Beaumont.E (7:00 AM)

Good morning!

So as an editorial assistant, will I assist with every step of the process, including formatting, cover design, and marketing, or just the editing phases? Also, I'm having a little trouble understanding the differences between the different editing phases. Developmental edits seem pretty straightforward, but I can't really figure out the rest.

O.Wheeler (12:48 PM)

If this were a bigger company, it would only be the editing phases, but since we're an independent press, it will be the entire process. I can send you a few things that will explain the other stuff.

Beaumont.E (12:48 PM)

Oh, I mean, I guess that works. Thanks.

Subject: Editorial Management

Oliver Wheeler <O.Wheeler@colemanpress.com>
To: Ezra Beaumont
3/26/2020 12:50 PM

Ezra,

Here is some more in-depth information about the different phases of the publishing process. I've also included a document with some links to a few webinars and online courses we have access to as part of our continuing education program.

Oliver Wheeler
Copyeditor, Interim Developmental Editor
Coleman Press

ATTACHMENTS
Editorial Management 1 - Acquisition to Publi-
cation.pdf
Editorial Management 2 - Publication and Be-
yond.pdf
Developmental Editing.pdf
Copyediting.pdf
Copyediting vs. Line Editing.pdf
Grammar for Editors.pdf
Continuing Education Resources.docx

Monday, April 6, 2020

ACTION CENTER

Outlook (O.Wheeler@colemanpress.com)
    Franklin.C.Hoffman@gmail.com
    RE: Ashes Of Autumn
    GeorgiaMeyersAuthor@gmail.com
    RE: The Secret Stranger

Outlook (submissions@colemanpress.com)
    372 unread emails

Skype
    E.Beaumont
    Hey I just had a question for you...

Ezra Beaumont
EDITORIAL ASSISTANT, Available - Video Capable

Monday, April 6, 2020

Beaumont.E: (7:30 AM)

Hey I just had a question for you when
you get a minute.

O.Wheeler (4:45 PM)

Sorry, I was dealing with an author that keeps fighting me on every edit I suggest. What's your question?

Beaumont.E (4:46 PM)

No worries!

It's about queries. So from what I gather, being a publisher's reader is a part of the editorial assistant position right?

O.Wheeler (4:48 PM)

Correct.

Beaumont.E (4:48 PM)

And that consists of reading the unsolicited manuscripts, right? But how do we decide what we want vs. what we don't want?

O.Wheeler (5:03 PM)

That part takes experience, but I'll send you some documents and examples.

Subject: Query Letter Basics

Oliver Wheeler <O.Wheeler@colemanpress.com>
To: Ezra Beaumont
4/6/2020 5:05 PM

Oliver Wheeler
Copyeditor, Interim Developmental Editor
Coleman Press
ATTACHMENTS
What is a query letter.pdf
What to look for in a manuscript.pdf
Query sorting.pdf

Good query examples.pdf
Rejected query examples.pdf

Friday, April 10, 2020

ACTION CENTER

Outlook (submissions@colemanpress.com)
236 unread emails

Skype

E.Beaumont
Morning! I have a follow-up question...

Monday, April 13, 2020

ACTION CENTER

Outlook (O.Wheeler@colemanpress.com)
Franklin.C.Hoffman@gmail.com
RE: Ashes Of Autumn

Outlook (submissions@colemanpress.com)
239 unread emails

Skype

E.Beaumont
Morning! I have a follow-up question...
E.Beaumont
Hey, just wanted to follow up...

Subject: RE: Ashes Of Autumn

FCH <Franklin.C.Hoffman@gmail.com>
To: Oliver Wheeler
4/13/2020 2:00 AM

Ok, I know I'm super late with the edits, but I just don't know if I agree with the content changes you suggested.

Can I have an extension to do a few more re-writes?

Thanks,

FCH

Subject: FW: RE: Ashes Of Autumn

Oliver Wheeler <O.Wheeler@colemanpress.com>

To: David Henry

4/13/2020 8:20 AM

David,

I'm forwarding you the chain of emails between Frank and me so that you can see what I've been dealing with.

I've gone through several rounds of developmental edits with him, and he's fighting me at every step. I haven't even been able to start the line edit because there are so many glaring problems with his manuscript.

Honestly, I think I'm a little out of my depth here with this one.

Help?

Oliver Wheeler

Copyeditor, Interim Developmental Editor

Coleman Press

David Henry <D.Henry@colemanpress.com>

To: Oliver Wheeler

4/13/2020 8:45 AM

Oliver,

Don't worry about it anymore. I'll knock some sense into him. I've worked with him before. He can be a pain in the ass. It's a real shame that his work is so popular.

Thanks,
David Henry
Manager, Editing and Design
Coleman Press

Oliver Wheeler <O.Wheeler@colemanpress.com>
To: David Henry
4/13/2020 8:50 AM

Thanks, David.

I've got enough on my plate between covering commissioning, getting through the slush pile, and training the new guy.

Oliver Wheeler
Copyeditor, Interim Developmental Editor
Coleman Press

Ezra Beaumont
EDITORIAL ASSISTANT, Available - Video Capable

Friday, April 10, 2020

E.Beaumont (7:18 AM)

Morning! I have a follow-up question about queries. So after we decide to pursue a manuscript, we go into commissioning editing. Would I handle that, too? And if so, how do I go about that?

Monday, April 13, 2020

E. Beaumont (7:25 AM)

Hey, just wanted to follow up from Friday.

Subject: Communicating with Potential Clients

Oliver Wheeler <O.Wheeler@colemanpress.com>

To: Ezra Beaumont
4/13/2020 10:50 AM

Oliver Wheeler
Copyeditor, Interim Developmental Editor
Coleman Press

ATTACHMENTS
Contracts, Rights, and Signing Authors.pdf
Communicating with authors.pdf
Contract writing.pdf

Thursday, April 16, 2020

ACTION CENTER

Outlook (O.Wheeler@colemanpress.com)
Franklin.C.Hoffman@gmail.com
RE: Ashes Of Autumn

Outlook (submissions@colemanpress.com)
302 unread emails

Skype
E.Beaumont
Morning!

Ezra Beaumont
EDITORIAL ASSISTANT, Available - Video Capable

Thursday, April 16, 2020

E.Beaumont (7:00 AM)

Morning!

So I was wondering when I was going to get started actually doing things? I feel like I've been reading about the job forever and I think I'm ready to do things more hands-on.

O.Wheeler (9:13 AM)

I hate to break it to you, but if you think that the stuff I've been sending you is a lot, that's kind of the job. It's a publishing company. There's a lot of reading involved.

E.Beaumont (9:15 AM)

I know that. I actually like reading.

What I'm trying to say is that I feel like I have a good grasp of the background stuff now and think I'm ready to start trying to implement what I've learned. I'm more of a hands-on kind of learner, anyway.

O.Wheeler (9:42 AM)

Alright. I'm not entirely sure you're fully ready to deal with authors yet, but I guess you could start getting familiar with the publishing software we use since that's where all the contracts, timelines, and payments get logged and processed. Did IT get you set up with a login when they set up your email and computer?

E.Beaumont (9:43 AM)

Yeah they did, but when I logged in, I didn't know what to make of all the menus.

O.Wheeler (9:43 AM)

I'll send you the manual for the

software. It's a little long, but it's pretty helpful.

Subject: PubPro Manual

Oliver Wheeler <O.Wheeler@colemanpress.com>

To: Ezra Beaumont
4/16/2020 9:45 AM

Oliver Wheeler
Copyeditor, Interim Developmental Editor
Coleman Press
ATTACHMENTS
PubPro 2018 manual.pdf

Ezra Beaumont
EDITORIAL ASSISTANT, Available - Video Capable

Beaumont.E (9:50 AM)

"A little long"? It's nearly 200 pages.

O.Wheeler (9:50 AM)

We get submitted manuscripts that are longer than that.

Beaumont.E (9:55 AM)

Okay, well, thanks.

5

Ezra

Thursday Morning, April 16, 2020

Ezra slammed his laptop closed a little harder than he meant to.

"What did that poor computer do to you?" Josie asked him from her end of the dining room table, looking up from the law textbooks that surrounded her.

"It's the guy who's been training me. Although, I say training in the loosest sense of the word because all he keeps doing is sending me document upon document to read. Then, every time I have questions about something, he just sends me another document instead of answering my question." Ezra shoved the laptop away and dropped his forehead to the table's surface. "I don't know what to do. I feel like I'm just wasting my time. Ryan's dad went out of his way to help me by hiring me, but it's been a month and I haven't done a single fucking thing."

"Hey, language," Josie scolded. Ezra lifted his head slightly to see her jerk her head to the living room where Willow was sitting cross-legged on the floor in front of the television, playing Animal Crossing.

Ezra grimaced. "Sorry."

"Have you talked to Ryan about any of this?" Josie asked. "This guy is a friend of his, right? So maybe he can help, or at least offer some advice…"

"Yeah, Oliver was his college roommate. I was actually excited to meet him and work with him because, from everything Ryan and Anna have ever said about him, he seemed like he'd be a good guy." Ezra sighed. "It's almost like he hates me."

"Well, I doubt he hates you. Didn't Ryan warn you that the team has been a little on edge since they've been short-staffed?" Josie pointed out.

"Yeah, but I've talked to a few other editors—you know, just to introduce myself—and they've all seemed nice," Ezra countered.

"Well, taking a few minutes out of your day to have a quick introduction chat is a lot less stressful than taking on training a new employee. Just talk to Ryan before jumping to conclusions."

"Okay, fine," Ezra said with a sigh.

"You're welcome. I'm so glad I could help," Josie said, deadpan.

He rolled his eyes, then Josie flashed a hint of a grin before turning back to her case notes.

Ezra pulled out his phone.

Ryan Coleman
April 16, 2020, 10:19 AM

Ezra Beaumont

Hey, question for you.

Ryan Coleman

Hey! How's the first month going?

Ezra Beaumont

Well, that's what I wanted to pick your brain about.

It's been a month, and I haven't actually started doing anything yet. All I've done is read what seems to be an endless supply of documents about the publishing process.

Ryan Coleman

Yeah, I should have warned you about that. I mentioned to Oliver that you didn't have any publishing experience, so he's probably trying to get you up to speed before getting you started with the real stuff.

Ezra Beaumont

Right. That's what Oliver said you'd said.

Ryan Coleman

There's no rush. Just take your time and ask Oliver questions if you have them. He's great at explaining stuff. He basically held my hand while I was on the editing team before Dad let me go into marketing.

Ezra Beaumont

Okay, but see, that's my problem. Getting him to answer a single question is like pulling teeth. When he sent me that first introduction email, he warned me he's swamped doing the jobs of three people so it might take him a while to get back to me when I had questions, which seemed a little rude but also understandable. But I thought that at least when he got back to me, he would answer my question.

Except he doesn't. I wasn't joking when I said he has an endless supply of publishing instructional documents. Every time I ask a question, even what should be a question with a straightforward answer, I get another email with like 5 documents attached.

Like I get that he's busy, but at this point it seems like he's just actively avoiding me.

Ryan Coleman

Okay, well I can guarantee you that Oliver isn't avoiding you. However, he can kind of get sucked into his work and has a hard time pulling himself out of it, so that might be what's happening.

How do you usually reach out to him?

Ezra Beaumont

Skype.

Ryan Coleman

Is that it?

Ezra Beaumont

Other than the emails with infinite attachments, yeah.

And here's the other thing: I messaged him today to ask when I could start trying to do some tasks I'd be responsible for because I'm more of a hands-on learner anyway, but again, all I got was a blunt response and a 200-page software manual.

Ryan Coleman

Yikes. Okay, maybe he's a little more overwhelmed than I thought. He can come across a little snippy via text when he's stressed.

Do you want me to check in with him to see what's up?

Ezra Beaumont

No, don't do that.

The last thing Ezra wanted was for Oliver to think that he went to Ryan to tattle on him for a few rude messages.

Ezra Beaumont

I can handle it. I just wanted to get your advice on what to do.

Ryan Coleman

I would try getting him on the phone. I'm assuming the software manual was for PubPro?

Ezra Beaumont

Yeah

Ryan Coleman

Okay, I would just ask if you two could get together on a Skype call or something so he can walk you through it. It'll be faster, and frankly easier because trying to figure out PubPro using solely the manual is a pain in the ass.

Oliver is better on the phone anyway. Sometimes it's easier just to call him because you know you'll actually get a

response and you'll have his full or at
least mostly full attention.

Ezra Beaumont

Okay, yeah, I'll try that.

Thanks

Ryan Coleman

No problem. But if you need me to talk
to him, just let me know.

Ezra Beaumont

I will.

Ezra locked his phone and set it on the table, then pulled his laptop toward him again. He opened the lid and waited for the screen to power back on.

"I take it Ryan had some advice," Josie said, glancing up from her notebook.

"Yeah. I'm just hoping it works," Ezra said. He typed in his password, then pulled up Skype.

Oliver Wheeler
COPYEDITOR, Available - Video Capable
Thursday, April 16, 2020

E. Beaumont (10:35 AM)

Hey, so like I said, I'm more of a hands-on kind of guy. And with learning practical skills or software, it helps if I watch someone else do it first. So is there any way you can just walk me through the software via a screen share on Skype or something? It would be a lot faster than me reading that document, having to ask you a bunch of questions, you giving me

> MORE reading, and then me just hav-
> ing more questions.

He drummed his fingers on the space next to the track-
pad, waiting for Oliver's response. Within a few moments, the little dancing bubbles that showed he was
typing appeared.

They disappeared.

Then reappeared.

After several minutes, Oliver's reply came through.

O.Wheeler (10:43 AM)

Fine. But I won't be able to block off any
time until Monday. Also, we'll have to
call on our phones because the audio
feature for the Skype screen share is awful.

E. Beaumont (10:43 AM)

Thanks, Oliver! I appreciate it.

Would around 9 am work? To give you
some time to wake up and check
emails and whatnot.

Oliver didn't message back after that, but a minute
later, Ezra's laptop pinged with an email notification
for a calendar invite at 9 AM on Monday. So that was
at least something.

Monday Morning, April 20, 2020

Ezra sat propped up against the headboard, his legs
crisscrossed and his laptop balanced on his right knee
and the notebook he stole from Willow to take notes

balanced on his left. He checked the time. There were about ten minutes until his call with Oliver. He tapped his pen on the open page.

He didn't know why he was so restless. It was just a phone call. But he hadn't been able to sit still since he woke up this morning—a good forty-five minutes before his alarm went off. He'd gone on a run, showered, and even made breakfast to help around the house, but nothing soothed the low level of anxiety that coursed through him.

He checked the time again. Eight minutes. Maybe he would just message Oliver to let him know he was ready on the off chance they could start early.

Oliver Wheeler
COPYEDITOR, Available - Video Capable
Monday, April 20, 2020

E. Beaumont (8:52 AM)

Morning!
Ready when you are!

Why he added an emoji, he wasn't sure.

Oliver didn't message back, but not even a minute passed before Ezra's computer blooped with the Skype call. His phone buzzed on the bed next to him a few seconds later. Taking a deep breath, he accepted both calls.

"Morning!" Ezra said.

"Morning." The voice on the other end was soft and low, a little hoarse like it was thick with sleep.

"It's good to actually meet you—well, get a voice to the name anyway," Ezra said. There was a hum of acknowledgment, but nothing else, so he plowed on. "Although it feels a little weird to be meeting you like this. I figured the first time I met all of Ryan's friends would be at his wedding, but here we are."

"Yeah," Oliver said, his voice still gravelly—almost pained. He cleared his throat and spoke again, only slightly more clearly this time. "Sorry, this is the first time I've spoken out loud in a few days."

Ezra let out a laugh. "Live alone?"

There was a brief pause. "Yeah. So, can you see my screen?"

"What?" Ezra blinked, then looked at his computer. On the screen was a small, grainy window reflecting the PubPro software-loading screen. "Oh, yeah, I can."

"Great. So, on the left side is the menu for each team. We all use the same software to make it easier to communicate. The sections you'll need to focus on are for contracts and manuscript information," Oliver said.

"Do the manuscripts get edited and formatted in here?" Ezra asked.

"No, we use InDesign for formatting. But you won't have to deal with that for now, and honestly, I don't really know how to use it," Oliver said. Ezra opened his mouth to ask whom he should get in touch with to learn that part of the process, as well, but Oliver continued on.

Over the next half-hour, Oliver went quickly through each menu and tool, explaining the relevant steps of the publishing process. Ryan was right; Oliver did really know his stuff, and he was good at explaining things. Anytime Ezra had a question, Oliver would quickly end up answering it before he got the chance to even ask. But even if that wasn't the case, he wouldn't have really got a question in edgewise. It was as if Oliver was trying his best to set the world record for the shortest software training session. Ezra had a hard time keeping up with his notes. He also couldn't help feeling like simply having this call was a major annoyance for Oliver. Ryan would probably tell him he was being paranoid, but he'd spent 18 years in a house where passive aggression was basically a third language. He'd gotten very good at figuring out the subtle hints that someone was annoyed. And Oliver seemed annoyed.

Finally, Oliver finished up his explanation and took a pause long enough for Ezra to actually get a word in. "Thanks, Oliver. All of that made a lot more sense than when I tried to go through that manual you sent," he said. "I spent all of Friday looking at it, but I'm not really great with technical manuals. You should have seen me in my high school chemistry lab. I'm pretty sure I would have blown up the school if it wasn't for Ryan."

He laughed, hoping the joke would break the ice, but all Oliver responded with was, "So, you don't have any questions?"

Yeah, Oliver was definitely annoyed.

"Not really—it seems pretty straightforward. I may have some later once I actually start messing around with things, but I think, for now, I'm good."

"Okay," Oliver said, sounding skeptical. "Feel free to get familiar with everything in there, but for now, I'll continue to handle writing contracts and dealing with scheduling just so we don't have any problems."

"Oh, yeah, that makes sense, I guess," Ezra said, deflating slightly. He was also quite familiar with the signs that someone didn't trust him, and it was becoming obvious that Oliver didn't. "What should I start with, then?"

"You can start managing the query box. I'll walk you through that, too," Oliver said. He switched from Pub-Pro to Outlook and navigated to the email inbox dedicated solely to submissions.

"Christ, that's a lot of unread emails," Ezra swore.

"Yeah. We're one of the few publishing companies that accept direct proposals from authors without literary agents, which means we get a lot of manuscripts that aren't ready," Oliver explained. "Half of the proposals are incomplete, too, which is the annoying part. There are instructions on the website, but they hardly ever get followed."

"So, what exactly do we do with these?" Ezra asked.

"We have to go through each one and read the query letter and check it for completion, then sort it into respective genres."

"What is the point of sorting by genre?"

"It helps us decide what to move forward with. It all depends on what genres are popular."

"And how do we know what's going to be popular?"

"Market research, but don't worry about that," Oliver answered tersely. "That's Andrew's area. He lets us know what genres to pursue and which to ignore for the time being."

"Right, okay," Ezra said. "So, I go through the inbox and read the query letters, then sort them. And once they're sorted, I read them to see what might be worth pursuing, and from there, I'd reach out to the authors to get a full manuscript?"

"Basically. But for now, just focus on getting familiar with the query letters themselves," Oliver instructed. "It's pretty easy to figure out that a manuscript isn't worth anything based solely on the pitch. I'll take care of reading the manuscripts and reaching out to potential authors."

"Are you sure?" Ezra asked. "I think I've got a handle on it, and I know you're busy with editing."

"It's fine. Just focus on getting familiar with query letters and the software." There was a pause, a shuffling sound, then a muffled groan.

"Are you alright, Oliver?"

"I'm fine," Oliver croaked. He cleared his throat after what sounded like another groan. "If you don't have questions…" He trailed off, and Ezra took the hint.

"No, I don't. I'll let you get back to work. Thanks for your help. I really appreciate—"

The Skype call disconnected, and Ezra pulled the phone away from his ear to see that Oliver had already hung up.

6

Oliver

Tuesday Afternoon, April 22, 2020

Notification Center

PHONE

> **Anna Reid -** 1 missed call (12:40 PM)

MESSAGES

> **Anna Reid -** 4 iMessages (12:50 PM)
> **Ryan Coleman -** 3 text messages (12:30 PM)
> **Mary Wen -** 7 text messages (10:07 AM)
> **Juliet Ríos -** 2 iMessages (9:32 AM)
> **Ezra Beaumont -** 1 iMessage (8:03 AM)
> **Dad -** 1 text message (7:45 AM)

Oliver groaned as he looked at the time, then at the barrage of missed text messages and phone calls. He hadn't meant to sleep so late, but his inability to do most of his low-impact exercises, which helped with his RA, had started to have an effect on his energy levels. The stress from work also wasn't helping, so since he had the day off, he figured he deserved to sleep in. If he was honest with himself, though, the main reason he'd snoozed his alarm this morning and gone right back to sleep was because it was his birthday, and he was spending it alone. And if he was asleep, then he didn't have to think about that.

But his hip was starting to hurt from being in one position for so long, so he sluggishly got out of bed, fed Fiona, and put on a kettle before sitting on his couch to go through his texts.

Anna Reid

April 22, 2020, 7:00 AM

Anna Reid

Happy birthday, Ollie! Love you bunches and I miss you already

April 22, 2020, 8:45 AM

Anna Reid

Okay, maybe you're just sleeping in a bit. Call me later?

April 22, 2020, 11:45 AM

Anna Reid

Ollie? Ryan is telling me you're probably just sucked into writing or something (Sorry I spilled the beans about your book, btw.) But I also know how you get sometimes, so please call me?

April 22, 2020, 12:43 PM

Anna Reid

I'm starting to worry. I know you took the day off, but it's not really like you to

go MIA like this. Are you feeling okay?
Are you having a flare-up? Just let me
know so I can try to help. Love you.

April 22, 2020, 2:47 PM

Oliver Wheeler

Shit, sorry. I was asleep. I'm not having
a flare—just catching up on sleep
since my sleep schedule has been all
kinds of fucked up because of work.

Anna Reid

Oh, thank God. But you're okay?

Oliver Wheeler

Yeah, I'm fine.

Ryan Coleman
April 22, 2020, 7:53 AM

Ryan Coleman

Happy birthday!!!!

Have a great day off. Try not to have too
much fun 😊

April 22, 2020, 12:30 PM

Ryan Coleman

Alright, Ollie, I know you're probably
just taking advantage of the day off and
writing or something and just got
sucked into a scene, but if you could at
least text Anna back so she knows
you're alive, that'd be great. Otherwise
she's going to want to storm over to
your apartment.

April 22, 2020, 2:48 PM

Oliver Wheeler

Sorry, I was asleep. I texted her back.

And thanks.

Ryan Coleman

Oh, thank god. You live.

Mary Wen

April 22, 2020, 10:07 AM

Mary Wen

HAPPY BIRTHDAY TO YOU

HAPPY BIRTHDAY TO YOU

HAPPY BIRTHDAY DEAR OLLIE

HAPPY BIRTHDAY TO YOU

AND MANY MOREEEEEEEE

Your present should arrive in the mail
sometime tomorrow.

Love you and miss you, you wonderful,
sarcastic, old man, you.

Oliver rolled his eyes but smiled. Mary had been calling
him an old man since they'd met and instantly became
best friends in home room his freshman year of high
school, but as he got up to deal with the now-whistling
kettle, he actually felt like it. The restrictions better
open up soon because the lack of even minor movement was really starting to wear on him.

April 22, 2020, 2:51 PM

Oliver Wheeler

Okay, wow. That was a lot. You're a
lot.

But I love and miss you, too, you lovely, crazy lady, you.

Juliet Ríos

April 22, 2020, 9:32 AM

Juliet Ríos

HAPPY BIRTHDAY YOU SEXY BITCH

Check your doorstep. Love you ♡

April 22, 2020, 3:01 PM

Oliver Wheeler

I don't know how you got into my building without buzzing me, but I don't care because there's cake. You're a saint, Jules.

Ezra Beaumont

April 22, 2020, 8:03 AM

Ezra Beaumont

Hey, Oliver! Ryan told me you're off for your birthday, so I just wanted to wish you a happy birthday and say that I hope you have a good day off.

Dad

April 22, 2020, 7:45 AM

Dad

Happy birthday, kiddo. Hope you're being safe. I worry about you in such a big city. Call me later, and maybe we can have a Zoom dinner. I finally figured out my webcam. Love you.

April 22, 2020, 3:03 PM

Oliver Wheeler

Thanks, Dad. I'm safe. I'll call you around 8 p.m. my time.

I love you, too.

Mary Wen

April 22, 2020, 3:05 PM

Mary Wen

He answers! Good, I was worried.

Oliver Wheeler

Sorry, I was sleeping.

Mary Wen

It's 3 o'clock in the afternoon.

Oliver Wheeler

Oh, really? I wasn't aware of that. It's not like I can tell time or read the clock on my phone.

Sorry, I'm just a little grumpy.

Mary Wen

No shit. I couldn't tell.

But seriously, are you alright? It's not like you to sleep this late. You wake up at the ass crack of dawn no matter what time you go to sleep.

Oliver Wheeler

I'm just tired, ok?

Mary Wen

Have you talked to your doctor? Cause seriously, if you're feeling extreme fatigue, you could be anemic again.

Oliver Wheeler

It's not anemia. I just haven't been

sleeping well lately because work fucking sucks, so I thought I would try to catch up on sleep since I took the day off. I mean, it's not like I can do anything else right now since I shouldn't leave my goddamn apartment.

Mary Wen

Oh, Ollie...You're not ok, are you?

Oliver Wheeler

I'll be fine.

Mary Wen

It's ok if you're not ok.

I know this can't be easy. I'm worried, too. So is Robin. I had to stop her from panic-buying apocalypse levels of canned food and toilet paper. So, if you aren't at your best right now, that's completely understandable.

Oliver Wheeler

I know. I'm trying.

Mary Wen

I hate that I can't be there with you. I don't like the idea of you just sitting in your apartment all alone on your birthday.

Oliver Wheeler

It's honestly not that big of a deal. I've never really cared about my birthday. Besides, it's not like 25 is a big birthday, anyway. Juliet dropped off a homemade cake, so I'm honestly ok.

Mary Wen

At the risk of sounding like Martin...

Please tell me you're eating something healthy and balanced before digging into that cake by yourself.

Oliver Wheeler

Well...it's a black forest cake, so technically, there's fruit on it?

Mary Wen

Oliver

Oliver Wheeler

Mary

Mary Wen

Honestly, Oliver. You can't survive on chocolate alone.

Oliver Wheeler

But it's my birthday.

Mary Wen

Don't make me order a salad delivery to your apartment.

Oliver Wheeler

Jesus Christ. You ARE my dad.

Mary Wen

Does that mean I'll be a DILF? Or MILF rather? Because if so, I take that as a compliment.

Besides, better your dad than my mom, and someone has to make sure you're eating from all the categories on the food triangle.

Oliver Wheeler

I'm an adult, Mary. I can take care of myself. Don't worry. I made soup yesterday, and it has plenty of vegetables in it.

Also, did you just call my dad a DILF? Because gross.

Mary Wen

No, Robin did, but she's not wrong.

And good. I know you probably think I'm a nag, but it's just because I love you. You're my best friend, Ollie.

Oliver Wheeler

I know, and I appreciate it.

Even if it's mildly annoying.

Mary Wen

Oliver Wheeler

♡

Juliet Rios

April 22, 2020, 4:27 PM

Juliet Rios

Wow, you slept in late. Must have had some wild night last night, huh?

Also, you're welcome for the cake

Oliver Wheeler

Oh, yeah. I had a completely wild all-by-my-lonesome.

Juliet Rios

Sexy.

I'm almost a little jealous.

Oliver Wheeler

Okay, take that energy over to Mark...

Juliet Rios

Love you, mean it

Anna Reid

April 22, 2020, 4:26 PM

Anna Reid

Idea: are you up for a video call with everyone later?

Oliver Wheeler

Who's "everyone"?

Anna Reid

Just Ryan, Juliet, Mary, your dad, and me.

Oliver Wheeler

You talked to Mary?

Anna Reid

It was her idea.

Besides, we actually talk regularly. We really hit it off when she was in town last year for Christmas.

Oliver Wheeler

Oh, god. That's terrifying. She has no filter. What has she told you?

Anna Reid

Oh...LOTS. 😊

Oliver Wheeler

Fuck. I'm going to go crawl under the covers and die now.

Anna Reid

Awww, Ollie! I'm just teasing. She hasn't told me anything super mortifying.

Oliver Wheeler

I'm sorry. The party you are trying to reach is no longer available in the realm of the living. If you would like to contact the spirit of Oliver Wheeler, please consult a ouija board or dial

*774748 to talk to a representative.

Anna Reid

Wow.

Just be back from the spirit realm by 7 for your virtual birthday party.

Oliver Wheeler

O.....K......

Ezra

Wednesday Afternoon, April 23, 2020

Ryan Coleman
ASSOCIATE DIGITAL MARKETING MANAGER, Available - Video Capable

Wednesday, April 23, 2020

E.Beaumont (3:53 PM)

Is there a possibility that I might have my training taken over by a different editor?

R.Coleman (3:53 PM)

Why? What happened?

E.Beaumont (3:53 PM)

Well, I'm pretty sure at this point that Oliver straight up hates me, so I think it would just be easier on everyone if I didn't have to work so closely with him.

R.Coleman (3:54 PM)

Okay, hold on. There's no way that's possible. Because in the 6+ years that I've

known Oliver, he's never hated anyone.
Oliver is almost painfully nice to nearly
anyone.

Well, unless you give him an actual reason not to be, but even then he usually
forgives people.

So you're saying that I made him hate
me?

I've known him for a month and we've
barely spoken. How TF would I have
done something already to make him
hate me?

No that's not what I'm saying at all.

What happened?

Well, like I said the other day, we've
barely spoken since I've started. Our
first exchange out of the gate was
cold, and every exchange after that
has gotten worse. You know how I
said that instead of answering my
questions, he would just send me
more documents? Well after a while
he wouldn't even send any text with
it. Just a blank email with attachments.

Then when I finally get him on the
phone to go over PubPro, it was like
he was trying to get off as quickly as
possible. I barely had time to get a
word in.

And yesterday, I tried to be nice and

text him for his birthday, but he left me on read. Then today, when I messaged to ask how his birthday was, he ignored me again.

Like...what the hell did I do? I mean, I know sometimes I can come on a little strong, but I haven't even had the chance to make an ass out of myself yet!

R.Coleman (3:59 PM)

Okay, wow. That was a lot. But I'm a little surprised because that doesn't sound like Oliver at all.

Ezra huffed and grabbed his phone to call Ryan. It only rang once before Ryan answered. "Hey—"

"Look, I know you're probably going to just tell me I'm being paranoid, but I really don't think I am," Ezra said, skipping a greeting entirely.

"No, that's not what I was saying. I believe you. I'm just completely baffled. This really doesn't sound like the Oliver I know," Ryan said.

"Well, I'm glad you believe me because I think by now I'm a pretty good judge of when someone wants nothing to do with me. I got that vibe enough from my family, so I recognize it when I see it. And I'm getting that vibe from Oliver." Ryan started to say something, but Ezra continued over him. "Like, on our phone call, for example, he sounded a little bit like he was in pain, so I asked if he was alright—you know, because that's what a nice person would do—"

"He sounded like he was in pain?" Ryan asked.

"Yeah. When he answered, his voice was really gravelly, but I thought maybe that was just what his voice was like. But then, toward the end, he kinda let out this pained groan, and when I asked him if he was okay, he straight up hung up on me. He completely shut me down," Ezra said, emphasizing the last sentence.

"Shit, he was probably in the middle of a flare," Ryan muttered, but Ezra still caught it.

"A flare?"

"Shit, has he not mentioned those before?" Ryan asked.

"Ryan, he hasn't mentioned anything to me before. The guy seems intent on ignoring me," Ezra said.

"Okay, well, pretend I didn't say anything because I probably shouldn't be talking about Oliver's condition without him. I just thought he would have said something. He's pretty open about it, usually. Oliver has an autoimmune disorder. It's not bad all the time, but sometimes it flares up, and when it does, he's pretty miserable. He tries to power through it but…" Ryan trailed off.

"Oh," Ezra said, not really sure what else to say.

"Yeah," Ryan echoed. "It gets worse with stress. And with work being the way it has been and being quarantined, I don't think he's particularly coping well."

Ezra sighed. "That really sucks, but I guess it makes sense." And he meant that. He didn't know a lot about autoimmune disorders, but he knew when they acted up, they could be pretty uncomfortable. So a flare, as Ryan called it, explained Oliver's behavior toward the end of their call the other day. Ezra probably wouldn't have wanted to admit his pain to a coworker either. However, that didn't give him free rein to be a dick in every one of their interactions. He wouldn't say that to Ryan though. Instead, he tried to be more diplomatic.

"What doesn't make sense is him not trusting me to do the job you hired me to do. I've been here for over a month, and he only just started trusting me to sort the query box. Not even read manuscripts, just sort through emails. You'd think that for someone so stressed, he'd want someone to take some things off his plate. OH, and speaking of the query box—it's like no matter how long I spend working on it, it never makes a dent. It's a nightmare!" Ezra exclaimed. He was in full rant mode now.

Ryan laughed. "Yeah, you're right. The way we deal with queries is shit. I got so sick of trying to go through them when Dad first had me start working during the summers in college."

"There has got to be a better way to accept manuscript queries than to just get a bunch of emails sent to an email address. A form on the website or something so that we don't have to spend as much time combing through to find completed proposals, and we can spend our time actually reading the proposals to get more authors added to our client list."

"Well, since Dad's been encouraging me to make more executive decisions for the company, I'd say, try to come up with a better way to accept queries, because you're right. The way we deal with queries is shit," Ryan said. "It was fine when we were smaller and only had like 10 submissions a year, but we've been way past that for a long time."

"Okay, I'll try to figure something out," Ezra said, and his head already started turning with potential ideas. "Maybe I can use it as an olive branch with Oliver to make him not hate me."

"He probably doesn't hate you. But even so, an olive branch wouldn't hurt," Ryan said before letting out a long sigh. "Also, I know you didn't want me to talk to him before, but I think I kind of have to now because you're right. It's been a month, and he needs to let you do your job."

Ezra groaned. "Yeah, okay. I know you're right. I

was just hoping to avoid it."

"Yeah, I know."

Ezra sighed and shifted his laptop off his lap so he could stretch his legs.

"Alright, well, I have a meeting in five, so I have to go," Ryan said.

"Thanks, Ryan," Ezra said.

"No problem," he replied. "Oh, and remember not to bring up the autoimmune thing until he does. I don't need him hating me, too, for telling you."

"Hey!" Ezra protested. "You just said that he doesn't hate me!"

"Gotta go, bye!" Ryan teased.

7

Oliver

Thursday Afternoon, April 23, 2020

Ryan Coleman
ASSOCIATE DIGITAL MARKETING MANAGER, Available - Video Capable

Thursday, April 23, 2020

R.Coleman (4:30 PM)

Hey, I wanted to talk to you about Ezra.

O.Wheeler (4:30 PM)

What about Ezra?

R.Coleman (4:30 PM)

Well, he thinks you hate him.

O.Wheeler (4:31 PM)

I don't hate him?

R.Coleman (4:31 PM)

I didn't think you did, but he says you will barely give him the time of day. So what's that about? You're usually a pretty friendly person.

O.Wheeler (4:32 PM)

I'm just swamped. That line-editing job I picked up when Molly left unexpectedly has been giving me a lot of problems, and I still have all of those contracts to write up and manuscripts to read, so excuse me for not wanting to make small talk.

R.Coleman (4:32 PM)

That brings me to my second thing. Why are you still reading proposals and writing up contracts when that's Ezra's job?

O.Wheeler (4:33 PM)

I don't know if he's ready yet, and we can't afford to lose out on any potential contracts right now. We're only just now recovering from the shit storm that was the last commissioning editor.

R.Coleman (4:33 PM)

That's completely different. Ezra is actually a competent human. Pat was a dumbass.

O.Wheeler (4:35 PM)

We thought Pat was competent, too. Ezra doesn't have any experience, and last time we had someone that didn't have experience in the position, I ended up having to do both jobs and fix half of his mistakes.

R.Coleman (4:36 PM)

I'll give it to you that Pat caused a shit ton of problems for us, but that's because he lied on his resume. It's completely different.

Ezra isn't claiming to be able to do
things that he doesn't know how to do.
He isn't anything like Pat.

O.Wheeler (4:37 PM)

Isn't he, though? Neither of them was
qualified for the job but got it anyway,
and both of them carry themselves
with the same arrogant "I can do anything I want" attitude.

R.Coleman (4:38 PM)

How do you even know how Ezra carries
himself if you have barely said two
words to him?

O.Wheeler (4:38 PM)

You've told me plenty of stories about
him. Besides, I know his type.

R.Coleman (4:39 PM)

His type? Look, you've got Ezra completely wrong. Yes, both of us got up to
some absolutely idiotic things when we
were in school together, and those are
the stories I tell because they're the
most fun. But Ezra is actually a really
smart guy. He's freaking brilliant when
he applies himself.

O.Wheeler (4:40 PM)

"When he applies himself" being the
operative phrase there. How am I supposed to know if he's going to apply
himself to this? I mean, the guy spent
three years hopping around Europe on
a whim. Has he even held down an actual job before?

Oliver felt his phone buzz next to him, and he pinched

the bridge of his nose. With a sigh, he picked it up and answered it.

"Seriously, Oliver, what is going on with you?" Ryan said without even waiting for Oliver to say hello. "You are usually the first person to give someone a chance, and that's what this is for Ezra. A chance."

"I just know his type," Oliver said.

"'His type?'" Ryan parroted back. "What does that even mean?"

"The rich, entitled type," Oliver said, exasperated. "I encountered enough of them in college to know what they're like. Look, I know he's your best friend—"

"So that's what this is about," Ryan interrupted. "Look, I know Nick messed you up—"

"This isn't about Nick."

"So your prejudice against rich kids has nothing to do with your freshman-year roommate who totally fucked you over?" Ryan asked pointedly.

Oliver let out a huff. "Not rich kids. Trust-fund kids. There's a difference." Ryan was silent on the other end of the line for long enough that Oliver let out a resigned sigh. "Alright, fine, maybe that's where it originated, but every single other trust-fund kid I had to deal with in my classes confirmed it. They were all the same. They come from family money and have trust funds, so they have no work ethic because they've had everything handed to them."

"Alright, look, Ollie, I'll admit that normally you're right, but in this instance, you're wrong," Ryan said. "Ezra has been my friend for ten years, so I can tell you that you're wrong about him. Yes, he was privileged. He will be the first person to admit that, but he hasn't had it easy. I won't go into details because, it's not my place to spill his darkest secrets, but he's been dealt a shit hand. If anyone is going to understand that, I would think it would be you."

Oliver slid the laptop off of his legs, and instantly Fiona jumped up to replace it. He scratched her head and frowned to himself. Ryan was right. He would understand that.

"So yes, my dad gave Ezra a chance by giving him this job even though he doesn't have experience," Ryan continued. "But he sure as hell is going to be applying himself because he needs it—not just for the money, but because he needs to prove himself."

Oliver also understood that well—too well.

"I'm not saying the two of you need to be best friends or anything, but I love both of you, and you're both going to be involved in my wedding, so it would be nice if you at least got along. To say nothing of the fact that it would make working together a-hell-of-a-lot easier."

"You're right," Oliver said. "I judged Ezra before I even met him, and he's frequently proved me wrong, but I still acted like a dick."

"Well, I never said you were acting like a dick," Ryan said.

"No, but I was," Oliver admitted. "I'll make more of an effort."

"Thank you," Ryan said, sounding relieved. "And give Ezra more responsibility. He can handle it. Besides, you're overworked, and I'm starting to seriously worry about you burning out."

Oliver couldn't help smiling to himself. "Yeah, okay, Andrew."

"Hey!"

"But you're right. I'll start transferring some of what I've been doing over to Ezra and have him work with the other editors, as well."

Ryan thanked him again, then they said their goodbyes and hung up.

Oliver dropped the phone next to him on the couch

and looked at Fiona. "Are you going to get up so I can get back to work?" Fiona chirped and tucked her head under her paw, an adorably manipulative move he could never ignore. He smiled and scratched her neck. "Okay, fine, I'll take a break."

Friday Night, April 24, 2020

Oliver stared at the recipe on his phone in one hand while stirring the bubbling sauce. *Simmer on low while you wait for the pasta water to boil and for the pasta to cook.* He swiped out of the recipe and went back to his podcast, pressing play. He could figure out the rest of this recipe on his own.

Oliver rarely used a recipe—only when he needed to learn a new technique. He loved to cook, and he'd been doing it since he was tall enough to reach the stove with a step stool, so he was pretty good at it. But he'd never made vodka sauce before, so he wanted to get the order of ingredients right, especially since cream was involved. He'd gotten a pot out and started to boil it before beginning the sauce, since it sometimes took upwards of twenty minutes to boil, and it was finally bubbling, so he tore open the box of pasta and dumped it in. Then he ducked down to pull a colander out from the back of one of the bottom cabinets.

He loved his apartment for many reasons—its adjacency to Prospect Park, the built-in bookshelves, the walk-in closet that was big enough to turn into a makeshift bedroom, the amount of light it got—but the kitchen was not one of those reasons. It was a tiny galley kitchen, with only three weirdly deep cabinets, minimal counter space, a stove, and a fridge. He'd gotten creative with space by using a baker's cart, but it was still almost impossible to use. He was almost constantly bumping into something, especially when he had to get into the lower cabinet where he kept his cookware because he usually had to position himself halfway into the cabinet just to reach the back of it. Which was exactly what he had to do now in order to reach the colander which had fallen off the precarious stack of cookware he usually tried to keep stacked in the front half.

Just as he was pulling the colander free, his phone rang, and since he'd had it at full volume to hear his podcast, it rang loudly, causing him to jump and knock his head on the cabinet frame. "Fuck!" he shouted and brought his free hand to the back of his head. Grumbling and swearing, he tossed the colander onto the counter above him, then pulled himself up off the floor, using the counter for leverage. He looked at his phone.

INCOMING CALL - Ezra Beaumont

Oliver stared at the phone for a moment, noting the time. Why was Ezra calling him at 9:00 PM on a Friday? Why was he calling at all? Confused and still clutching the sore spot on the back of his head, Oliver accepted the call.

"Hello?"

"Hey, Oliver," Ezra's smooth voice rang through the phone. "Sorry to call you at—Jesus, it's later than I thought. I had something for work I wanted to run by you, but I didn't realize how late it was. It can just wait until Monday. You're probably busy."

After his conversation with Ryan yesterday, Oliver was a lot more aware of the anxiety in Ezra's voice. His stomach churned as the guilt set in. It was as if Ezra was afraid that he would bite his head off, and that wasn't the feeling he wanted to inspire in someone—

especially a coworker and Ryan's oldest friend. So he took a deep breath, let it out, and forced a more welcoming tone into his voice. "No, it's fine. I'm cooking dinner, but I can multitask."

"Oh, okay. Cool," Ezra said, still seemingly wary. "Do you always eat dinner this late?"

"Often. Sometimes, I get stuck on something, then I forget to eat until late," Oliver admitted. "Do you always work this late?"

"Yeah," Ezra said. "My cousin Josie is in law school and has a seven-year-old, and when I started, Ryan told me that hours were pretty flexible as long as work got done. So I'll work for a few hours in the morning, then take the afternoon and early evening to help her daughter with her schoolwork so she can study."

"That's really nice of you," Oliver said.

"I figure it's the least I can do since she and her husband gave me a place to stay," Ezra said, shrugging off the compliment.

There was a slightly awkward silence, so Oliver changed the subject. "So, you wanted to run something by me?"

"Right," Ezra said as if suddenly remembering. "It's about the way we handle query submissions. I think we can both agree that the submission mailbox is like a circle of hell. Specifically, the one where they're condemned to push boulders for the rest of their life."

Oliver let out a surprised laugh. He hadn't expected Ezra to have read Dante's *Inferno*, much less remember enough to make specific references to it. "God, that is such an accurate description. I feel like Sisyphus every time I open it."

"Right?" Ezra said with a laugh. "So, I started thinking: there has to be a better way to do this."

"I've been thinking the same thing. It's been on my long-term to-do list for months, but I haven't been able to do anything about it because I'm too busy putting out fires, and unfortunately query management isn't even smoldering." Speaking of fires, Oliver checked the noodles and found them to be done, so he flicked off the burner and turned to put the colander in the sink.

"Well, I have a potential solution, so maybe you'll be able to cross it off your list now," Ezra said. "Since our fundamental problem is sorting through emails to gather all the relevant information, I thought that maybe if we had some sort of form on our website, that might speed up the process."

"That's a good idea. Although, our IT department isn't the best with web design, seeing as it's not even an actual department. It's just a marketing guy with slightly more technical experience than anyone else in the company," Oliver said as he shoved the phone between his ear and his shoulder so his hands would be free. Then he grabbed a towel to protect his hands and turned back to the stove to get the pot.

"Yeah, that's what Ryan said. So I was going to look into doing it myself since I took a web design class one summer while at Trinity so I could stay in Ireland instead of coming back to the States. Then that way, someone would just have to copy the code into the website host. But then, I found a program that already—"

Oliver stopped short in front of the sink. "Did you say Trinity? Like as in Trinity Dublin?"

"Yeah, why—"

"No way!" Oliver blurted out. In his excitement, his hand slipped, sloshing some of the still-hot water. "Jesus! Shit! Fucking hell!" He flinched and dropped both the pot and his phone. Thankfully, he'd dropped the pot directly into the colander, so at least he didn't ruin his dinner. Sucking on the quickly reddening burn on his hand, he bent over to pick up his phone from the floor. No cracks, thank God.

"You alright, Oliver?" Ezra tentatively asked once Oliver brought the phone back to his ear.

"Fuck," Oliver whispered under his breath, staring at his hand. "Yeah, sorry, I'm apparently just a massive klutz today because I smacked my head on the underside of the cabinet right before you called, and now I just splashed scalding water on my hand."

"Do you need to go?"

"No, it's fine. I'm fine," Oliver said quickly. "I'm going to put you on speaker, though." He put his phone on speaker and set it on the counter while he got to work straining the pasta.

"So, I'm guessing you're familiar with my alma mater?" Ezra said with a slight hint of teasing in his voice.

"The school that's responsible for educating Bram Stoker, Oscar Wilde, and Samuel Beckett? Of course I am. You couldn't not be with a mother who was an English literature professor." With the pasta strained, Oliver flicked off the burner heating the sauce and turned to reach for a bowl from one of the upper cabinets.

Ezra laughed. "Well, you'll probably be disappointed to hear that despite me going to the same school, I'm not really that familiar with any of their work."

"Not even Dracula?" Oliver asked as he portioned out pasta and sauce.

"Okay, well, I've read Dracula, obviously. I don't think you can make it out of high school without reading Dracula," Ezra said defensively. "And I was supposed to read something by Beckett once, but honestly, I didn't much care for it. It just seems a little depressing to me. A little too... existentialist."

"How can you not care for Beckett?" Oliver asked incredulously. "He was instrumental in the Theatre of the Absurd!" He grabbed his bowl of pasta and carried it into his small living room to eat it on the couch. "I mean, *Waiting for Godot*? What an amazing commentary on the absurdity of existence, the uncertainty of time, and the purposelessness of life. Also, Beckett wasn't really an existentialist; he was just commonly labeled as one. And yeah, on the face, his works are a little depressive, but they're actually about despair and the will to survive despite that despair, even in the face of an uncomprehending and incomprehensible world. And you've read nothing from Wilde? *The Importance of Being Earnest*? *A Picture of Dorian Gray*?"

The other end of the line was silent, so Oliver carried on, gushing about the aestheticism of Oscar Wilde and the social commentary in *The Importance of Being Earnest*. After a few minutes, he stopped and felt his face heat.

"Sorry," he said, laughing nervously. "You probably don't care about any of that. Ryan tells me all the time that I get carried away talking about literature."

It wasn't just literature—he often got like this, overexcited about one of his unusual obsessions. He could talk for hours about baking or plants if someone let him. He often could keep it in check, especially around new people, but never when literature was involved. There was a reason he went into publishing.

Ezra chuckled, but it was strained—like it was forced or uncomfortable, not at all like the carefree laugh from a few moments ago. "No, it's fine," Ezra said. "You seem to know what you're talking about. Maybe if you'd been at Trinity with me, I'd have read more."

"Still, you didn't really call to hear me talk about a bunch of dead Irish authors. You were saying something about a query form?" Oliver prompted, then took a bite of his pasta, which wasn't as hot as he would have liked since he'd abandoned it for his rant.

"Right, yeah," Ezra said, sounding absentminded. There was a brief pause before he continued. "So I was doing some research on some other independent presses and literary agents and found Query Manager. It's free, and it has everything we'd need. The title, author, genre, and word count would be front and center instead of us having to search for it. It keeps track of things like if someone has queried us before and when. We'd also be able to send out automatic rejections or requests for the full manuscript."

"Wow, that sounds a hell of a lot easier. You said it's free?"

"Yeah, and I looked at the approval criteria. I'm pretty sure we meet all of it."

"Well, I think it sounds like a great idea. We'll need Andrew's approval before continuing with it, but I think he'll go for it." Oliver took another bite of his pasta.

"Okay. So I guess I'll send you the information so you can pitch it to Andrew?" Ezra asked.

Oliver swallowed and set his fork down. Ryan had told him to give Ezra more responsibility. This would be the perfect opportunity. "Actually, could you do it? It was your idea, and that author who's been giving me a hard time is supposed to get me his latest draft on Monday, so I'll probably be busy with that." Ezra didn't answer right away, so he continued. "Just send him the information, and tell him everything you told me."

"Yeah, I can do that," Ezra said after another brief pause. "Should I say I ran it by you, as well?"

"It wouldn't hurt," Oliver said. "When you get approval, you can start setting it up and just let me know if you need anything from me."

"Okay, will do," Ezra said. "Well, I'll let you get to your dinner."

"Thanks," Oliver said. He picked up his fork again and started pushing his pasta around. "Also, thank you for coming up with this idea. Now I'll be able to clear one of the million Post-its off my wall."

Ezra laughed, and Oliver smiled to himself. "Thanks, Oliver. Have a good weekend."

"You, too."

8

Ezra

Friday Night, April 23, 2020

Ryan Coleman

April 23, 2020, 9:45 PM

Ryan Coleman

So based on the text I just got from Oliver, I take it the idea went over well.

Ezra Beaumont

He texted you?

Ryan Coleman

Well, I kinda laid into him a bit, so I'm glad it took.

Ezra Beaumont

You did? I mean, yeah, it did. He told me to pitch it to your dad and get it set up when I get approval.

But what did you say to him?

Ryan Coleman

It's not that important. Just as long as

he's stopped being a dick.

Ezra Beaumont

It was definitely a shift. We actually had a bit of a non-work-related conversation, which was unexpected. Nice though.

Ryan Coleman

Good. I knew you two would hit it off if given a chance.

Ezra Beaumont

Yeah

Ryan Coleman

What?

Ezra Beaumont

Alright, I'm fully aware this is going to sound completely crazy

Like full-blown insanity

And you're probably going to either murder me or want to have my head examined

Ryan Coleman

Jesus Christ, spit it out

Ezra Beaumont

I'm TRYING

I'm still processing over here

Ryan Coleman

Processing WHAT? What happened?

Ezra Beaumont

Alright

Okay

Um, I think I might possibly like Oliver

Ryan Coleman

Well, he is a likable person

Wait, like, as in LIKE?

Ezra Beaumont

I don't know, but, yeah, maybe.

Ryan Coleman

So you're telling me you have a crush on my and Anna's best friend.

Ezra Beaumont

It's not a crush. I'm not twelve.

Okay, maybe it's a crush. It's very confusing, given I thought he hated my guts not even an hour ago.

Ryan Coleman

Well, the line between hate and love is very thin or else the enemies-to-lovers trope wouldn't be so popular.

Side note: if you come across any manuscripts with enemies to lovers while you're reading through queries, move those to the top of the list.

But back to Oliver.

What happened?

Ezra Beaumont

Alright, so after helping Willow with her homework and dealing with dinner, I got back to work on the query thing, and I finally figure it out, so without thinking or checking the time, I call Oliver. I catch him making dinner, so I tell him I can just talk to him Monday, but he keeps me on the phone, saying it was fine, which is already a better interaction by a mile.

So I'm telling him about my idea, and for once, he's actually talking to me,

like full sentences and not at all in
that clipped tone he has.

Ryan Coleman

I'm familiar with the tone.

Ezra Beaumont

Right, so we're talking, making jokes
about Dante's Inferno, and I mention
Trinity. Then, suddenly, and I mean literally out of nowhere, he lets out a
stream of curse words because he's
still cooking and he burned himself on
something, or dropped something, I
don't know.

Ryan Coleman

Oh yeah, Oliver may look like a cinnamon roll and a librarian had a baby, but
he swears like a sailor.

Ezra Beaumont

Well, that sounds completely endearing and doesn't help my crush at all.
Thanks for that.

Ryan Coleman

Sorry, continue.

Although you've seen pictures of him.
It's a spot-on description.

Ezra Beaumont

Actually, I don't think I have, thinking
about it. Or if I have, I don't remember
what he looks like.

But NOT the point.

Until then, he's still been a little reserved, but then he does a complete
180. When most people hear I went to
school in Dublin, they ask me if I was

at pubs every night or if I kissed the Blarney Stone, which is not even in Dublin. It's in Cork. But no. Oliver goes on about these authors that went to Trinity, and he sounds so passionate about it. One minute he's screaming obscenities, and the next he's going on about symbolism in Waiting for Godot.

Ryan Coleman

Oh my God

You fell into the trap.

Ezra Beaumont

Trap?

Ryan Coleman

And from what it sounds like, you fell hard. I haven't seen someone fall this deeply into the trap since our junior year of college.

Ezra Beaumont

What on Earth are you going on about? Is this a thing Oliver does?

Ryan Coleman

Not knowingly.

He pulls people in with his nearly infectious enthusiasm for the written word. I swear, in college, Ollie had more girls after him than the guys on the football team. No one was safe from the enthralling nature of the trap.

Again, not that he noticed. He's kind of oblivious.

Anyway, we started calling it "Ollie's Literary Trap." And it looks like you fell into it.

Oh, wait until I tell Anna and Jules.

Ezra Beaumont

DON'T YOU DARE

Ryan Coleman

Were you grinning like an idiot?

Ezra Beaumont

Maybe

Ryan Coleman

And did you stay silent long enough, just listening to him go on, that he stopped himself and apologized for babbling like an idiot?

Ezra Beaumont

I couldn't help it! It was the most he'd ever said to me. And dammit, it was just so endearing.

And I don't even like Beckett!

It took me a few seconds to catch back up once he stopped talking, too. I completely forgot why I'd called.

Ryan Coleman

Yup. Sounds about right.

Ezra Beaumont

In your infinite wisdom, how long are people usually stuck in "Ollie's Literary Trap"?

Ryan Coleman

Not very long. Just don't get into another conversation with him about literature.

Ezra Beaumont

Ryan

We work at a freaking publishing

company. That's going to be impossible.

Ryan Coleman

Welp. Then...You're doomed?

Ezra Beaumont

I hate you.

End of April 2020

Oliver Wheeler
COPYEDITOR, Available - Video Capable

Monday, April 27, 2020

E.Beaumont (12:34 PM)

Hey, I don't know if you saw Andrew's
reply, but I got his approval for Query
Manager, so I applied for it.

O.Wheeler (12:59 PM)

I did. That's great. I would have messaged and said something sooner, but
I've been going over the final structural
edits for that book from hell.

Do you know how long it will take for us
to be approved for an account?

E.Beaumont (1:01 PM)

I don't know. I'm able to experiment
with it a little, but I think they need to
verify that we meet the requirements
before I can really start building the
form and adding tags and automated
responses and whatnot. So is there
something I can do in the meantime?

Also, can you send me some examples

of rejection emails so I can start drafting those for the auto reply?

O.Wheeler (1:05 PM)

Yeah, I've got plenty of rejection emails,
but let me dig through my emails to find
some that I sent requesting the full
manuscript. It's been...a while since I've
gotten to send one of those.

E.Beaumont (1:06 PM)

Are all the submissions really that
bad?

O.Wheeler (1:07 PM)

Not all of them. I also haven't had a lot
of room for new projects. A lot actually
have promise, but simply weren't ready
to be queried yet. If that's the case, I
usually send a slightly different email
with comments on what they could im-
prove.

I'll send you some of those emails, too.

E.Beaumont (1:07 PM)

Thanks, I appreciate it.

O.Wheeler (1:09 PM)

No problem. In the meantime, if you
want to read through the queries still in
our email box, that would be great.

E.Beaumont (1:09 PM)

I can do that. Any tips?

O.Wheeler (1:11 PM)

I usually send rejections/requests in
batches, so I'll move them into corre-
sponding folders as I read, then draft
several emails at a time.

E.Beaumont (1:11 PM)

Makes sense.

O.Wheeler (1:12 PM)

For now, leave the requests to me though, since I have a better idea of what we can actually pursue. So you can just sort those into a maybe pile, and I'll sort from there. But you can send rejection emails without checking in with me. I feel you'll easily be able to determine what we won't want to pursue.

E.Beaumont (1:12 PM)

Okay, that also makes sense.

Thanks, Oliver!

O.Wheeler (1:13 PM)

You're welcome

Wednesday, April 29, 2020

E.Beaumont (2:30 PM)

Okay, I think I got everything set up as best I could. I went through the inbox and input all the unprocessed queries into the system so we can deal with them easier.

O.Wheeler (2:35 PM)

Oh, wow, really? I mean, it will definitely make things easier, but that must have taken ages.

E.Beaumont (2:37 PM)

It wasn't too bad. I put the TV on in the background. Also, I ignored the ones that didn't follow our website's instructions, which was over half of them.

Do you want me to give you a virtual tour of everything, or just the login so you can look at it on your own time?

O.Wheeler (2:38 PM)

I think a virtual tour may be better. Would you be comfortable presenting at the weekly staff meeting tomorrow so the other editors are on the same page?

E.Beaumont (2:47 PM)

Oh, yeah, I can do that.

O.Wheeler (2:47 PM)

Great.

Also, don't worry. You'll do fine.

9

Ezra

May 2020

Ezra Beaumont

"She was always in the back of his mind, like a bruised ankle from a razor scooter that he'd kicked in haste."

Oliver Wheeler 📚

I'm sorry, what?

Ezra Beaumont

It's my favorite line from the proposals I read today.

Or I guess I should say my favorite bad line from the proposals I read today.

Oliver Wheeler 📚

Oh, thank God

Ezra Beaumont

Worried for a moment?

Oliver Wheeler 🗒

A smidge, yeah

Ezra Beaumont

Haha no need to worry, it's already in the reject pile

May 7, 2020, 7:43 PM

Ezra Beaumont

"She fiddled with the seam of her dress with anxiety ridden phalanges."

I really thought you were exaggerating when you said how bad most of these were.

Oliver Wheeler 🗒

I wish I was.

Ezra Beaumont

This manuscript reads like the person went through line by line with a synonym finder. I can't even figure out what some of these sentences used to be.

Like, it's okay. You can just say fingers.

Oliver Wheeler 🗒

Agreed. Sometimes simple is better.

May 8, 2020, 7:15 PM

Ezra Beaumont

"And in that moment, Eric could've sworn the pigeon spoke to him."

Oliver Wheeler 🗒

What did it say?

Ezra Beaumont

No idea. The sample pages end with
that line.

Oliver Wheeler 🖥

Why would you leave me on this cliff-
hanger?

Ezra Beaumont

Listen, if I have to suffer knowing that
I will never know what the pigeon
said, you will, too.

Misery loves company, Oliver

May 11, 2020, 5:23 PM

Ezra Beaumont

I've officially started delving into the
thrillers, and I'm so glad I did.

"Samson waddled forward, careful not
to get his flipper in the puddle of vermillion hemoglobin and plasma leak-
ing out of the body of the mayor that
laid before him in the middle of the
floor."

Oliver Wheeler 🖥

I'm almost afraid to ask, but by flipper
they mean…?

Ezra Beaumont

He's a penguin.

Oliver Wheeler 🖥

And is the mayor also a penguin?

Ezra Beaumont

Yes.

Oliver Wheeler 🖥

Is everyone a penguin?

Ezra Beaumont

I don't think so. The mayor's secretary seems to be human. I think this might be a Detective Pikachu situation.

Can we request the full manuscript because I think I need to know if the hardened penguin detective learns to love.

Oliver Wheeler 📖

There's a romantic subplot?

Ezra Beaumont

According to the pitch

In all seriousness though, this one is actually pretty good. Yeah, the premise is a little campy, but the writing isn't bad.

Oliver Wheeler 📖

Can I direct you back to "the puddle of vermillion hemoglobin and plasma"?

Ezra Beaumont

I thought that was the most profound bit. Very vivid imagery.

Oliver Wheeler 📖

Please tell me you're screwing with me

Ezra Beaumont

A little

Oliver Wheeler 📖

Oh, thank fuck.

May 13, 2020, 6:15 PM

Ezra Beaumont

"The penguin stopped, then stared

into my soul as if it knew my inner-
most secret."

Oliver Wheeler 🗎

Are we still on the penguin detective
novel?

Ezra Beaumont

Nope!

Oliver Wheeler 🗎

You're telling me there is another book
about penguins.

Ezra Beaumont

Yes

Oliver Wheeler 🗎

God help us

May 14, 2020, 7:42 PM

Ezra Beaumont

"It's like my momma always said: Life
is like a box of saltines. Crummy,
bland, and only good for soup."

Oliver Wheeler 🗎

Well, that's a whole ass mood.

Ezra Beaumont

Is it? I've been staring at this line for
30 minutes and I still can't parse out
what it's supposed to mean.

Oliver Wheeler 🗎

Life sucks unless there's soup, which is
a mood.

Ezra Beaumont

Soup fan?

Oliver Wheeler 🗎

Soup can fix everything.

Ezra Beaumont

I'll take your word for it haha

Oliver Wheeler

Wait, don't tell me you're one of those soup-hating people.

Ezra Beaumont

I don't hate soup, I just never eat it outside of being sick.

Oliver Wheeler

See, that's your mistake. Soup is an all-the-time food. There are so many varieties for any occasion. Cream-based, broth-based, cold, hot, noodles, veggies, etc. etc.

Ezra Beaumont

Well, what is your favorite soup?

Oliver Wheeler

Probably French onion. It's really simple to make, but it took me forever to master because I was always too impatient when caramelizing the onions.

Ezra Beaumont

I've never had it, but I'll trust your judgement.

If I try it and hate it though, it's on you.

Oliver Wheeler

Where do you live?

Ezra Beaumont

Astoria. Why?

Oliver Wheeler

Order from Cafe Triskell. It's the best French onion soup in Astoria. It won't be as good delivered as it is in the

restaurant, but seeing as we still can't
go out to eat...

Ezra Beaumont

How do you even know that?

And I know. I really thought this would
be over by now. I miss restaurants.

Oliver Wheeler 🗐

Me, too. I'm kind of a food person. I love
to eat out, cook, and bake. Basically, if
there's food involved, I'm happy.

Ezra Beaumont

Noted. So if I ever need a restaurant or
recipe recommendations, I can come
to you?

Oliver Wheeler 🗐

If you don't mind wallet-friendly, hole-
in-the-wall restaurants, then yes.

Ezra Beaumont

Mind them? I prefer them.

And so does Josie, so maybe I'll convince her to order from Cafe Triskell
tomorrow. We usually order takeaway
once a week anyway.

Oliver Wheeler 🗐

Well, let me know what you think.

Ezra Beaumont

Will do 😊

May 15, 2020, 8:35 PM

Ezra Beaumont

Okay, you were right. Soup is not only
good for when you're sick.

Oliver Wheeler 🖥
So you liked it?

Ezra Beaumont
I did 😊

Oliver Wheeler 🖥
I'm glad

May 18, 2020, 8:17 PM

Ezra Beaumont
"I'll say this: she may be completely tone deaf, but she has an ass that sings like an angel."

Oliver Wheeler 🖥
Oh, no, have you started in on the romance novels?

Also, how does an ass "sing like an angel?"

Ezra Beaumont
I have. Get ready, because if today is any sign, there will be some doozies

Oliver Wheeler 🖥
I'll be waiting with bated breath.

Ezra Beaumont
Hopefully I won't disappoint.

Also, to answer your question, I have no idea.

May 20, 2020, 6:43 PM

Ezra Beaumont
"And then they had sex."

Oliver Wheeler 🖥
Is that it?

Ezra Beaumont

"And it was awesome."

Oliver Wheeler 📇

Wow. That's a whole new level of fade-to-black.

Ezra Beaumont

You have to give them points for simplicity I guess.

Also, "fade-to-black"?

Oliver Wheeler 📇

It describes the level at which intimacy is described in romance. There's a lot of different terminology revolving around romance novels.

Ezra Beaumont

Well, I guess I know what I'm researching tomorrow.

May 21, 2020, 7:53 PM

Ezra Beaumont

"Her breasts smiled as he walked into the room. God, he was handsome."

Oliver Wheeler 📇

No. Just...no.

Breasts are not capable of independent movement.

Ezra Beaumont

They aren't? Because in the ones I've read today, they have also "lunged", "quivered with anticipation", and "leapt".

Oliver Wheeler 📇

The lack of knowledge that some people

have about anatomy scares me.

Ezra Beaumont

Me, too, Oliver. Me, too.

Also, you were right. The bookish world has its own language. So many acronyms.

Oliver Wheeler 📇

Welcome to publishing 😊

May 22, 2020, 11:53 PM

Ezra Beaumont

"She made his heart beat faster than Uncle Glenn's couch-on-wheels, and the memory of choking on bugs while driving it seemed an apt description for the way his breath caught in his throat."

Ezra's phone buzzed before he could even set it down to continue reading.

Oliver Wheeler 📇

Well, that's definitely...an image.

Actually, that's a very familiar image.

Why are you reading rejected manuscripts in the middle of the night on a Friday? Why are you working at all?

Shit, Oliver had texted back. He hadn't expected Oliver to actually text him back. They'd never texted late at night before. And Ezra was tipsy. Tipsy texting the person you mildly fancy at midnight was probably a recipe for disaster, but that didn't stop Ezra from answering.

Ezra Beaumont

Feeling restless, so I thought that maybe getting tipsy and reading rejected manuscripts might keep me entertained.

I thought I'd just text so you woke up to this wonderful, provoking image of Uncle Glenn's couch. Sorry if I woke you up.

Oliver Wheeler

You didn't. I can't sleep, so I thought I'd at least try to get some work done.

Ezra Beaumont

Working in the middle of the night? A little hypocritical of you, dear Ollie.

Oliver Wheeler

Ha. Ha. I'm working on my own terrible manuscript, not publishing stuff.

Shit. Pretend I didn't say that.

Ezra Beaumont

Wait, you're a writer?

Oliver Wheeler

I don't really broadcast it, but yeah, I am.

Or trying to be, anyway. It's what I went to NYU for, but then I got into publishing, and I've had the worst writing block for the past six months so it's slow going.

Ezra Beaumont

Well, thank you for telling me about it. I'll keep the intel under lock and key.

Oliver Wheeler

I appreciate that

Ezra Beaumont

I'd love to hear about the book, too, if you're up to sharing.

Oliver Wheeler

Maybe once I've got a better handle on how to get myself out of this plot hole I've written myself into.

Ezra Beaumont

No worries 😊

So, your degree is in Creative Writing, I'm guessing?

Oliver Wheeler

My minor is, at least. I did generic English as my major. Thought it would be more easily marketable career-wise.

Ezra Beaumont

Yeah, that makes sense

Oliver Wheeler

Oh, that reminds me. I meant to ask what you studied at Trinity.

Ezra Beaumont

Well, for my first semester, I studied business, but it bored me out of my mind, so I switched to history. I also got the Trinity equivalent to a double minor (because they don't exactly have a major/minor system like they do in America) in photography and anthropology.

Oliver Wheeler

Really?

Ezra Beaumont

Is that surprising?

Oliver Wheeler 🗐

No, sorry

Well, a double minor is a little surprising because that sounds like a lot in addition to a major

Ezra Beaumont

I needed something to occupy my summers so I could stay in Ireland full-time.

Oliver Wheeler 🗐

It's just that Ryan said we'd have a lot in common. My dad is a history professor at Portland State.

Ezra Beaumont

What's his area of focus?

Oliver Wheeler 🗐

Medieval England.

Ezra Beaumont

Oh, my second favorite period behind the Italian Renaissance.

Oliver Wheeler 🗐

Why the Italian Renaissance?

Ezra Beaumont

I think it's mostly the art. It was just such a fervent period of cultural growth. I can't really explain it, but it speaks to me.

Oliver Wheeler 🗐

I can see that. So I'm guessing you spent a lot of time in Rome?

Ezra Beaumont

Not as much as I would have liked, but yeah. That's actually where I was when all of this shit started going down. Thankfully Ryan could get me out and back here before things got too bad.

So, your dad is a history professor, and I remember you saying your mom is an English Literature professor.

Oliver Wheeler

Was, yeah.

She passed away 6 years ago. But that was how they met. Teaching.

Ezra Beaumont

Oh, I'm sorry.

Oliver Wheeler

Thanks.

Ezra Beaumont

Was your name her doing, then?

Oliver Wheeler

What?

Ezra Beaumont

Oliver Twist. I figured English literature...

Oliver Wheeler

Actually, yeah. No one usually picks up on that.

Ezra Beaumont

My nanny read it to me a lot as a kid.

Oliver Wheeler

You had a nanny?

Ezra Beaumont

More like an au pair, but yeah. At least until I went to boarding school, which is when I met Ryan.

Ezra stared down at the screen, his lower lip pulled between his teeth. A few minutes had passed without a response, and as much as he hated to admitted it, that set him on edge. Was he bothering Oliver? He'd said he was up late because he was writing. Was that a subtle hint that maybe Ezra should leave him alone?

He tapped out the question before he could stop himself.

> Sorry, am I distracting you? Should I leave you to write?

Oliver Wheeler 🗐

No, sorry, my best friend Mary was texting me with her nightly reminder to tell me to "go the fuck to sleep", which I should probably do.

Ezra Beaumont

> I guess I should try to sleep too.

Oliver Wheeler 🗐

Thank you for keeping me company while I struggle through plot holes, though.

Ezra couldn't help smiling. **I can't think of a better way to spend a Friday night.** He read the text back, then immediately erased it. Too strong. **Always**. He erased that, too.

Ezra Beaumont

> Of course. I'll happily keep you company any time.
>
> Goodnight, Ollie

Oliver Wheeler 🗐

I'd like that.

Night, Ezra.

May 26, 2020, 6:57 PM

Ezra Beaumont

"And suddenly, his flesh pillows were on her ear lobe, and she was melting into his touch."

Oliver Wheeler 🗐

Was that supposed to be arousing? Because I'm just a little scared.

Ezra Beaumont

Right? Again, this is one of those situations when synonyms are not your friend.

Oliver Wheeler 🗐

I'd argue that in this case, synonyms were, in fact, the enemy.

Ezra Beaumont

Hahaha

I think I'd have to agree.

May 27, 2020, 8:15 PM

Ezra Beaumont

"A tempest of tears fell from her eyes. 'I wish I'd never met you,' she screamed."

Oliver Wheeler 🗐

Okay, that one isn't actually that bad.

Ezra Beaumont

I did actually like the alliteration of "tempest of tears"

It's more the context that made it bad.

Oliver Wheeler 🗐

Who is she screaming at?

Ezra Beaumont

*what

Oliver Wheeler 🗐

Oh no.

Ezra Beaumont

She is, in fact, screaming at a cat

Oliver Wheeler 🗐

What did the cat do to her?

Ezra Beaumont

I'm not really sure. The book opened with that then flashed back in time 6 months.

Oliver Wheeler 🗐

Oh, flash-forward hooks are one of my least favorite tropes in writing.

Also, you may appreciate the impeccable timing of my cat, who jumped in my lap the moment you mentioned a cat as if she somehow had a sixth sense we were talking about a cat that wasn't her.

Ezra Beaumont

Aww, you have a cat?

Oliver Wheeler 🗐

Fiona. She's five. I adopted her from an elderly neighbor right after graduation. Or, rather, she sort of adopted me. Fiona kept escaping my neighbor's apartment to follow me home, then the neighbor had to move into an assisted living that didn't allow pets, and her son hates cats, so I got full custody.

I still occasionally send Ms. Valerie pictures.

Ezra Beaumont

Okay, well that's one of the cutest things I've ever heard.

What kind of cat is Fiona?

Are there types of cats? Or is that just a dog thing?

Oliver Wheeler 📧

There are breeds of cats. Most people don't bother finding out like they do with dogs, but Ms. Valerie did one of those pet DNA things. Fiona is a Himalayan rag-doll mix.

Do you want to see a picture of her?

Ezra Beaumont

Yes!

Oliver Wheeler 📧

[picture message]

Ezra Beaumont

Holy shit she's huge.

Oliver Wheeler 📧

Yeah, that's the rag-doll. They're fucking huge and very floppy, hence the name.

Ezra Beaumont

She's also gorgeous. Majestic as hell.

Oliver Wheeler 📧

I will tell her you think so.

Ezra Beaumont

Thank you 😊

May 28, 2020, 6:47 PM

Ezra Beaumont

"He stood there, mouth gaped open, his velvet wrapped steel pulsing as he watched her undress."

I think it's officially time I stepped away from the romance novels. I'm all for a good euphemism, but I think "velvet wrapped steel" is where I draw the line.

Oliver Wheeler

You think that's bad? I once read a book set in a magic school. There were so many uses of the word "wand".

And this wasn't for work. This was an already published novel.

Ezra Beaumont

Well, I guess both are magical wood...

Oliver Wheeler

Jesus fuck

I just choked on my tea. Fiona was not pleased.

Ezra Beaumont

Sorry!

Couldn't help it. It was right there.

Also, my apologies to Fiona.

Oliver Wheeler

No, it was a good joke. And I needed her to get up so I could refresh my tea, anyway.

Ezra Beaumont

Well, then I'm glad I could assist.

So, do you read a lot? Outside the job, I mean.

Oliver Wheeler 📚

Not as much as I'd like to, but more so now with the quarantine. My TBR pile has been getting blissfully smaller over the past two months.

Ezra Beaumont

I know what you mean.

My to-be-watched list is getting pro-gressively shorter. I didn't get around to watching a lot of television while I was abroad, but now I've got nothing but time.

What are you reading now?

Oliver Wheeler 📚

A Dance with Dragons.

Ezra Beaumont

That's the book series that Game of Thrones was based on, right?

I've been debating whether to watch it.

Oliver Wheeler 📚

How have you never watched Game of Thrones? You have to be one of the few people on the planet who hasn't.

Ezra Beaumont

Hey!

Like I said, I haven't had a lot of time for the past 6 years to sit and watch television.

Oliver Wheeler 📚

Ah yes, you were too busy traipsing

around Europe, staying in fancy hotels
and partying in bars and clubs. 😊

Ezra Beaumont

Actually, judgy pants, I stayed mostly
in hostels or couch surfed. I'll give you
the bars and clubs thing, but I was
bartending at them so I wasn't actually partying.

I was trying to stay off the grid.

Oliver Wheeler

"Judgy pants"?

Ezra Beaumont

How did I know THAT was what you'd
pick out of that sentence?

In my defense, I spend most of my day
with a 7-year-old.

So is the show worth watching?

Oliver Wheeler

Overall, I'd say so. The first 6 seasons
are outstanding. And season 8 had one
of the best episodes, in my opinion. The
rest of the season is complete shit,
though.

Ezra Beaumont

I'll have to add it to my list then.

Once I finish Riverdale with Josie,
that is.

Oliver Wheeler

You mean the show meant for teenagers
on the CW?

Ezra Beaumont

SO JUDGEMENTAL.

10

Ezra

Friday Afternoon, May 29, 2020

Ryan Coleman

May 29, 2020, 3:22 PM

Ryan Coleman

Hey, so Anna and I did a lot of thinking. It doesn't look like the restrictions for events are going to be lifted in time for August, and we don't want to risk anyone getting sick or anything. So we're postponing the wedding until next year.

Ezra Beaumont

God, Ryan, I'm so sorry.

I mean, it makes complete sense and it was probably the right decision, but fuck, that really sucks.

What do you need me to do?

I can help reach out to vendors if you

need me to. Or literally anything else you need.

Ryan Coleman

Thanks. Juliet (Anna's MOH) is taking care of a lot, which is good because Anna isn't in the right place to be dealing with it right now.

She helped with a lot of the planning anyway.

Ezra Beaumont

How is Anna?

Ryan Coleman

Anna held it together while she was on the phone with her parents and then with Juliet, but the second she hung up...

Ezra Beaumont

Poor Anna-Banana. Give her a hug for me.

Also, give Juliet my number in case she needs help.

Ryan Coleman

I will for both.

Ezra Beaumont

And how are you doing?

Ryan Coleman

I'm okay. Anna's taking it a lot harder than I am.

I mean, I'm upset, don't get me wrong. But we've also been agonizing over this decision for a month now, ever since the stay-at-home order was put in place. So part of me is relieved?

Like, at least we've decided, you know?

Ezra Beaumont

Yeah, that makes sense. I'd be upset too. But you have a point. At least now you know what's going on.

Fuck, I hate this for you guys.

Ryan Coleman

Yeah, I hate it too.

I was just so excited to get married this year. I mean, I knew after our first date that I wanted to marry her.

Ezra Beaumont

Yeah, I remember that phone call. You were absolutely smitten.

Ryan Coleman

Still am.

God and 4 years later I get so close to being able to do just that, and a stupid pandemic gets in the way.

Fuck.

Okay, maybe I'm not handling this as well as I thought.

Ezra Beaumont

Who says you can't still get married this year?

I mean, you can't have the big fancy reception this year, but you can still get married. At some point small gatherings of people will probably be okay.

Ryan Coleman

You think?

Ezra Beaumont

Yeah.

Everyone would understand.

I'm sure lots of people are doing the same thing.

You can still stand up in front of the priest and say your vows, and just have the big party next year when everything's calmed down.

Ryan Coleman

Well, technically the original plan was to stand up in front of Oliver, but I get your point.

I'll propose the idea to Anna once she wakes up. After she calmed down a bit she passed out in my lap.

I couldn't care less if we had a big ceremony as long as I get to call her my wife.

Ezra Beaumont

Make sure you say that when you propose the idea.

Oliver was going to officiate?

Ryan Coleman

Yeah. Anna wanted him to be a bridesman and I wanted him as a groomsman, so he offered to officiate instead as a compromise.

Ezra Beaumont

Of course he did.

That is such an Oliver thing to do.

Ryan Coleman

You're still nursing that crush, aren't you?

Ezra Beaumont

...Maybe.

> But we can talk about that later.

Ryan Coleman

I don't mind. Honestly, a distraction
would be kind of welcome right now.

Wait, I think Anna is waking up.

Ezra Beaumont

> No, it's fine. Go comfort your fiancée
> and good luck with your second pro-
> posal.

"Archie, did you hear me?"

"What?" Ezra looked up from his phone and blinked at Willow, who sat on the floor in front of the TV.

"I asked if you could help me with this." Willow used the controller to gesture at the TV, where Link was standing at the entrance of a glowing blue-and-orange shrine. "I've died twice trying to beat it."

"Oh, yeah. I'll see what I can do. Sorry, I was—"

"Texting," she finished for him, teasing. Then she frowned. "You look sad. Why do you look sad? Normally when you're on your phone, you're smiling."

Ezra half smiled at that. Usually, if he was on his phone, he was smiling, because usually when he was on his phone, he was texting Oliver. Josie had commented on it once or twice, but he didn't realize it was so obvious that even Willow picked up on it.

His slight smile faded, then he sighed. "I am a little sad," he admitted because while Willow was only seven, that didn't mean that he couldn't talk to her like she was an adult—at least to a certain extent.

"Why?"

"That was my best friend Ryan. He's the one who's supposed to be getting married this year, but for the same reason you're going to school online, he and his fiancée Anna had to postpone the wedding," he explained. "So I'm sad for them."

"That sucks," Willow said, and it took everything Ezra had not to burst out laughing at her frankness. He had a feeling that she wasn't supposed to use that word, but Josie and Ted weren't around to correct her, and she wasn't wrong.

"Yeah, it does," he echoed.

Willow scrunched her face into what Ezra learned was her thinking face—which looked eerily similar to Josie's thinking face. "They should get married anyway," she said after a moment. "Mommy and Daddy didn't have a big wedding."

"That's what I told them, too," Ezra said. "I'll tell Ryan and Anna you agree."

Willow nodded, then got up off the floor to join Ezra on the couch. She handed him the controller. "Here. Video games usually cheer me up when I'm sad."

He smirked at her. "You just want me to beat the shrine for you."

"Things can have two purposes," she said, and Ezra laughed.

"Well, I can't argue with that logic."

One completed shrine and some light Hyrule exploration later, Ezra's phone buzzed in his lap. He looked down to see Oliver's name flash on the screen. His stomach flipped. Oliver had never texted him first. He was always the one to instigate their conversations with his bad query quotes.

Ezra handed the controller back to Willow. "Here, you can take over for a bit," he said, then picked up his phone.

Oliver Wheeler 🖥

May 29, 2020, 4:03 PM

Oliver Wheeler 🖥

Hey, so I'm guessing Ryan has probably talked to you about the wedding.

Ezra Beaumont

Yeah, he did. He texted you too?

Oliver Wheeler 🖥

Juliet called me. She's already putting me to work.

Ezra Beaumont

This sucks. I hate this for them.

Oliver Wheeler 🖥

I know. Me, too.

Ezra Beaumont

What is Juliet having you do? Is it anything I can help with?

I feel useless. I wasn't around at all during the planning part so I just want something to do now to help.

Oliver Wheeler 🖥

Well, unless you know calligraphy, I'm not sure you'd be of much help. Juliet's got me drafting the "change the dates" since I was the one who did the original invitations.

Ezra Beaumont

Wait, those were you?

They were so good!

Did you just do the calligraphy or did you do the artwork for it too?

Oliver Wheeler 🖥

Art too, but it's not that big of a deal. It

was just a bit of watercolor.

Ezra Beaumont

So you're a writer and an artist? Anything else I should know about you?

Oliver Wheeler 🖥

I wouldn't really call myself an artist.

Ezra Beaumont

I would. Those invitations looked
amazing! I thought they profession-
ally ordered those.

Do you have any pictures of other stuff
you've done?

Oliver Wheeler 🖥

I mean, there's some on my Instagram,
but honestly, none of it is that good and
probably isn't worth looking at.

And I'm already regretting saying that.

Ezra Beaumont

Welp, too late. Already searching for
your profile.

Okay, can we talk about your handle?

"olliehotwheeler"? Really?

Oliver Wheeler 🖥

Ryan is to blame for that. He made it for
me, and I haven't bothered changing it.

Ezra Beaumont

Also, how are there absolutely no photos of you on here? Lots of coffee and
books, but not you.

Oliver Wheeler 🖥

I don't really take photos of myself.

Ezra Beaumont

Okay, finally found some of your art.

Ollie, this stuff is amazing.

Oliver Wheeler 🖼

It's really not. I hardly get the chance to practice anymore because my wrists are shit, so my more recent stuff is even worse.

Ezra Beaumont

What's wrong with your wrists?
If you don't mind me asking.

Oliver Wheeler 🖼

No, it's ok.

I have Rheumatoid Arthritis. It's an autoimmune disease that basically makes all of my joints inflamed. I have the most problems with my hips and wrists, but sometimes it's everything.

Ezra Beaumont

Oh. That's...I'd say I'm sorry, but I'm sure you're probably sick of hearing things like that.

Oliver Wheeler 🖼

So fucking sick of it.

Ezra Beaumont

Well, then I'll just say that you're crazy if you think you're not still a talented artist just because you occasionally have wrist problems, seeing as you did those invitations recently and they were beautiful.

Oliver Wheeler 🖼

Oh. Well, thanks.

Ezra Beaumont

You're welcome 😊

Oliver Wheeler

Oliver

Monday Afternoon, June 1, 2020

Oliver read over his editorial letter one more time, making sure everything made sense, then attached it to the email draft and hit send. He checked the time. 4:37 PM. There was more work he could do, of course, but he'd been up since 7 AM working, and he was making a better effort at having a work-life balance—especially now that the nightmare manuscript had officially been passed off to a different copy editor. Ryan had been right when he said that he was barreling toward burnout at the rate he was going. If he was honest with himself, he was already burned out. Even with Ezra starting to take on some of his workload, he was still stressed, and his sleep schedule was all sorts of fucked up, which meant that he was flaring up more than usual. So Oliver shut his work laptop and set it aside.

Out of habit, he pulled his personal laptop into his lap before Fiona could jump up and claim the spot and opened the Scrivener file for his novel. Oliver wasn't sure what to do with himself now that he wasn't working like crazy, and he was still in hyper-productive mode, so he figured he might as well channel that energy into his book. Although, if he were smart, he would take a real break. One where he could turn off his brain, which didn't include writing.

Sighing, Oliver closed out Scrivener, then went to close his laptop. But before he closed the lid, the

computer started ringing, letting him know he had a
FaceTime call. He lifted the lid again and saw Mary's
name flash in the top right corner. She always had impeccable timing.

Oliver pressed accept, and Mary's face filled the
screen. "Hey—holy shit, your hair!" he exclaimed.

"Oh, you noticed?" Mary said, looking like she was
fighting a grin.

He wasn't usually one to notice things like hair
changes—any appearance changes, really—something
Mary always teased him about because otherwise he
was a pretty observant person. But this change was
hard to miss because instead of the long, stick-straight
black hair she'd sported since high school, it barely extended past her chin and was neon blue. "It's blue.
How could I miss that?"

"Well, what do you think?" she asked.

"I think your mother is going to kill you," he said.

"Eh, she'll get over it," she said, waving her hand.

"Did you forget about Christmas 2015?" Oliver
countered.

Mary grimaced. That was the year she'd brought her
first girlfriend home, but that wasn't what made that
year grimace-worthy. The girlfriend had been a surprise
for her parents, but only because until that point, they'd
sort of assumed she wasn't interested in dating anyone
since she hadn't until that point, despite her coming out
to them as a lesbian junior year of high school. The
nose ring Mary had gone home with was a different
story though. "It's just hair. It'll grow out. Besides, I'm
stuck at home. What family photos am I ruining?"

"I'm just saying," Oliver said with a shrug. "It looks
good, though. I approve. Did Robin do it?"

"Yeah, we got bored this morning. She's rocking an
undercut now."

"Well, I'm glad you're keeping productive during the

quarantine. How are you two, otherwise?" he asked. Mary was a wedding photographer, and her girlfriend, Robin, was a tattoo artist, so they were both temporarily out of work until things got more under control.

Mary sighed. "We're doing…alright. We've been talking about setting up an Etsy shop so we can sell some of my non-wedding or event shots and some of Robin's sketches and watercolors—the ones that aren't for clients, anyway. But almost every freelance artist is doing that right now, so the market is probably too over-saturated for it to make a difference."

"You should do it," Oliver said.

"You think?"

"Absolutely. You're both crazy talented and have pretty impressive Instagram followings, so I bet people would love to own prints of your work."

She smiled. "Thanks, Ollie. But what about you? How's work?"

"Finally slowing down," he said with a sigh of relief.

"How's the new guy?"

"He's good."

Good was a bit of an understatement, but for some reason Oliver didn't feel like elaborating past that. Ezra had really taken to being a publishing assistant, actually. He was naturally smart, a quick learner, and creative. He also had great instincts for potential manuscripts. Every single one of the "maybes" he marked was solid or could get there with some reworking, and he marked the latter with a tag of some sort, indicating his thoughts on that. It made Oliver regret not trusting him with more responsibility sooner, because if he had, maybe he would have been able to climb out of the work hell-hole a lot sooner.

"That's all I get?" Mary asked, indignant. "A month and a half ago you wouldn't shut up about how annoying it was to have to train him, and how he's spoiled and unqualified, and now all I get is 'he's good,'?"

"Okay, I was wrong about that, and I feel bad. But he's picked everything up quickly, and he's nice. Charming," Oliver said with a shrug.

"Charming?" she repeated.

"I don't know. He's charismatic."

She gasped. "You like him!"

"I do not," Oliver protested.

"Yes, you do! You're blushing."

"I am not," he said, but even as he denied it, he felt his face heat.

His phone buzzed next to him, and the comedic timing didn't escape his notice as he immediately reached for it. He knew who it was already, of course, and what the text was likely about. There was only one person it could be, because there was only one person who texted him with any sort of regularity anymore, and that was Ezra. But he smiled regardless as he read that day's bad query quote.

The verisimilitude of his character struck her like a blow to the chest, a tester dummy crumpling against a brick wall at 50mph.

"Oh, my God, that's him, isn't it?" Mary exclaimed, forcing Oliver to look up.

"Okay, fine, it was," he admitted, then added, "but don't read into it."

"Ollie, your entire face just lit up."

"He sends me these terrible quotes from the queries that he's been reading every day. They make me laugh."

"He texts you every day?"

Oliver huffed. "Well, not every day, but most days."

"And is it just the quotes, or do you talk about other stuff?" Mary asked.

"We have a lot in common, that's all," Oliver said.

"Like the fact that you clearly have a crush on each other?"

"We don't—" Oliver closed his eyes and pinched the bridge of his nose. "Can we please stop talking about this? I don't have a crush, and neither does he. We're friends, and that's it."

"Okay, okay, fine. But for the record, me thinks the Ollie doth protest too much," Mary sing-songed.

"Don't misquote Shakespeare at me," Oliver fired back before promptly changing the subject.

11

Oliver

Monday Night, June 8, 2020

Oliver glanced up from his book for what must have been the sixtieth time that night to look at his phone. It was nearing 11 PM, and he hadn't heard from Ezra yet, which—as much as he hated to admit it—bothered him. It was bordering on pathetic, but he couldn't help it. Nearly every night, Oliver found himself waiting by his phone for Ezra to send the day's bad query quote, wanting some excuse to talk to him but too scared to send a text first. He'd only gotten the courage to text first once, and that was only after a 15-minute debate with himself and because he had the excuse of wanting to talk about Ryan and Anna postponing their wedding.

But if he texted Ezra first without some sort of reason, then he would be admitting that he wanted to text Ezra to talk to him, and that would prove that Mary was right about him having a crush. It was fine. He could go a day without talking to him. Maybe Ezra was just—Oliver's phone buzzed next to him, and he jumped for it, dropping his book, losing his place, and nearly dropping his phone in his haste to answer it. That probably proved Mary right, too, but that didn't stop him.

He took a second to calm himself, taking a deep breath and curling his knees into his chest, before holding the phone to his ear. "Ezra, hi," he said, wincing at the eagerness in his voice.

"Ollie, sorry, I know it's late, but I think I've actually found a winner," Ezra said, skipping a greeting entirely. It had been nearly a month since their last phone call, and this was only their third phone call in total, so Oliver didn't know his voice very well, but it sounded different. He sounded like he was almost buzzing with excitement, and though that was a stark contrast to the hesitation in his voice during their last two phone calls, Oliver didn't think that was it. It almost sounded like—

"I know it's probably too early to say that seeing as we only have the first three chapters, but God, they're perfect," Ezra said.

Oliver furrowed his brow. He had to be hearing things because that couldn't be a faint English accent he was hearing. He would have remembered if Ezra had an accent.

"It's just so immersive. The imagery, the world-building, the characterization. I'm obsessed. I've already read it twice," Ezra continued in a rush.

Oliver's mouth dropped open. He definitely wasn't hearing things. The longer Ezra spoke, the more pronounced the accent became. What the fuck?

"Ollie? You there?"

Oliver shut his mouth and shook his head to clear it. "Yeah, sorry," he croaked. He cleared his throat. "Um, Ezra, why are you putting on an English accent?"

"Oh, crap," Ezra muttered, a nervous laugh escaping him before he cleared his throat. "That happens sometimes."

Oliver stayed silent, confused, so Ezra continued.

"My mother is British, so I was actually born in London. My whole family still has an accent—even my dad did before he died, although I'm pretty sure it was fake because he was American. Anyway, we moved to New York when I was ten when my grandfather died, and my dad had to take over company operations in the US. When we got here, I lost the accent," he explained, his vague American accent returning as he spoke.

"Oh," Oliver said, swallowing hard. "But it's coming back?"

Ezra cleared his throat again, and when he spoke again, the accent was almost completely gone. "Like I said, most of my family still has the accent, so since I've been living with my cousin Josie, mine creeps back up when I'm not paying attention."

"Josie is your cousin on your mother's side, but she lives in the US?" Oliver asked.

"Yeah. She moved to New York with her now-husband when she found out she was pregnant with Willow," Ezra said.

"Ah," Oliver said, then he paused for a moment, trying to figure out how to word his next question. "I didn't say anything when you first mentioned it because I didn't want to pry, but I assumed, based on what Ryan said, that you were kind of on the outs with your family."

Ezra laughed wryly. "That's one way to put it. But I am with everyone except Josie. She's the other black stain on the otherwise impeccable pedigree of the Beaumont-Carmichael family."

Oliver couldn't help the laugh that escaped his lips. He clapped a hand over his mouth. "Sorry, I don't mean to laugh. That just sounds so—"

"Dramatic?" Ezra supplied, laughing, as well. "I wish I could say that I was kidding, but honest to God, that's what my family is like. A bunch of posh bigots, the lot of them. Josie and I are not, so they disowned us."

"Disowned?" Oliver said, flabbergasted. "People do that still?"

"Rich, powerful families like mine do. One wrong move they can't ignore, and you're out. For Josie, it was getting knocked up out of wedlock, then eloping and moving to New York."

"Your family kicked her out for that? How old was she?"

"Twenty-three, I think? So a grown-ass woman. It was complete bullshit. Although Josie's disownment was rather tame compared to mine. Her mother still talks to her on holidays—although I'm pretty sure her father doesn't know about that. But Caroline—my mother…" Ezra sighed.

"It's okay," Oliver said. "You don't have to talk about it."

"No, it's fine," Ezra said, a little too casually. "My mother was more vicious about everything. Within a matter of hours, she completely disinherited me, revoked my shares in Beaumont-Carmichael Holding, and banned me from all family functions and from having any contact with anyone."

"So it wasn't just that you got cut off. Your parents cut you out of their life?"

"I'm guessing that's what Ryan told you?" Ezra asked with a hollow laugh. "That my mother cut me off?"

"He didn't say a lot, to be honest. But I kind of assumed…"

"Yeah, that makes sense. Explains why you were a bit of a jerk at first. You thought I was just some rich kid that spent too much of mommy's and daddy's money, so they were teaching me a lesson."

Ezra's tone was light and teasing, but Oliver still felt

a wave of mortification wash over him. He pulled his knees tighter into his chest. He was the worst. The actual, literal worst. "I'm so sorry—"

"Don't worry about it. I figured Ryan hadn't filled you in on what happened. He knows I don't really like to talk about my family."

"No," Oliver said firmly. "I operated under a completely false assumption of who you were and treated you accordingly. I acted like a dick, and that wasn't fair to you at all."

"Ollie, it's fine," Ezra said with a laugh.

"Still," Oliver insisted, "I'm sorry. I don't normally jump to conclusions like that, but—" He sighed. "Honestly, I've had some unpleasant experiences with rich, trust-fund kids, so I wasn't acting like myself."

"Well, most kids with a trust fund are the worst—and I was surrounded by them, so I'd know—so I don't think I can blame you." Ezra laughed.

They fell silent for a long moment until Ezra spoke up again. "So, you didn't ask me what I did to get the boot."

"Didn't want to pry," Oliver said. "You said that you don't enjoy talking about your family."

"I don't with strangers, but you're not a stranger."

"So, what did you do then?"

"Well, it was more of a 'who' I did," Ezra said cheekily.

Oliver's hand gripped the phone a fraction tighter. He didn't even need Ezra to say the words to know what he was about to say.

"Caroline must have been sick of me hiding from her in Europe, so she sent a PI to drag me home, and… Well, I guess she simply couldn't ignore the fact that I'd been shacking up with a guy."

"She disowned you because you're gay?" Oliver croaked.

"Well, bi, but yeah."

"Sorry. But that's—that's— It's 2020. Who cares who you sleep with?"

"Caroline Beaumont."

"Well, if I didn't think she was a raging bitch before, I do now."

Ezra let out a surprised laugh. "Bloody hell."

Oliver's traitorous stomach fluttered again as the accent slipped back into Ezra's voice for a split second. "Sorry, I know she's your mom, but—"

"No, the shoe absolutely fits," Ezra said. "Your foul mouth continues to surprise me, though."

"Sorry, Anna yells at me for it constantly," Oliver said sheepishly.

"Don't apologize," Ezra said in a rush. "I like it."

Oliver smiled. "Can I ask you another question?"

"Shoot."

"Why do you try so hard to suppress your accent?"

Ezra sighed. "It's going to sound stupid, but I thought it would make me less like them. I lost the accent pretty quickly once I was at boarding school, and whenever I was home on break, I could see how annoyed it made my mother that I had a 'dirty American accent,' so I worked harder to make sure I kept it."

"That doesn't sound stupid. It makes sense."

"Yeah?"

"Yeah. I mean, your family sounds like they're a bunch of complete dicks." Ezra laughed, then Oliver continued, "But I don't think your accent makes you like them. Where you came from is part of you. So, if your accent is coming back, what's wrong with that?"

"I guess that's true," Ezra mused.

"Besides," Oliver ventured, "I think it suits you."

"You think?"

"I do."

"Well, thanks."

"You're welcome."

They were silent again for a long moment, then, Ezra broke it. "Oh, wait, I actually had a reason to call you. The manuscript." Ezra laughed, and Oliver forced a laugh back. Right. Work. Ezra hadn't called him simply to talk. "I think it's a winner. I put it in the maybe pile already, but I wanted to give you a heads-up so you might prioritize reaching out to the author."

"You should do it," Oliver said.

"Really?" Ezra asked, surprised.

"Your instincts have been spot on, and you were excited enough about this one to call, so yeah. Go for it," Oliver said.

"Okay. Thanks," Ezra said. "Well, it's late. I'll let you go."

Oliver checked the time. It wasn't that late, but it was still a Monday. "Yeah. Well, thanks for calling."

"Of course. Goodnight, Ollie," Ezra said, almost softly.

"Goodnight," Oliver said.

He hung up and stared at his phone for a moment before pulling up his text thread with Mary.

Mary Wen
June 8, 2020, 11:38 PM
So, he's bi.

Mary Wen

OMG Hot new co-worker guy?

OLLIE

I KNEW you had a crush on him. Why else would you be freaking out over finding out that he's bi?

Oliver Wheeler

I'm not freaking out.

Okay, fine. I'm freaking out. But I don't think it's a crush.

Mary Wen

What else would you call it?

Oliver Wheeler

I think I'm just lonely, and Ezra's new, so I'm confusing whatever this is for actual feelings.

Mary Wen

Sure, he's new, but he's also "charming", "charismatic", "funny"...

Oliver Wheeler

Ugh. I really need to stop telling you everything.

Mary Wen

And I get the loneliness. But the two aren't mutually exclusive. You can be lonely and have a crush on your new, tall, dark, handsome, guitar-playing, tattoo-covered coworker who texts you bad literary quotes daily.

Oliver Wheeler

He also has a British accent.

Mary Wen

And he just gets hotter.

But wait, I thought he was from New York?

And you've talked on the phone with him before. How are you just now noticing it?

Oliver Wheeler

He was born in London and moved to New York when he was a kid, which is why he didn't have an accent. But, he's living with his cousin, and she still does, so his is coming back.

Wait. He plays guitar? He has tattoos? Fuuuuck. And how do you even know that?

Mary Wen

Stalked his Instagram.

Oliver, are you telling me you don't know what this man looks like?

Oliver Wheeler

Not really. I mean, I have a vague idea. White. Dark hair. Taller than Ryan, although that's not that hard. But that's from a glimpse of some photos I saw on Ryan's wall in college.

Mary Wen

So you have a crush on this man, and it's based purely on your conversations with him?

Robin says that is adorable and quite possibly the most Oliver thing she's ever heard.

Oliver Wheeler

Have you been telling her everything I've been saying???

Mary Wen

No, we're cuddling so she's reading over my shoulder

Oh, also, re: Ezra, she says that if you don't hit that ASAP, she has half a mind to fly to New York and hit that herself, and honestly, I wouldn't blame her. He's hot as fuck

Oliver Wheeler

I regret introducing you two

Mary Wen

No you don't

But here

Ezra Beaumont
(@ezrawandering)
Instagram photos and videos
Instagram.com

You're welcome

Oliver Wheeler

Yeah, I know what his Instagram is. He followed me the other day.

Mary Wen

And you didn't follow him back? Or check his feed at all?

Oliver Wheeler

Of course I followed him back. I just didn't look at his profile at all. He was straight, or so I thought. I didn't want to stalk his Instagram lest my inappropriate crush get worse.

Mary Wen

Ah ha! So you admit it's a crush!

Oliver Wheeler

...

Mary Wen

You're hopeless.

So how did him being bi come up?

Oliver Wheeler

We were talking about his cousin, and he off-handedly mentions that they were both disowned by their family.

Mary Wen

Is that even a thing still? It's 2020.

Oliver Wheeler

That's what I said.

Mary Wen

Wait, did his family really disown him
for being queer?

I'm guessing that's what it is. Makes
sense based on context.

W the actual F?

Oliver Wheeler

Yeah. They did. It's a lot worse than
that, too. I won't get into the details,
but his family is fucking awful.

I just feel like I completely misjudged
him. At first, I thought he was this
over-inflated rich boy with a desperate desire to rebel for no reason, but
now... Idk. I mean, with a family like
his, no wonder he wanted to rebel
against them. There's just a lot more
to him than I initially thought.

Mary Wen

This isn't just a crush, is it? You really
like him.

Oliver Wheeler

I don't know. Maybe.

Mary Wen

Wait, question. When did you talk to
him? Was it right before you texted me?

Oliver Wheeler

Yes

But don't read into it. He texts me
about work at night all the time. It's

when he does the majority of his reading. Also, just because he's bisexual doesn't automatically mean he likes me.

Mary Wen

You don't know that unless you do something about it.

Oliver Wheeler

And how am I supposed to do something about it in the middle of a fucking pandemic? It's not exactly prime conditions for dating.

Mary Wen

Okay, but this won't be forever. Things will go back to normal, and in the meantime, you can have Zoom dates.

Oliver Wheeler

Except we have no idea when things are going to go back to normal, Mary. And even if they go back to normal for the rest of the world, I'll still need to be more cautious than everyone else. It's not fair to saddle someone with having to be overly careful just for me.

Mary Wen

Where is this coming from, Ollie? You've never let your RA stand in the way of you dating before.

Oliver Wheeler

Things are different now. Before, I was just in pain all the time and a depressed mess because of it, but now I can't even go to the grocery store for myself. Shit's fucked, Mary. Shit's fucked.

Mary Wen

This is just temporary, though. It won't always be like this.

Oliver Wheeler

You can't know that!

Mary Wen

Fine. You're right. I DON'T know that. But that doesn't mean you don't deserve to be happy. And who says that lover boy wouldn't happily take extra precautions for you? I mean, you're a catch.

Oliver Wheeler

You have to say that. You're my best friend.

Mary Wen

I mean it. Honestly, if I had any romantic interest in men, I would have scooped you up a long time ago. But sadly, our emotional bond was destined to be platonic.

Robin agrees. She says if you hadn't brought me into your tattoo appointment for moral support, she would have absolutely hit on you.

Oliver Wheeler

Mary...Look, I get that you're trying to cheer me up, and I love you for it. And thank Robin for the compliment. But there's no amount of ego-boosting that you can do to make me feel better about this.

Mary Wen

Ollie...

Oliver Wheeler
Please Mar? It's late, and I'm tired.

Mary Wen

Okay. But for the record, I think you should give this a chance.

Oliver Wheeler

I'll take your thoughts into consideration.

Mary Wen

Love you, you stubborn old man, you.

Oliver Wheeler

Love you too, you equally stubborn crazy lady, you.

Oliver threw his phone on the charging pad on his nightstand with a sigh. It hadn't been just some lie to get Mary off his back; he really was exhausted. However, he knew that even if he shut off the lights, lay down, and tried to do that deep-breathing exercise he'd read about online that was supposed to induce sleep, he wouldn't be able to sleep. Not even the comforting sounds of Fiona purring on the pillow next to him would do it. He was too wired, which was almost his constant state of being at this point. Fucking exhausted, but too awake to sleep.

It wasn't the what-he'd-come-to-accept-as-usual pandemic dread that was keeping him up, though. It was Ezra. He kept running through that conversation over and over. And even though he didn't want to, his mind was also trying to put together a mental picture of what Ezra looked like in relation to what he already knew about him. Charismatic. Charming. Funny. Helps his little cousin with her homework. Lived in Europe for seven years. Bar tends. Dark hair. Indeterminable height. Tattoos. Plays guitar. Has a fucking British accent.

Bi.

Screw it.

Oliver grabbed his phone from the charging pad and pulled up Instagram.

Almost the instant Ezra's profile loaded, Oliver's breath left him in a sharp exhale. Mary was right. Ezra was fucking gorgeous with dark, curly hair that fell just past his shoulders, a slight tan to his skin that hinted how often he was outside, the most brilliant blue eyes he'd ever seen, and tattoos. God, the tattoos. He had at least three that he could see in the first picture of him sitting on the floor playing Mario Kart with a little girl Oliver assumed was his cousin's daughter. Well, that wasn't adorable at all.

Oliver was in trouble. He needed to stop, because if one picture was threatening to send him careening over the edge into full-blown feelings, then a complete Instagram stalk would likely end him. That didn't stop him, though. One picture wasn't enough. Besides, he already knew that Ezra stalked his Instagram because he'd told him as much and had even liked a few photos of artwork he'd posted well over a year ago. A return Instagram stalk was expected, right?

So he scrolled. He scrolled past beautiful travel photography, pictures of Ezra sightseeing—always with what looked like a Canon DSLR dangling from his shoulder—and closeups of freshly done tattoos. From Oliver's count, Ezra had at least six, including a creation of Adam's silhouette on his ribs; a phoenix covering most of his right arm and some of his chest and shoulder blade, with a quote in French under it that Oliver didn't understand; a camera aperture opening on his forearm; and a Magnolia just behind his ear. Oliver also thought he glimpsed a full-back tattoo of a tree in a few photos, but there wasn't a full shot of it he could see.

There were also a few videos of Ezra busking on the street that Oliver initially scrolled past, but then curiosity got the best of him, and he went back to watch. And Ezra was good. Of course he was. So was the girl that was in half of them performing with him, who, based on their chemistry, had likely been a girlfriend of some sort—not that Oliver was jealous. He had no right to be. Ezra wasn't his to be jealous over, especially since this deep social media dive made one thing perfectly clear: Ezra was completely out of his league.

12

Ezra

Mid-June 2020

Oliver Wheeler 🖥
June 11, 2020 - 7:32 PM

Ezra Beaumont

"Well, I can't eat muffins in an agitated manner. The butter would probably get on my cuffs. One should always eat muffins calmly. It is the only way to eat them."

Oliver Wheeler 🖥

The Importance of Being Earnest?

Ezra Beaumont

Well, you went on about it for a good 45 minutes so I thought I'd give it a read.

Oliver Wheeler 🖥

Okay, I did NOT go on for 45 minutes. It

was more like five. But anyway, what did
you think?

Ezra Beaumont

I LOVED it.

Also, I've basically been a Bunburyist
my entire life haha.

Oliver Wheeler 🖥

Is it really Bunburying, though, if you're
throwing it in your parents' faces?

Ezra Beaumont

Oi! You make it sound as if I was just
some common rebel.

I like to think of it as me commenting
on society by escaping what they considered "proper" and "decent".

Although, it was immensely satisfying
watching Caroline fume at the ears.

Oliver Wheeler 🖥

Very Algernon of you.

Ezra Beaumont

Why thank you.

High praise since he's the best character in the play.

Oliver Wheeler 🖥

Of COURSE, you think that. :P

Ezra Beaumont

What? I'm guessing you're more of a
Jack fan?

Oliver Wheeler 🖥

Well, he is the title character of the play,
after all.

Ezra Beaumont

Also, Speaking of Algernon, another

quote of his I thoroughly enjoyed and would have quoted in response to you calling my mother a raging bitch had I not waited until yesterday to read the play:

"My dear boy, I love hearing my relations abused. It is the only thing that makes me put up with them at all. Relations are simply a tedious pack of people who haven't got the remotest knowledge of how to live, nor the smallest instinct about when to die."

Oliver Wheeler 📖

I think I would have about died if you'd quoted that to me.

But as for Jack, I think there's a lot to learn from his journey. I kind of identified with him when I first read it—the desire to escape from real life while still maintaining his honorable image. Then how he eventually reconciles the two and figures out who he is.

Ezra Beaumont

Are you telling me that you have a secret wild side that I don't know about?

Oliver Wheeler 📖

Well, if I did, it wouldn't exactly be in my best interest to tell you, would it?

Ezra Beaumont

Cheeky.

Jack may be the title character, but Algernon is a stand-in for Wilde himself, which means that he's clearly the better character.

Oliver Wheeler 📧

Becoming a Wilde fan now?

Ezra Beaumont

Again, you went on for 45 minutes.

I put Dorian Gray on digital hold at the library to read next.

Oliver Wheeler 📧

You know, there's actually a movie about Wilde.

Ezra Beaumont

Wait, really?

Ooooh. Hold on, googling.

Stephen Fry and Jude Law?

Oliver Wheeler 📧

Yup, that's the one.

Ezra Beaumont

We should watch it!

Oliver Wheeler 📧

Haha ok.

June 12, 2020, 10:30 AM

Ezra Beaumont

Okay, so I couldn't find Wilde anywhere to stream, but I may or may not have found a copy of it online in some capacity.

Oliver Wheeler 📧

You Torrented it, didn't you?

Ezra Beaumont

Maaaybe.

So when do you want to watch it?

Oliver Wheeler 📇

Oh, you were serious?

Ezra Beaumont

I was.

Do you not want to?

Oliver Wheeler 📇

No, I do.

I just have such a vibrant social calendar right now. I'll have to check my calendar to see if I have any availability.

Hmm...it appears I was mistaken. I am not doing anything on any night for the foreseeable future.

Ezra Beaumont

Well, lucky me then.

7 tomorrow work?

Oliver Wheeler 📇

Yeah, that works for me.

Ezra Beaumont

Alright, great.

Looking forward to it 😊

Oliver Wheeler 📇

Me, too 😊

Ezra looked at the clock on his computer for probably the fiftieth time in five minutes, desperately wishing that time would move faster. Five more minutes until he could start the call with Oliver. Five more minutes until he could put a face to the voice and personality that he'd grown to like so much.

It was a little weird, thinking about it—having feelings for a person he'd never actually seen. Well, having a crush on a person. Ezra wasn't sure how he could consider how he felt toward Oliver to be a crush anymore. Crushes were silly and juvenile. They were shallow and something you had when you didn't really know someone. Crushes were more about the idea of a person. And Oliver wasn't really an idea anymore. He was this whole person who cursed like a sailor, read constantly, loved plants and baking, was sarcastic and witty in a way that snuck up on you. Oliver had a cat that he absolutely adored and was opinionated.

Ezra knew and liked all of this about him, but the only thing he knew about his appearance was that he looked like a cinnamon roll and a librarian had a baby, which didn't quite inform Ezra's mental picture of Oliver other than guessing that there was probably a surplus of cardigans. Sure, he could have probably gone onto Ryan or Anna's Facebooks and found Oliver to get a picture, but something about that felt like cheating. Anyway, Ezra decided it didn't matter what this man looked like. He liked him. He liked him a lot.

That didn't make him any less nervous to see him in person—well, virtually but visually. That nervousness probably wasn't helped by the fact he'd gotten the follower notification from Oliver a few days ago. So he knew that Oliver now knew what he looked like because while Oliver's Instagram was completely void of any picture of himself, Ezra's was full of them. He also knew that after over a week since Ezra stalked his Instagram, Oliver had chosen the moment they'd gotten off the phone to stalk Ezra's back. He couldn't help but feel like that meant something.

But this wasn't a date. He didn't even know if Oliver was into guys. They were just watching a movie together because they were friends and that's what friends do, especially when they're both stuck at home and in need of social interaction. But even though he kept telling himself that, he still had changed his shirt four times and spent several minutes longer than normal taming his thick curls.

Two minutes until seven, Ezra opened a new Chrome window and logged into Kast to see that Oliver was already online. He chewed on his lip for a moment as the cursor hovered over the "start call" button, then he sucked in a deep breath, held it, and clicked. Within a few seconds, Oliver's face filled the screen, and Ezra's jaw nearly dropped. There was no way Ezra could have conjured a mental picture that did him justice. Oliver had sandy-brown curls that stuck up in all directions and were just long enough to hang in his soft green eyes. Green eyes that were accentuated by the oversized forest-green sweater he was wearing. Freckles dotted his pale skin, mostly focusing on a patch across his nose. Something about Oliver felt warm, sweet, and safe, and that combined with the sweater even in June… Well, Ryan's incoherent assessment was completely spot-on. A cinnamon roll mixed with a librarian was the perfect way to describe him.

And then Oliver smiled, and the breath Ezra had been holding left him in a rush. Bloody hell, that smile. Slightly shy but also bright, and which lit up his entire face. "Hi," Oliver whispered.

Ezra swallowed and forced what he hoped looked like an effortless smile on his face. "Hey."

"How are you?"

"Good. And you?"

"Good." Oliver bit his lip, then brought a sweater-sleeve-covered hand and tucked it under his chin.

"It's good to put a face to your voice," Ezra said.

"Yeah. Same," Oliver said.

Ezra smirked. "I already know you Instagram-stalked me, Ollie."

A faint blush crept onto Oliver's cheeks, somehow making him even more adorable. "Well, photos are different. I hear you're not trying to hide your accent anymore."

"Oh, yeah, well…" Ezra shrugged and ran a hand through his hair, then cursed himself for it. "It was getting exhausting trying to avoid it when I talk to Josie so often. And you had a good point."

"Well, I'm glad I could help."

Ezra smiled, which Oliver returned. "So, *Wilde*?"

Oliver nodded, so Ezra started the screen-share, which unfortunately minimized Oliver's face to a small window in the corner, and pulled up the already queued window to press play.

They stayed mostly silent as they watched the movie until about halfway through when Ezra let out a scoff. "Oh, well, that's just not fair," Ezra said, exasperated. "Why does Jude Law have to be able to sing and be so hot?"

"Fuck, I know," Oliver said with a sigh. "He's so hot. Based on the number of times I watched Sherlock Holmes in high school, I should have realized I was bi a lot sooner."

Ezra nearly choked. Oliver was bi.

In retrospect, Ezra probably could have guessed that earlier. He'd been picking up the vibes, but he'd honestly thought that was just wishful thinking. It wouldn't have been the first time. But now…

He quickly tamped down that train of thought. The last thing he needed was unrealistic hope. Just because Oliver was interested in men didn't mean that he would be interested in Ezra. Still, whatever focus Ezra had on the movie was now gone.

"So, if Jude Law wasn't your big queer awakening, who was?" Ezra asked.

"Oh, that's a shit show of a story," Oliver said with a hollow laugh.

"Sorry, didn't mean to pry," Ezra said.

"Oh, no, it's okay. So, it was my freshman year at NYU," Oliver started.

Ezra paused the stream, then made the window with Oliver's face take up more room on his computer screen. "Guy on your dorm floor?" Ezra offered.

"Specifically, my roommate."

"Oh, no," Ezra whispered.

"Oh, yes," Oliver said. "So, I started having feelings that one simply does not have for their roommate, and of course, I panic. So I text my best friend, Mary, who's still in Portland, because she came out as gay in high school, so in theory, she could talk me through it."

"That's good that you had someone to talk to who had experience."

"I'm guessing you didn't?" Oliver asked.

"Not really. I mean, Ryan was, but I'll tell that story once you're done," Ezra said, gesturing for Oliver to continue.

"Right, so Mary talks me through it, and I realize I'm bi. Then, one night around Halloween, I came back to my dorm room tipsy because Juliet had gotten some older student to sneak her some crappy alcohol—"

"Oh, no," Ezra whispered again, already guessing where the story was going.

"So, I got back to my room, and I decided I was going to take a shot and at least come out to Nick—that was the guy's name. I didn't really make a move on him; I just needed to tell someone else besides Mary, and I thought—" Oliver shook his head. "I don't even know what I thought."

"Did he react badly?" Ezra asked tentatively, still waiting for the part of the story that qualified it as a "shit show."

"No, actually. He asked how I realized I was bi, and, in another alcohol-induced moment of confidence, I admitted I had started having feelings for—well, I didn't mention him, but I was drunk, and it was obvious I was talking about him. That was when he kissed me."

"Oh!" Ezra felt his eyes widen in surprise.

Oliver laughed. "Weren't expecting that, huh?" Ezra shook his head. "Well, neither was I. But I went with it, and we started dating in secret. And it was nice. It wasn't just hooking up. We did couple-y things together, too."

"So, where does the 'shit show' part of this story come in?"

"Ah, yes." Oliver bit his lip and wrapped his arms around his torso as if to comfort himself, and for a moment, Ezra couldn't help but wish he was the one wrapping his arms around Oliver in comfort. "Well, one night, about two weeks before the end of the spring semester, I came back early from a study group session to find Nick with some random girl's mouth around his cock," Oliver said bitterly.

"Oh, Olls…"

"He then denied that he had ever had feelings for me to begin with—said I was imagining things, that he was just bored, that we were just having some fun, and insisted that he was straight."

A surge of anger pulsed through Ezra. "That prick. What did you do?"

"Well, first, I withdrew my roommate request form for the next year—because we'd planned to continue living together—and put in for a random roommate. Then I slept in Anna and Juliet's room for the rest of the semester," Oliver said too casually. "Of course, I had to tell them what happened, but they were supportive, so at least that was good."

"I'm sorry. That really sucks."

Oliver shrugged. "It is what it is. That random roommate ended up being Ryan, so I think I was better off for it. But for reference, when I said I had unpleasant experiences with rich, trust-fund kids, he was the start of it. It's your turn, though. What was your big queer awakening?"

Ezra frowned for a moment, wanting to say something else, but clearly Oliver didn't want to dwell on it, so he let it go. "Alright, I'll tell you, but you can't tell Ryan that you know because I'm pretty sure he would kill me if he knew I told you."

Oliver's face lit up, and he sat up a little straighter. "Oh, this has to be good."

Ezra grinned. "It's entertaining, to say the least. Alright, so Ryan and I…we're fifteen at boarding school, and it was a holiday weekend, but neither of us was going home for it. We were bored out of our minds, so we did what any normal teenager at a boarding school would do." Oliver raised an eyebrow in question. "We bought some beer off an older student with a fake ID and got trashed."

"Ah, yes, of course," Oliver teased.

"And, well, I had been thinking I might like guys for a while then, so I admitted that to Ryan. And Ryan surprises me by admitting that he was feeling a little curious, too. So…"

Oliver stared at him for a moment, patient glee written all over his face as he waited for Ezra to continue. "So, in our drunken stupor, we decided that the only way to see if we were interested in blokes was to fool around a bit—and it wasn't just like, one quick kiss either, because that would have been bad science."

Oliver clapped a sweater-covered hand over his mouth, and his eyebrows shot up, so they were hidden in his curls. "Oh, my God."

Ezra couldn't help but laugh. God, he was too cute.

"So, after about twenty minutes of heavy making out, we pull apart, and Ryan says to me, 'You're a fantastic kisser and all, but I think I'm going to stick with girls.'" Ezra paused as Oliver let out a surprised laugh. "And I realized that although I most definitely did not—and still do not—have any feelings for Ryan, I enjoyed kissing a bloke way more than I would if I were straight."

"Oh, my God. Oh, my God."

"You can't say anything. We swore never to talk about it again," Ezra said in a rush. "I don't think he's even told Anna this story."

"I won't, but, oh, my God," Oliver said again. "This is literally the best information. Thank you for telling me this. I think you just added five years to my life."

Ezra laughed, and Oliver simply grinned back at him. After a long moment, Ezra cleared his throat. "So, continue with the movie?"

"Sure." Oliver settled farther into his pillows, and just as Ezra was about to pull up the screen share again, a flash of white moved into the frame.

"Oh, is that Fiona?" Ezra asked, excited.

Oliver laughed, but it was muffled as the giant cat brushed against his face and tried to settle on his chest. "Yes, this is her. Hold on—Fiona, pretty girl, I can't see through you."

Ezra nearly melted as he watched Oliver scoop the cat up and cradle her like a baby.

"There we go." Oliver gave her chin a scratch, then turned his attention back to the camera. "Sorry, she's a little co-dependent. She'll end up falling asleep like this."

"Adorable," Ezra said, unable to suppress the smile on his face.

"I'm good to go now."

Ezra nodded, then pulled up the stream, thankful that Oliver's picture became smaller again because he wasn't sure how much of Oliver cuddling his cat he could stand to watch and still pretend to be focused on the movie.

When the credits rolled, and Oliver's face once again filled Ezra's screen, Fiona was gone.

"So," Oliver said. "This was nice."

"It was good to know what the person I've been talking to for three months looks like," Ezra said.

"Yeah, it was good to talk to you, not over text. I didn't realize, but it's kind of lonely being cooped up here by myself," Oliver admitted.

"Would—would it be alright if I suggested doing this more?" Ezra asked.

Oliver smiled. "I'd like that."

13

Ezra

Summer 2020

Oliver Wheeler 🗐
June 15, 2020, 8:32 PM

> Ezra Beaumont
>
> Hey so I was thinking of starting to watch Game of Thrones. Would you maybe want to watch it with me?

Oliver Wheeler 🗐
Oh, I don't know. I'm still a little mad at the ending.

> Ezra Beaumont
>
> Oh yeah. That's fine.
> I just thought I'd offer.

Oliver Wheeler 🗐
Ezra, I'm kidding. I'd like to watch it with you.

> Ezra Beaumont
>
> Oh. Ok then 😊

You know you aren't making me want to watch this show anymore by complaining about how bad the ending was 😊

Oliver Wheeler 📇

Or am I making you want to watch it more because now you're curious about what made it so bad?

Ezra Beaumont

How do you know me so well already?

Oliver Wheeler 📇

It's a gift 😊

Ezra Beaumont

Are you busy now?

Oliver Wheeler 📇

Not at all.

June 16, 2020, 8:20 PM

Ezra Beaumont

I'm a little hesitant still, but I need to figure out what Littlefinger is up to because I don't trust that guy.

Oliver Wheeler 📇

Oh, just you wait.

Give me fifteen?

June 20, 2020, 4:03 PM

Ezra Beaumont

Alright... I'm still mourning the loss of Drogo but I need to see what happens next for Dany.

Are you busy?

Oliver Wheeler 🗐

Nope 😊

June 21, 2020, 3:37 PM

Oliver Wheeler 🗐

Busy?

Ezra Beaumont

Never too busy for the Moon of my Life.

Oliver Wheeler 🗐

You and your Dany obsession.

Ezra Beaumont

She has dragons, Ollie.

DRAGONS.

June 26, 2020, 7:13 PM

Ezra Beaumont

Ready to finish season 3?

June 27, 2020, 12:18 AM

Oliver Wheeler 🗐

Hey, you're probably asleep, but I just wanted to say sorry about earlier. I had a sudden burst of creative energy to work on my book, and when I get stuck in work mode, I forget about the outside world a little.

Ezra Beaumont

It's fine, Ollie. I understand.

Your passion for your work is one of my favorite things about you.

Oliver Wheeler

Raincheck for tomorrow night?

Ezra Beaumont

So...

I may or may not have watched an episode without you.

Oliver Wheeler

Oh, no. You watched the Red Wedding without me, didn't you?

Ezra Beaumont

I have almost no impulse control. You should know this by now.

But yes. I did. And I'm DEVASTATED.

I'm never watching without you again.

Oliver Wheeler

Watching with me won't prevent bad things from happening, you know.

Ezra Beaumont

Yes but you can console me when my heart is ripped out.

Oliver Wheeler

Oh, well, I think I can manage that.

July 3, 2020, 7:25 PM

Oliver Wheeler

Free?

Ezra Beaumont

No. This show keeps killing my favorite characters.

But yes, give me 20 minutes.

Oliver Wheeler

Want me to warn you next time?

Ezra Beaumont

> No, I think I'm just going to assume that anyone is going to die at any moment.

Oliver Wheeler 🖼

It might be safer that way, to be honest.

July 4, 2020, 2:17 PM

Oliver Wheeler 🖼

Happy Fourth of July!

As a British-American dual citizen, is this a conflicting holiday for you?

Ezra Beaumont

> Very clever.

Oliver Wheeler 🖼

I thought so. But really, are you doing anything to celebrate?

Ezra Beaumont

> Set off sparklers with Willow in the backyard, and Josie's husband Ted is grilling. You?

Oliver Wheeler 🖼

I'll probably watch the televised fireworks and continue reading Red, White & Royal Blue.

Ezra Beaumont

> What's it about?

Oliver Wheeler 🖼

The first son of the first female US president having his bi awakening and falling in love with the Crown Prince of England.

Ezra Beaumont

Very patriotic of you.

Oliver Wheeler 📇

I thought it fit the theme of today.

Ezra Beaumont

Would you still want to watch GOT tonight?

Oliver Wheeler 📇

Sure. 9 pm work?

Ezra Beaumont

Sounds perfect.

July 7, 2020, 7:03 PM

Ezra Beaumont

Please tell me you're done with the final copy edits for the manuscript you wanted to finish by today, because I'm quite literally dying to find out what happens to Jon.

Oliver Wheeler 📇

You know he's in the last season, right?

Ezra Beaumont

I did not, but thank you for that spoiler. But for all I know he could be a white walker.

Oliver Wheeler 📇

Haha.

Ezra Beaumont

So are you free?

Oliver Wheeler 📇

Yeah, I'm free

July 11, 2020, 2:15 PM

Ezra Beaumont

Want to start season 7?

Oliver Wheeler 📇

Sure. Let me just finish this scene I'm working on. I only need maybe 10 minutes.

Also, fair warning, this is the season things start to go downhill. They ran out of books so it gets...rough.

Ezra Beaumont

If you want to wait until later, that's fine

Also, the books aren't finished yet?

Oliver Wheeler 📇

It's okay, I want to keep watching. I need to take a break anyway.

And no, at this rate, I'm worried they're never going to be finished.

Ezra Beaumont

Oh, well I was thinking of starting those next after finishing Red, White & Royal Blue, but maybe not if you think they'll never get finished.

Oliver Wheeler 📇

You're reading Red, White & Royal Blue?

Ezra Beaumont

You mentioned it and it sounded interesting. I'm only about a chapter in so far though.

So do you want to start around 3?

Oliver Wheeler 📇

Sounds perfect.

July 17, 2020, 8:33 PM

Oliver Wheeler 🖿

Are you ready for the last episode?

Ezra Beaumont

I guess

Sorry, I'm still mad. They just did the Moon of My Life so dirty.

Oliver Wheeler 🖿

I'm sorry, I warned you.

Ezra Beaumont

I know.

Although, if I'm honest, I might have thought that you were exaggerating. But you weren't.

It's so bad. Like, bad enough that I'm questioning why you wanted to watch this again with me.

Oliver Wheeler 🖿

I thought it might be better on a re-watch. Also, I thought your reactions would be fun, which they were, so no regrets there.

Ezra Beaumont

Oh, well I'm glad I could entertain you.

So, want to hop on?

Oliver Wheeler 🖿

Yeah

July 18, 2020, 2:17 PM

Ezra Beaumont

So, I know we finished GOT last night, but did you maybe want to watch something else?

Oliver Wheeler 📇

Sure, but since you made me rewatch that finale, I'm picking the next show.

Ezra Beaumont

I thought you said you didn't mind because my reactions were entertaining

Also, may I point out that I technically picked GOT because you're the one that mentioned it and mocked me for never having watched it before

Same with Wilde's work

Come to think of it, half of our interactions are you mocking me for the media I haven't consumed

Oliver Wheeler 📇

Alright, alright, you've made your point.

What do you suggest then?

Ezra Beaumont

Have you ever seen Psych?

Oliver Wheeler 📇

I have not.

Ezra Beaumont

Well, then I guess I know what we're watching. It's the perfect palette cleanser.

Oliver Wheeler 📇

What's it about?

Ezra Beaumont

A fake psychic detective. It's a little older, but it holds up well. And there's a musical episode and 2 movies. One just came out the other day, but I haven't had time to watch it yet.

Oliver Wheeler 🖥

So, The Mentalist.

Ezra Beaumont

Except better and a comedy. Although, they do poke fun at the Mentalist frequently on it.

Oliver Wheeler 🖥

Alright, well, if you recommend it, I trust you. I can be ready in like 15?

Ezra Beaumont

Sounds great 😊

July 24, 2020, 6:18 PM

Oliver Wheeler 🖥

So, I don't think that I'll be able to watch tonight. My best friend, Mary, wants to have a catch-up call. Tomorrow though?

Ezra Beaumont

Tomorrow works 😊

That gives me some time to play Breath of the Wild with Willow.

Oliver Wheeler 🖥

You play Zelda with her?

Ezra Beaumont

More like watch and beat the shrines or lynel when she can't, but yeah.

Oliver Wheeler 🖥

That's sweet. Is this before or after you let her braid your hair?

Ezra Beaumont

Saw that picture Josie tagged me in, did you?

Oliver Wheeler

Possibly...

She's pretty good for a seven-year-old

Ezra Beaumont

Well, don't pretend that I didn't totally pull it off

Oliver Wheeler

I will admit, it looked good

Ezra Beaumont

😊

Oliver Wheeler

😊

Oliver

Tuesday Evening, August 4, 2020

Ezra Beaumont

August 4, 2020, 5:12 PM

Ezra Beaumont

Okay, baking question.

How does one "cream butter"?

Oliver Wheeler

Is your butter softened?

Ezra Beaumont

Uhhh, no. It's been in the fridge.

Oliver Wheeler

Okay, first you want to soften it in the microwave, but be careful not to let it melt because then you get air bubbles and whatever you're making will get all greasy.

What are you making, by the way?

Ezra Beaumont

Cake. It's Josie's birthday so Willow and I are making a cake.

Or attempting to anyway.

Okay, so once the butter is soft, what's next?

Oliver Wheeler

Okay, so to cream butter, you put it in your mixer along with your sugar and beat them at a moderate speed for about 2-3 minutes until it's well blended, fluffy, and a pale yellow.

Ezra Beaumont

And what is a moderate speed?

Also, would there be a difference between using regular sugar and brown sugar?

And how does one separate eggs?

Also, Willow is on dry ingredients and wants to know if there is a difference between baking powder and baking soda.

Oliver Wheeler

Oh, God. Step away from the mixer. I'm calling you.

The camera jostled as he presumably set it down on the counter propped up against something so he had use of both of his hands. Then Ezra backed away, giving Oliver a fuller view of not just the kitchen but of Ezra. After two months of daily video calls to watch television together, Oliver should have been used to how hot

Ezra was—and in a tiny window in the bottom right corner of his screen with a not very well-lit Ezra lounging in bed, he was…mostly. But nothing could have prepared him for Ezra wearing a sleeveless shirt showing off almost all of his tattoos and a "World's Best Dad" apron that had to be Josie's husband's, with his hair in a braid that wrapped around his head like a crown.

"So, we may be a little in over our heads. Josie said she would have been okay with a box mix, but Willow insisted—"

"You insisted, too!" a child's voice called from out of frame.

"Okay, fine," Ezra said as he brushed a few wisps of hair that had fallen out of his braid away from his flour-covered face using the back of his hand, which was also covered in flour. "We insisted on making one from scratch. Willow, say hi to my friend, Oliver."

A small child with similar bone structure to Ezra and strawberry-blond hair popped her head into view of the camera. "Hi, Oliver!" Then she looked at Ezra. "Archie, is this the friend you're always texting and watching TV with?"

"Yeah," Ezra said with a small smile. For a split second, Oliver thought he saw a hint of pink creep up onto Ezra's cheeks but quickly dismissed it.

"Archie?" Oliver asked.

"Oh, yeah, it's, uh, short for Archibald," Ezra explained, and this time Oliver was sure that he was blushing. "It's a family name."

"So Ezra is your—"

"Middle name," Ezra finished.

"So your full name is Archibald Ezra Beaumont," Oliver said, deadpan.

"I know, it's so posh, and I hate it. I started going by my middle name at the first opportunity I could, but

Josie's been calling me Archie since I was a toddler, so…"

Oliver tried to suppress the smile threatening to creep onto his face.

Ezra pointed a finger at him. "Don't start, you."

Oliver held up a hand in surrender. "I said nothing."

"You didn't have to. I can read your face," Ezra said, narrowing his eyes, and Oliver grinned innocently. "Oh, just tell us how to bake this bloody cake."

Thirty minutes and only one mixer mishap later, the cake was in the oven.

"Hopefully, it turns out okay," Ezra said, frowning slightly.

"I'm sure it will," Oliver said.

"And if it doesn't, it's the thought that counts, right?"

"Unless you all get food poisoning."

"Oi!" Ezra exclaimed, indignant, and Oliver smiled. He opened his mouth to say something else, but another voice cut him off out of frame.

"What on Earth happened here? Did the cake explode?" Oliver heard a hint of an English accent, a little stronger than Ezra's, which meant that it was probably his cousin, Josie.

"A little," Willow said, also out of frame. "But Oliver helped us fix it."

"Don't worry, Jose, we'll get it cleaned up. Ollie, this is my cousin, Josie," Ezra said. He pivoted the camera, revealing a woman in her early thirties with short, blond hair standing a few feet behind him.

"It's nice to meet you," Oliver said.

Josie smiled and waved. "Hi, Oliver. Thank you for helping my cousin and daughter not make an irreversible mess of my kitchen."

Oliver laughed. "It's no problem. Once Ezra texted me asking what the difference between baking soda and baking powder is, I knew I had to step in before he made something completely inedible."

Josie let out a loud laugh. "I like him." Then she looked at Ezra with a raised eyebrow and said something Oliver couldn't quite understand.

Was that French?

Ezra didn't respond, so she continued until Ezra cut her off, firing something back in warning.

That was definitely French.

Josie spoke again, still in rapid-fire French, and Ezra huffed before pivoting the camera so she was no longer in frame and looking at Oliver. "Sorry, Olls, can you give me a second?"

Oliver nodded, dumbfounded.

Ezra spoke French.

Because, of course he did. He wasn't already sexy enough, so he had to speak one of the sexiest languages on the planet.

Ezra propped the phone back up, bringing Willow back into the frame, then whirled around to face Josie.

Willow leaned in close to the camera and sighed. "I hate it when they do that," she murmured.

Whatever Willow said next, Oliver didn't quite catch, but he mumbled something in acknowledgment anyway. Ezra and Josie utterly mesmerized him conferring in rapid-fire French in the background. He couldn't understand any of it, of course, but—wait, was that his name? And if he wasn't mistaken, he also thought he heard the word for "date." Or was it "meeting?"

Either way, he heard his name, which meant they were talking about him. But in what context, he didn't know.

They got off the phone once the cake came out of the oven, and Oliver gave them the seal of approval to let it cool before icing. Later that night, after he'd eaten dinner, Oliver's phone pinged with a text.

Ezra Beaumont
August 4, 2020, 9:03 PM

Ezra Beaumont

Thank you so much

You really are the best

Oliver Wheeler

It wasn't a problem. I'm glad I could help.

Ezra Beaumont

Willow adored you, by the way. I'm pretty sure she loves you more than she loves me now.

Oliver Wheeler

Well, I am great. And Willow is adorable. Your cousin Josie is nice, too. You both look a lot alike. Does everyone in your family have the same gorgeous bone structure, or is it just you guys?

Ezra Beaumont

Everyone on my mother's side at least. It's the only thing I'm grateful to her for.

Are you calling me gorgeous, Oliver?

Oliver Wheeler

As if you don't already know what you look like, Archie.

Ezra Beaumont

No

Dear, God, no.

I let Josie call me that because she has since I was a toddler, and by extension, Willow. But that's it.

Oliver Wheeler

Aww, but I think it's sweet.

Ezra Beaumont

Absolutely not.

Oliver Wheeler

I'm just messing with you.

I like Ezra better anyway. 😊

14

Oliver

Monday Evening, August 17, 2020

Ryan Coleman

August 17, 2020, 6:58 PM

Ryan Coleman

Hey, are you able to hop on a group zoom call really quick?

Oliver Wheeler

I have plans in about half an hour, so it'll have to be quick.

Ryan Coleman

Ezra will be on the call too. So don't worry about that.

Oliver Wheeler

How did you know my plans are with Ezra?

Never mind. What's up?

Ryan Coleman

The same way I know you two have

talked every day for nearly three and a
half months.

Oliver Wheeler

Ryan, what are you implying?

Ryan Coleman

Nothing. I'm just glad you two are hit-
ting it off. Do you want me to be implying something?

Oliver Wheeler

Forget I asked. Why are we having an
impromptu group zoom call?

Ryan Coleman

Wedding stuff, but I won't say more until
everyone is on the call. I sent you an
email with the link.

Oliver pulled up his email to click on the Zoom link
Ryan had sent him. Almost instantly, Anna's bright face
filled his screen.

"Ollie!" Anna exclaimed. "Oh, how I've missed your
adorable face. Your hair has gotten so long!"

"Yeah, well, that's what happens when I haven't
been able to get a haircut in five months," he joked.
"Yours is getting long, too."

Anna ran a hand through her blond hair, which now
fell well past her shoulders instead of barely grazing the
tops like it usually did. "Ugh, I know. I don't know how
Jules deals with hair this long daily. Oh! Speaking of—
"

Suddenly, the screen split as Juliet joined the call.
"Hello, beautiful people!"

"Hey, Jules," Oliver said.

"'Hey, Jules,'" she parroted back. "He hasn't seen
my beautiful face in well over a month, and all I get is
a 'Hey, Jules.' Honestly," she scoffed.

"Oh, my bad," Oliver said sarcastically. "Hello, oh wonderful, Juliet, the love of my life."

"'Love of my life?'" Ryan repeated, his face coming into the frame with Anna. "Someone is going to be jealous."

"Why would someone be jealous?" Juliet asked. "Oliver! Do you have a new beau?"

"No," Oliver said, a little too quickly. "I think he's talking about your boyfriend, Mark. Remember him?"

"Oh, right," she said with a shrug.

"So, what is this call about?" Oliver asked, wanting a change of subject. "Not that I'm not happy to see you guys."

"Hang on," Ryan said. "Ezra is logging into the call now."

"Oh, do I finally get to meet the dark and mysterious high school friend?" Juliet asked.

"Dark and mysterious?" Ezra repeated as his face popped up on the screen. "Sounds like an interesting guy."

"Oh, and he has an accent," Juliet cooed, leaning forward and tossing her long, brown hair over her shoulders, and Oliver had to fight not to roll his eyes. "Hi, I'm Juliet." She gave a little wave at the screen.

"Nice to meet you, Juliet. I've heard a lot about you from Ryan and Ollie," Ezra said with a smile. "Also, hi, everyone."

"Hey, Ezra!" Anna chirped. "Now we can share the news. Ryan, do you want to tell them?"

Ryan wrapped his arm around her shoulder and pressed a kiss to her temple. "No, you tell them, sweetheart. You're clearly excited about it."

"Are you sure?" she asked, looking up at him fondly.

"Jesus Christ, someone tell us something," Juliet demanded.

"Okay, okay," Anna said with a laugh. "Ryan and I

have decided that we're still getting married on the twenty-ninth."

"We don't want to wait until next year. We talked it over with our parents, and they were super supportive," Ryan continued.

"Oh, I'm so glad!" Juliet exclaimed. "What about the reception?"

"That's still happening next year. Don't worry, all of your planning won't go to waste," Anna assured her.

"Oh, thank God."

"So, where are you having it?" Ezra asked.

"Well, now that the parks are open again, we were thinking of having it outside," Ryan said. "That way, our parents can be there, and Ezra and Juliet, you guys, too, if you're comfortable with it."

"Well, there's no way I'm missing my best mate's wedding," Ezra said.

"Ditto," Juliet added. "But wait, Oliver was supposed to officiate."

"I still can," Oliver chimed in.

"But, Ollie, it's still too dangerous out there," Anna protested.

"What, so you don't want me there?" Oliver challenged.

"Of course, we want you to be there!" Anna said. "And we still want you to officiate. I was talking with Ryan, and we thought maybe we could FaceTime you in and—"

"So, like I'm some sort of Bubble Boy," Oliver said bitterly.

"We just don't want you to get sick," Ryan added.

"You're high risk, and we're just trying to be cognizant of—"

"I get that!" Oliver snapped. "Anna, you act as if I don't know that I'm sick. If anyone fucking knows that, it's me!"

"Ollie—"

"No! Look, I know you care about me, and you want to protect me, but you don't understand what this has been like for me. You guys talk about being stir-crazy, but at least you get to leave to go to the grocery store or go on walks. I haven't set foot outside in four months! I need to get out of this stupid fucking apartment, or I'm going to lose my ever-loving shit."

Everyone was silent after his outburst until Ezra broke the silence. "I think it should be up to Oliver. I mean, yeah, he's high-risk, but he's also an adult. He can make his own decisions, and he's right. It would be outside, and it would only be us, Andrew and Bridget, and Anna's parents. It should be fine. We've all been careful."

Oliver relaxed into his pillows and looked gratefully at Ezra. "Thank you, Ezra," he whispered.

Ezra sent a soft smile at the camera that Oliver somehow knew was only for him.

Oliver took a deep breath. "The numbers are looking okay, and like hell am I missing my two best friends getting married."

Ryan sighed and looked at Anna. "It wouldn't feel right not having Ollie there in person," he said gently.

"No, it wouldn't. Alright"—Anna sighed—"but we're meeting in the park by your apartment, Oliver, so you don't have to go too far."

"Oh, there's a gorgeous spot in Prospect Park that would be perfect," Juliet offered.

Oliver nodded in agreement, and they spent the next fifteen minutes making plans. When they were done, Oliver left the call and instantly grabbed his phone to text Ezra.

Ezra

Monday Night, August 17, 2020

Ezra had barely exited the Zoom call when his phone buzzed on his bedside table. He picked it up and saw several texts from Oliver come in rapid succession.

Oliver Wheeler 🗃
August 17, 2020, 7:30 PM

Oliver Wheeler 🗃

Hey

Thank you for agreeing with me back there.

And before you say that it was nothing, or it wasn't a big deal, it's not nothing. I know they mean well, but sometimes everyone gets so caught up with the fact that I'm sick that they treat me like I'm made of glass. So I appreciate you not doing that.

Ezra Beaumont

Like I said, you're an adult, and they weren't treating you like you could make a decision for yourself. Sure, it's a risk, but if anyone should assess that, it's you.

Oliver Wheeler 🗃

Still, you could have kept silent, but you didn't, so thank you. I honestly can't tell you how much that means to me.

Ezra stared at his phone for a long moment. If there

were ever a moment for him to just pluck up the courage and tell Oliver how he felt, it was now.

He could do it.

He should do it.

He was going to do it.

He took a deep breath, held it for a moment, then let it out slowly before typing out, **You mean a lot to me, so of course I have your back. I care about you, and honestly, I really didn't want to miss out on an opportunity to see you in person, even if it will be physically distanced.** His finger hovered over the send button.

He couldn't do it.

He erased the text and started over. **You're my friend, and I care about you. So, of course, I've got your back, Ollie.** He pressed send and let his head fall back against the headboard with a groan.

God, he was a coward.

Seconds later, his phone pinged, and he read the incoming texts. The first was Oliver thanking him again, then under that, something that gave Ezra slight hope despite him chickening out. **I care about you, too.**

15

Ezra

Friday Night, August 28, 2020

Ryan Coleman

August 28, 2020, 10:43 PM

Ezra Beaumont

So mate, tomorrow is the big day.

Are you nervous?

Ryan Coleman

Actually, not at all. I think it's because I know tomorrow is going to be so casual.

We don't have to worry about anyone getting too drunk and making a scene, or the caterer not showing up on time.

Tomorrow is literally just about Anna and me.

Ezra Beaumont

So no cold feet then?

Ryan Coleman

None. I've been waiting for this day

since our first date.

Ezra Beaumont

You're such a sap.

But I'm really happy for you.

Also you're making this whole best-man thing really easy.

I literally had two jobs: talk you down from getting cold feet and throwing the bachelor party.

First one I clearly don't need to do, and the second one... Well I'm still doing that eventually.

I don't care if you're not technically a bachelor anymore. You're getting a stag night dammit.

Ryan Coleman

I would be offended if I didn't, seeing as I know Juliet still intends on throwing Anna a bachelorette party.

Ezra Beaumont

Yours will be better.

Ryan Coleman

You sure about that? I think I heard them mention a cruise.

Ezra Beaumont

Oh man.

That sounds fun...

I'll come up with something. I've got another entire year to plan 😊

Ryan Coleman

Oh dear...

So, are YOU nervous about tomorrow?

Ezra Beaumont

Why would I be nervous?

Ryan Coleman

You're going to be seeing Ollie in person
for the first time.

Have you told him how you feel yet?

Ezra Beaumont

Ugh. Can we not?

Yes. I'm nervous, but I don't want to
talk about it.

Tomorrow is about you, not about me
and my crush on literally the cutest
man on the planet.

Go spend time with your soon-to-be
wife.

Ryan Coleman

Can't. She banished me to the spare
room so I won't see her until she's ready
and dressed up.

We're even arriving separately tomorrow.

Ezra Beaumont

Then get some sleep. It's a big day tomorrow.

Ryan Coleman

Not tired.

Ezra Beaumont

Take a melatonin

Ryan Coleman

Don't have any.

So you won't give me even the littlest
detail about how things are going?

Ezra Beaumont

There's nothing to tell because I haven't said anything to him yet.

Ryan Coleman

Yet? So you're going to then?

Ezra Beaumont

I don't know, okay?

I almost did the other day, but then I chickened out.

Ryan Coleman

Are you afraid he doesn't like you back? Because if that's it, I can tell you I'm pretty sure he does based solely on the way he looked at you on our Zoom call the other day.

Ezra Beaumont

It's not that exactly.

Ryan Coleman

Then what's holding you back?

Ezra Beaumont

Well, we work together and he's one of your best friends, which complicates things. But that aside...

I don't want to mess this up. Yeah, I'm fairly certain he likes me back because we've at least texted almost every day since May and FaceTimed every night for the past 2 months to watch tv together. But what if I'm wrong? What if he doesn't like me back and me saying something ruins our friendship? Or what if he does like me, but he hasn't said anything because he doesn't want to date me, so me saying something also ruins our friendship?

Ryan Coleman

Oh, wow, you really like him.

Ezra Beaumont

Yeah, we've been out of crush territory for a while now.

There's just something about him. He makes me feel good about myself and I didn't realize how much I needed that after all the shit with my mom. I know it'll probably sound crazy, but it feels like he came into my life at the right time. His friendship is important to me so what if I'm wrong? I don't want to lose him. I'd rather only ever be friends than have nothing at all.

Ryan Coleman

Well, look, for what it's worth, it takes a hell of a lot to lose Oliver as a friend once you have him, and from what it sounds like you've got him. So don't write off telling him how you feel just yet.

Maybe take tomorrow to test the waters. It'll be much easier to figure out if he actually likes you back in person.

Ezra Beaumont

Thanks. That helps.

Now, it's late. Get some sleep. Can't have you looking all puffy and sleep-deprived in pictures.

Ryan Coleman

Oh, speaking of, can you bring your camera? It's better than anyone else's.

Ezra Beaumont

I was already planning on it.

Ryan Coleman

Thank you. You're the best.

Ezra Beaumont

I know

Ryan Coleman

Night

Ezra Beaumont

Goodnight!

Saturday Afternoon, August 29, 2020

Ezra pulled Josie's car into the first spot he saw on the street across from the entrance to Prospect Park that Juliet had given him directions to. After straightening out and checking that he was close enough to the curb—which took longer than he would have cared to admit since it had been several years since he had to parallel park—he cut the engine and sighed. He was happy that Anna and Ryan were still able to get married, despite everything, but he wished that things were different. They deserved a big celebration, not a small, socially distanced ceremony in a park in the middle of a pandemic. It didn't feel right.

Ryan's wedding day was supposed to be a big affair with drinking and dancing. It was selfish, and he knew it, but he'd looked forward to learning what Ryan's life had been like for the past seven years. He wanted to make up for all of that lost time that he'd been floating around Europe like he was in limbo. He'd looked forward to meeting all of Ryan's new friends and maybe even meeting someone to take home that night because as every rom-com he'd ever watched had taught him, that was what the best man did.

Although, if he thought about it, there would still technically be a person there that he'd like to take out. Someone cute. Someone with sparkling green eyes, freckles dusted across his nose, and a smile that made him weak in the knees. Someone that he had no right being nervous to see—but he was. The prospect of seeing Oliver for the first time in person had his stomach twisted in knots. What if the chemistry he'd picked up on in video chats was suddenly not there anymore? Or, worse, what if he had been imagining it, and Oliver didn't feel anything toward him besides friendship? The conversation with Ryan last night didn't help, which is why Ezra hadn't wanted to talk about it in the first place, but Ryan always had a way of pulling information out of a person. So, there he sat, fiddling with the keys in his lap as he tried to deep-breathe away the nervous anticipation.

Ezra checked his reflection in the rearview mirror and ran a hand through his hair nervously before taking his mask and looping the elastic around his ears. He stared ahead for a moment longer, fiddling with the rolled-up sleeves of his Oxford shirt, then he took a deep breath to steel his nerves, grabbed the strap of his DSLR, and opened the car door.

The park was huge, but it still didn't take long for him to find the giant tree near the edge of the lake that Juliet had suggested would make the best backdrop for photos while still being close to an entrance so Oliver and Ryan's parents wouldn't have to hike halfway across the park. When he got there, he found Juliet— or at least who he assumed was Juliet—attempting to string up some paper lanterns in the tree. He'd only seen her once on the video call a few days prior, but her long, brown, curly hair was pretty recognizable.

"Do you need help with that?" Ezra asked as he approached.

"Oh!" Juliet jumped and whirled around. "Jesus, Ezra, you scared the shit out of me. Oh, hold on, let me put my mask back on." She set down the lantern she was fighting with, reached into the pocket of her red maxi dress to pull out her mask, then looped it around her ears. "Okay. It's nice to meet you in person. Wait, you are Ezra, right? I'd assumed based on the accent, tattoos, and frankly gorgeous hair, but it's hard to recognize people with these masks. I guess that's how superheroes keep their identity safe, though, huh?"

Ezra laughed. "Although, normally superheroes cover their eyes instead of their mouth. But yeah, I'm Ezra. It's nice to meet you." He instinctively went to reach a hand out to shake hers, but caught himself and settled on an awkward wave.

"I keep doing that, too," she said with a laugh. "But, to answer your question, yes, I could use help. I forgot to bring a step ladder, and I was just going to wait for Oliver—because he's a giant—but he's running behind." She swept her hair over her shoulder and looked him over. "You look strong, tall, and capable, though."

"I'll see what I can do," Ezra said, setting his camera down by a mini speaker in the grass. He took the lantern from her and got to work stringing the lanterns in the tree branches while Juliet turned her attention to setting up several blankets spread a few feet apart from each other with some boxed lunches and mini champagne bottles on each, which they thought would be the best socially distanced alternative to a traditional garden picnic.

"So, what time is everyone else getting here?" he asked after a few minutes of silent work.

"Ryan and his parents should get here in a few minutes, Anna sometime about ten minutes after that with her parents so she can enter, and"—she pulled her phone out of a pocket in her dress and checked it—"Oliver just texted that he's coming down the path now, so he should only be a few minutes."

Ezra's hands stilled for a moment on the knot he was tying to secure the last lantern. "Oh, cool," he said, trying to sound as casual as possible. Just as he said it, he heard a shout from across the park.

"Hey! Ezra!"

Ezra smiled, tightened the last knot, and turned to Ryan, strolling toward him, Andrew and Bridget Coleman following afterward. Ezra went to meet him halfway, and nearly pulled him into a crushing hug on instinct, but stopped himself. The two of them stood awkwardly at a distance from each other. "Hey, Ryan. Looking snazzy."

Ryan looked down at the casual linen suit he was wearing, then looked back up and shrugged like it was nothing, but Ezra could see the grin in his eyes.

Ezra smiled, then looked to Ryan's parents. "Hi, Andrew. Bridget."

"Oh, my sweet boy!" Bridget cried, gripping her husband's arm as if to prevent herself from hurrying forward to sweep him into a big hug. "You've grown up so much since I last saw you! Look how long your hair has gotten."

"I know, it's been a long time. Sorry, I haven't been back to visit in so long," Ezra said.

"Oh, don't let my wife guilt-trip you, son," Andrew said with a laugh. "You were experiencing culture! I want to hear all about your—"

"Oh, wait, I think I see Oliver," Ryan said, bringing a hand up to block the sun so he could squint into the distance.

From a distance, Oliver sent their group a wave. Ryan waved back enthusiastically before turning back to look at Ezra, not that he noticed. Ezra was too busy watching Oliver walk toward him—them. It was like time had slowed and everything else faded into the background. All he could hear was his own heartbeat thundering in his ears. Ezra had thought Oliver was gorgeous on a video call, but it didn't compare to seeing him in person.

"Hey, everyone," Oliver said as he reached the group, stopping a good six feet away from them.

Oliver was a little taller than Ezra had imagined him to be, taller than him, properly earning the "giant" title Juliet had given him. The sunlight brought out the gold in his hair and eyes and made the freckles scattered on what was visible of his face even more noticeable. His corduroy pants hugged his legs and were cuffed at the ankles, and, for once, he wasn't wearing some oversized jumper and instead had put on a fitted, dark green collared shirt with the sleeves rolled up.

It was a very good thing that Ezra was wearing a mask since he was pretty sure his mouth had dropped open because peeking out from underneath Oliver's rolled-up sleeve was a tattoo. Ezra couldn't see the whole thing, but from what he could see, there were books and some watercolor shading that was absolutely beautiful. It wasn't until he noticed the tattoo that Ezra realized Oliver was also using a cane. Nearly every square inch was covered in stickers, which made Ezra smile slightly. It was so Oliver.

"Hey, Olls," Ezra said, shoving his hands into the pockets of his black skinny jeans. If he thought not getting to hug Ryan, Andrew, and Bridget was hard, being ten feet away from Oliver without being able to even get near him was downright torture.

"Hi," Oliver said, sending him what must have been a smile based on the way those sparkling green eyes of his crinkled slightly. It was probably good that Oliver was wearing a mask, too, because he wasn't sure he'd be able to stand seeing Oliver's smile.

"I ran into Anna on my way in," Oliver said, turning his attention to Ryan. "So, we've probably got about ten more minutes to set up."

"Thanks, Ollie," Ryan said.

"I'll go make sure Anna is ready," Juliet called, then faint acoustic instrumental music started playing out of the tiny speaker, making Ezra jump. "Ezra, I saw you brought a camera. Do you want to get a few photos of Ryan and his parents before we get started?"

Ezra blinked for a moment to bring himself back to the real world and looked behind him to see Juliet with a bouquet in her hand. He needed to focus. His best mate was about to get married. "Yeah, I'll do that."

Ryan walked with Ezra to grab his camera, giving Oliver a moment to chat with Andrew and Bridget.

"So, still doing alright there, Ryan?" Ezra asked as he started fussing with the settings of his camera.

"I couldn't be happier," Ryan gushed.

"I'm beyond happy for you, mate. Anna is a good one. Honestly, the best," Ezra said.

"I know," he said, smiling. "And how are you doing?"

"I'm—" In the distance, Ezra heard Oliver laugh— probably at some corny dad pun Andrew was telling— and he couldn't help but look over for a split second. He snapped a quick test shot of the moment, then stopped short as Oliver glanced in his direction. Ezra shoved a hand through his hair, turned back to Ryan, and busied himself with checking that the exposure was right. "I'm great. Now come on, let's get some pictures before you get hitched."

Five minutes later, and a few dozen socially distanced family photos later, everyone was in place under the tree's shade, waiting for Anna to enter. Ezra stood next to Ryan, poised with his camera, ready to fire away. He glimpsed Juliet and knew Anna wasn't far behind, so he faced Ryan, ready to capture that first look.

Ryan's face lit up, which was easy to see, even with the mask on. Ezra turned and fired off a few more shots as Anna walked toward them, escorted by both of her parents. She looked stunning, her blond hair wound into a simple half-updo with flowers weaved into it that matched the flowers covering the white, lace sundress she was wearing. Juliet took her bouquet from her as she reached Ryan, who pulled her in for a hug.

"You are beautiful," Ryan whispered, resting his forehead against Anna's.

Anna let out a watery giggle. "And you are quite handsome."

They stood in their embrace for a moment longer, then stepped apart and held each other's hands.

Oliver pulled out his phone to read from, then cleared his throat so he could begin. "Friends and family, we are gathered here today to join together Ryan and Anna in the ultimate bonds of marriage. I've known Anna and Ryan for a long time, and it is an honor that I get to marry you both today."

"Couldn't have imagined anyone else doing it," Ryan said.

Oliver looked from Ryan to Anna, sending her a fond look before continuing. "Anna, from that first day of orientation at NYU seven years ago, you've treated me like family. You are so kind and so strong. I am in awe of you. And Ryan, you are the fiercest friend I have ever had. You care so deeply, and I don't know what I would do without you. I love you both so much, and it has been one of the greatest pleasures in my life watching my two best friends go from bickering hall mates to reluctant friends to one of the best couples I know. You both are so different and headstrong, but I think that's why you work so well together.

"Despite your differences, you make things work. Not because you need each other but because you chose each other, and I think that's even more of a testament to the love you have for each other more than anything else like fate or destiny could be. Now, I believe you two have prepared your own vows?"

Anna sniffed and nodded as a few tears rolled down her cheeks, disappearing beneath her mask.

"I'll go first," Ryan said. A breeze kicked up, and he reached a hand up to brush a few wisps of Anna's hair back behind her ear. "Anna, I could list all the reasons that I love you, but then we'd probably be here all day, and I'm pretty sure Oliver would kill me, so I'll keep it short. You are the best person I have ever met, and every moment that I spend with you makes me a better person, too. You are my best friend"—he turned to look at Ezra—"sorry, Ezra."

Everyone laughed.

"No problem, mate," Ezra said as Ryan turned back to Anna.

"You are my best friend, and I can't imagine spending the rest of my life with anyone but you."

Anna sniffed again. "Okay, I guess it's my turn. Ryan—" She let out a shuddering breath. "No, I can do this. Okay—Ryan, back in May, when we had to decide to postpone our wedding, it had to have been one of the most disappointing moments of my life, because for so long I have been looking for someone like you to spend forever with. But then, you looked at me and said, 'To hell with the big ceremony; all that matters to me is that I get to call you my wife,' and that reminded me of why I wanted to marry you. You were there for me like you always are, and you were right. At the end of the day, it doesn't matter to me where we are, as long as I get to call you my husband."

Ezra watched a tear escape the corner of Ryan's eye, which threatened to bring forth the tears welling up in his own eyes. He blinked and focused on continuing to take photos.

"Shit, guys, you're going to make me cry," Oliver said, laughing thickly.

"Oliver, could you maybe refrain from cursing in the middle of my wedding?" Anna scolded.

"Fuck, sorry. Ugh, dam—" Oliver stopped himself. "Sorry, sorry!" Everyone laughed. "I'll get that under control for the one next year. Okay. Anna, do you take Ryan to be your husband?"

"I do."

"And Ryan, do you take Anna to be your wife?"

"You bet, I do."

Oliver looked between them both, visibly beaming even behind the mask. "Well, by the power vested in me— Oh, wait, the rings. Jules, do you have—?"

Juliet nodded and took a few steps in and handed off the rings to Anna and Ryan. They placed the rings on each other's left ring fingers, then looked at Oliver.

"Alright, now, by the power vested in me by the State of New York and the online certification I took while I was bored during jury duty, I now pronounce you, husband and wife. Ryan, you may practice very poor social distancing and kiss your wife."

Ryan let go of Anna's hands, and after they both reached up to take their masks off, he swept Anna into his arms and kissed her.

16

Oliver

Saturday Night, August 20, 2020

Juliet Ríos

August 29, 2020, 5:03 PM

Juliet Rios

Okay, I have two things.

Oliver Wheeler

Yes?

Juliet Rios

One, beautiful speech. If I ever get married, I want you to officiate.

Oliver Wheeler

Great. That can be my thing now.

Juliet Rios

Two, WHAT WAS THAT VIBE BETWEEN YOU AND THE SEXY AS FUCK TATTOOED BRITISH MAN?

Oliver Wheeler

I have no idea what you're talking about.

Juliet Rios

Don't play coy with me, bitch. There was a vibe.

I thought I picked something up in that Zoom call the other day, so today I thought I'd test it by flirting my ass off to get a reaction, you know, as I do, and he was not paying me any mind.

Oliver Wheeler

So, because he wasn't flirting with you, you assume something is going on between us? That's a bit of a leap, Jules.

Juliet Rios

No, I assumed something was going on between you because you turned into a blushy mess the moment you saw him.

Oliver Wheeler

I was wearing a mask. How could you tell if I was blushing?

Juliet Rios

One, I know you. Two, you had to take your mask off to eat and were STILL BLUSHING every time he even looked at you.

I also know what I saw, and trust me when I tell you that Ezra definitely likes you.

Oliver Wheeler

Do you really think so?

Juliet Ríos

He froze like a deer in the headlights
when he saw you, and his voice got all
soft when he spoke to you.
He also couldn't keep his eyes off you.
So yeah, I'm confident he likes you too.

It had been hours since Juliet had texted Oliver, but he couldn't stop thinking about what she said about Ezra. It was one thing for him to believe that there had been a moment between them in the park, but it was another thing if Juliet noticed it. He wasn't making it up. And if he hadn't been imagining the energy between them at the wedding, maybe he hadn't been imagining the same energy during all of their video calls and text exchanges.

There was something there, but that didn't mean that Ezra wanted to pursue it. Ezra had never given him any sign that he wanted anything more than friendship, at least not directly. Oliver let out a frustrated groan and tossed his book onto the nightstand. He wouldn't be able to focus anyway, not with Mary's voice ringing through his head. *You don't know that unless you do something about it.*

Fuck it.

He grabbed his phone off the nightstand, checking the time. It was almost ten-thirty, so not too late, but later than he'd ever called before. He sucked in a deep breath. No, he couldn't chicken out. He navigated to his favorite contacts to find Ezra's name, and, before he could talk himself out of it, he tapped the call icon. He curled his knees into his chest as the phone rang.

It felt like forever before Ezra picked up. "Oliver?" Ezra asked, his voice sounding thick with sleep.

Fuck, Oliver had woken him up. Shit. And damn him, why did he have to sound even sexier when he was all groggy?

"Olls, is everything alright?"

"Shit. Sorry, I didn't mean to wake you up. I just— fuck—I can just talk to you tomorrow."

"No, it's okay, you didn't— Well, you woke me up, but I fell asleep reading. My lights are still on and everything, so I would have had to get up eventually," Ezra explained. "Is everything alright? You sound…"

"No, everything is fine," Oliver croaked, closing his eyes to collect himself. "Sorry, I didn't mean to call you out of the blue so late. I just figured— Well, I didn't know when you would get back from spending time with the Colemans, and I know you haven't seen them in a while, so I didn't text you earlier because I wanted to let you— Never mind. It's not important. I can let you get back to sleep."

"Ollie… You can call me out of the blue, no matter what time it is," Ezra said. "I enjoy talking to you."

"I enjoy talking to you, too, Ezra." He bit his lip as they both fell silent. He could do this. Maybe. "It was nice seeing everyone today," he said, breaking the silence.

"It was. I bet it was nice for you to get out of the apartment, too."

Oliver laughed nervously. "Yeah, it was. Although I'm pretty sure I got a sunburn."

Ezra laughed. "You weren't even outside that long!"

"Yeah, well, not everyone tans as easily as you do," he teased, and Ezra laughed again. "It was also nice seeing you. In-person, I mean."

Ezra was silent for a moment, and when he spoke again, his voice came out soft and unsure, as if he were nervous. "It was nice. Really nice. Harder than I expected, though."

"What—?"

"Sorry, that didn't come out right," Ezra blurted. He

muttered something to himself before continuing. "It's just—I expected it to be hard seeing Ryan, and Anna, and Andrew, and Bridget, and not be able to hug them or anything, but seeing you…"

"Ezra…" Oliver started, but Ezra continued speaking so fast that Oliver almost didn't understand him.

"I didn't think that the first time I got to meet you in person would be from six feet away with masks. I pictured it being when all of this mess was over, and everything was back to normal. And part of me wishes I could pretend that today didn't count because I'd built it up in my head so much and—"

"Ezra," Oliver said, more firmly this time. "I—"

"Sorry, I know I'm rambling, it's just—"

"I like you," Oliver blurted out, unable to stop himself. He heard Ezra's sharp intake of breath and clapped a hand over his mouth, even though he knew it wouldn't take the words back.

"I'm—wait, what?"

Oliver took a deep breath and let it out slowly. "Sorry, I didn't mean to blurt it out like that, but—fuck, there it is. I like you, Ezra. A lot. As more than just a friend."

The silence that greeted him was deafening, and Oliver was about to hang up the phone in embarrassment when Ezra let out a breathy laugh. "Oh, thank God."

Oliver let out the breath he'd been holding in a rush. "What?"

"I like you, too. I like you a lot—have for a while now. Since our second phone call. It's why I kept sending you all of those random quotes. I just wanted an excuse to talk to you."

Oliver laughed in relief. "Fuck, thank God. Wait, you mean the phone call when I burned my hand and lectured you about literature for twenty minutes?"

Ezra let out a strangled groan that sounded like it

was being muffled by his pillow. "It was the most you'd ever said to me, and it was just cute, okay?"

Oliver felt his face flush, and he hugged his knees tighter to his chest.

"Ryan teased me mercilessly about it, too," Ezra said with a laugh. "He couldn't believe that I'd fallen into Ollie's Literary Trap."

"I'm sorry, the what, now?"

"Shit, I don't think I was supposed to tell you about that. Apparently, it was something Ryan, Juliet, and Anna came up with in college. Forget I said anything."

"Oh, I will definitely ask them about that later," Oliver promised, and Ezra laughed.

"But, yeah. So, I've liked you for months, even though you were a bit of a jerk at first."

"Hey, I said I was sorry about that," Oliver protested. "And I changed my mind about you once I got to know you better."

"I know, I'm just teasing you," Ezra said.

"I still feel bad, though."

"Don't. If you hadn't been a jerk, I might not have tried so hard to get you to change your mind, then we wouldn't be here."

Oliver smiled. "Well, I'm glad you did. I've never been happier to be wrong about a person."

"Can we—can I FaceTime you? I know I saw you already today, but I want to see you again."

Oliver swallowed hard. "Yeah, okay. I mean, yeah, I want to see you, too." He heard the call-disconnecting sound, only for a ringing sound to replace it as Ezra started a FaceTime call. Oliver hugged his knees and positioned the camera to answer the call. "Hi," he said, sending a shy smile at the camera.

"Jesus, you're cute," Ezra breathed.

Oliver felt his cheeks heat, and he let out a nervous laugh.

"Sorry, did I say that out loud?"

Oliver nodded. "Yeah, you did."

Ezra smiled, then shrugged. "Well, I stand by it. Oh, also, can I just say how entirely unfair that I did not know you have a tattoo until today?"

"Unfair?" Oliver asked.

"Yes, unfair. How could you not mention that you have a tattoo? A forearm tattoo, at that."

"It never came up?"

"'Never came up,' he says."

"I still don't get how this is unfair," Oliver said, smiling at Ezra's mock outrage.

"Tattoos are very attractive."

"Says the man who has six."

"Eight, actually. But, see, the difference is you knew about those beforehand. I, on the other hand, was completely blindsided today," Ezra teased.

"Oh, well, now you know how I felt the other day when you just broke out in French. As if you weren't sexy enough with the aforementioned tattoos and the British accent, you have to be fluent in another fucking language?" Oliver fired back. "And French, at that."

"Ah, so you like when I speak French, do you?" Ezra grinned slowly, and Oliver felt his cheeks heat again. "*Merde, tu es si mignon.*"

"Ezra," Oliver groaned, earning a laugh. He was silent for a beat. "You know, I nearly said screw it today when I saw you. It took every bit of restraint I had not to just walk right up to you and—fuck, I don't even know—hug you, I guess?"

The camera jostled as Ezra shifted onto his side and grabbed a pillow to hug to his chest. "God, I know."

Oliver groaned again and buried his face in his knees. "I hate this. I fucking hate this."

"Olls—"

He lifted his head. "I just hate this. I hate being sick.

As if it's not bad enough that I'm sometimes in so much fucking pain that I need a cane to walk, or that I lose feeling in my hands when it gets too cold, but now...my body feels like a prison half the time, and now, because of it, my apartment's a prison, too," Oliver vented.

"I can't even imagine how hard this is for you."

"And at first it was fine—well, not fine, but I didn't mind it so much. I'm a homebody anyway, but— Dammit, I want to see you. Like actually, see you. But I can't leave my apartment without worrying about getting the damn coronavirus." Oliver sighed and buried his face in his knees again. "I'm sorry. I don't mean to be such a mess."

"What if I came to you?" Ezra asked.

Oliver lifted his head again.

"I've been doing a lot of reading on risk mitigation and incubation periods, and other than today, I've been good about staying home. We get groceries delivered, and the only time I leave the house is to go out for runs, and I go really early in the morning, so I don't encounter anyone. So I could get tested, and when the test comes back negative, I could come over."

Oliver opened his mouth to say something, but Ezra cut him off.

"I wouldn't even have to come in. I'd honestly be content with just sitting in your hallway and talking to you through a crack in your door but—"

"If you think that the next time you're within ten feet of me, I'm not touching you, then you're mistaken," Oliver interrupted, then he laughed nervously and added, "with your consent, obviously."

"You have it," Ezra said, smiling.

Oliver sighed. "But I don't know if I can ask you to go through the trouble of getting a test just to see me."

"You aren't asking," Ezra said, matter-of-fact. "It

was my idea."

"I know, it's just that we don't know how long this situation will last—"

"So we keep doing the same thing until it's safe—"

"But what if it's months? I don't want you to change your life because of me—"

"I would continue to social distance despite the city lifting the order because it's the smart thing to do, not only because it would be safer for you." Ezra took a deep breath, then softened. "If you don't want to take the risk because you think it's not safe yet, I understand that. But please don't say no just because you don't want me going through the trouble. My wanting to take these precautions has just as much to do with me as it does with you. I want to see you."

Oliver took a deep breath and let it out shakily. "Okay."

"'Okay' as in, we're doing this?" Ezra asked hopefully.

He tucked his his knees under his chin and nodded. "Fuck. Yes. I want to see you, too."

Ezra grinned, and Oliver couldn't help but blush. God, he'd never blushed so much in his life. It was almost embarrassing.

"*Si mignon*," Ezra breathed. "I'll make an appointment to get tested in a few days."

"Okay." Oliver smiled. "How fast is the turnaround for the results?"

"Last time, it took about a week, but they're getting faster, so I'm not sure."

"So not in time for next weekend," Oliver said with a small sigh.

"No, but probably by the weekend after next," Ezra said.

Oliver smiled again. "So, September 12th, then?"

Ezra nodded. "It's a date."

17

Oliver

Saturday Afternoon, September 12, 2020

Ezra Beaumont

September 12, 2020, 1:43 PM

Ezra Beaumont

Just parked.

Oliver swore under his breath and tossed his phone on the nearby chair. Ezra was early.

Shit, shit, shit.

Ezra was early, and he was nowhere near ready. The sourdough loaf he'd made that morning had taken a lot longer to bake than usual, which meant that he hadn't been able to clean when he'd originally intended. Then, of course, cleaning the apartment had taken a lot longer than he'd planned for, which led to him only getting out of the shower five minutes ago. So now, he only had about five minutes to get dressed, and he didn't know what he was going to wear.

None of this would have been a problem if he'd been able to clean the apartment the weekend before like he'd intended to. But his body had decided that the walk from his apartment to Prospect Park for Ryan and Anna's wedding was an overexertion—despite it being less than a mile and a half round trip and him using his cane as a precautionary measure—and his knees flared up for a week and a half. Perfect timing, really. But he didn't have time to dwell on it or panic because Ezra was only a few minutes away, and he wasn't wearing pants.

Oliver went over to the dresser that doubled as a TV stand and pulled out a T-shirt and the pair of corduroy pants he wore to the wedding—also his first date pants because Juliet had always said they made his legs look great even though he didn't think so. Then he went over to the entryway closet and yanked a random maroon cardigan off of a hanger. He slid it on and shut the closet door just in time for the buzzer by the front door to go off.

He jumped and ran over to the call box, then stopped short and waited a beat before pressing the intercom button so as to not seem like he was waiting by the door. "Hello?" he said into the speaker.

"Hey, it's me," Ezra's voice came through the speaker.

Oliver pressed the button to let Ezra in, then less than a minute later, since his apartment was on the first floor, there was a knock at the door. After taking a beat to take a deep breath, he opened the door. He smiled at Ezra, who stood on his doormat with his hands shoved into his pockets. He'd dressed relatively casually, too—just black jeans with a slight rip in the knee, a white T-shirt, and an open flannel rolled up to his forearms since the weather had started to cool down.

Oliver hadn't been nervous when he woke up, which

was likely because the number of tasks he had to cram into a short time period had preoccupied his brain. But now that Ezra was standing in front of him—looking effortlessly handsome at that…

"*Bonjour*," Ezra said, his eyes crinkling at the corners in a smile that Oliver couldn't see because of the mask he was still wearing. Cocky fucker.

"Hi," Oliver breathed. They stood there for a moment before Oliver shook his head to clear it and stepped out of the way. "Sorry, come in."

"Thanks." Ezra stepped through the doorway and glanced around the small apartment while Oliver shut the door.

"You can kick your shoes off there," Oliver said, pointing to the mat next to the door, "and the bathroom is just through there so you can wash your hands."

"Great, thanks." Ezra toed off his shoes, then followed Oliver's directions to the bathroom.

Oliver wasn't sure what to do with himself while Ezra was washing his hands, and the apartment wasn't all that big, so he took a few steps away from the door and leaned against the back of the couch to wait. Less than a minute later, Ezra walked back out, took off his mask, and shoved it in his pocket.

Oliver stood again and smiled nervously. "Hi."

Ezra smiled back, almost nervously, as well. "Hi."

"So, I would give you a tour, but this is kind of all there is, apartment-wise." Oliver gestured around the living room, which was taken up by his brown plushy couch. "You passed my barely functional kitchen on the way to the bathroom, and my bedroom is through that door"—he pointed to the set of French doors flanked by bookshelves—"well, I call it a bedroom, but it's sectioned off with pressure walls and not legally big enough to be considered a bedroom."

"I was going to ask how you found a one-bedroom in this neighborhood all on your own on an editor's salary," Ezra said with a laugh.

"Yeah, they have to list it as a studio. Also, Andrew's friend from college is the building owner, so I got a discount."

"Gotta love nepotism."

"Well, you would know," Oliver teased.

Ezra gasped in mock indignation. "Rude."

Oliver laughed and shifted his weight.

Ezra smiled, then took a tentative step toward him. "Can I—?" He held out his arms.

Oliver nodded and closed the distance between them, wrapping his arms around Ezra's waist while Ezra's arms circled his shoulders. He'd meant to keep the hug short since it was only the first date, but—fuck, it had been six months since someone had hugged him, and he couldn't help it. He let out a small sigh and pulled Ezra tighter into his chest, smiling when Ezra squeezed him just as tightly back. They stood there for a few beats, then Oliver pulled away. He kept his arms around Ezra's waist but allowed enough space for him to step away if he wanted. He didn't.

"Sorry, this is the first hug I've had in months, not counting Fiona," Oliver admitted, heat creeping into his cheeks.

Ezra simply smiled and pulled him back in for another tight hug, although shorter this time. "Don't apologize. But speaking of Fiona, where is that beautiful creature?"

Oliver laughed. "Probably hiding under my bed, which is what she does when someone new comes—" A trill interrupted him, and he looked down to see Fiona weaving between his and Ezra's legs. "Or not."

Ezra's face lit up as he looked down between them, then his arms dropped from around Oliver's shoulders in favor of crouching down to greet Fiona. "Well, hello, ma'am," he said, holding out a hand for her to sniff.

Oliver watched, expecting Fiona to look at Ezra's hand with mild disinterest, then walk away—which was what she usually did with anyone who wasn't him—but to his surprise, she rubbed her cheek on Ezra's out-stretched hand.

Ezra looked up and grinned. "I think she likes me."

"It looks like it," Oliver said, unable to help returning the grin.

After a few more head pats, Fiona trotted away, and Ezra straightened back up. "So, movies?"

"Yes. If you want to make yourself comfortable, I can get drinks first. I have water and some iced mint tea, but I could also make some hot tea if you'd like."

"Iced mint would be great, thank you," Ezra said.

Oliver nodded and walked toward the kitchen while Ezra made his way around the couch to sit. He quickly poured two glasses of iced tea, then headed back out to the main room to find Fiona already settling in Ezra's lap.

Ezra looked up and smiled, which was impossibly endearing. "I've been claimed."

"Okay, do you have tuna in your pockets or something?" Oliver asked as he set the glasses down on coasters on the leather trunk that served as his coffee table. "Because she usually never warms up to a person this quickly."

"I may or may not have watched a few Jackson Galaxy videos on how to make cats like you," Ezra admitted.

Oliver let out a surprised laugh and sat next to him. "Really?"

"Well, I had to make sure I made a good impression," Ezra said as if it was obvious. "If your cat hated me, it wouldn't be a good sign that this date was going to go well, would it?"

Oliver stared at him for a moment, then smiled. "What?"

"I think that might be the cutest thing I've ever heard."

They shared a soft smile, then Oliver leaned forward to grab the remote off the coffee table. When he settled back onto the couch, he scooted close enough that their legs could brush if they shifted, but not too close as to make things uncomfortable. "So, what are you in the mood for?" he asked as he clicked the TV on.

"You can pick. I'll watch almost anything."

"Would you judge me if I suggested a romcom?"

Ezra's face lit up. "Oh, my God. Oliver Wheeler—the same man that reads Faulkner and Wilde, and watches period dramas on the BBC—watches romantic comedies?"

"It's a guilty pleasure, okay!" Oliver said, elbowing him in the ribs.

Ezra squirmed and laughed, disturbing Fiona and making her get up. "Oh, sorry, Fiona," he called after her. "I think it's endearing. I like romcoms, too. I didn't use to, but my college roommate loved them, and she made me watch them all the time."

"New or old?"

"Old."

"Oh! What about *Dirty Dancing*? It's more of a dramedy, but—"

"It is a classic, though," Ezra said. So Oliver smiled, selected the title, and pressed play.

Oliver did his best to focus on the movie, but couldn't help getting distracted every time their shoulders and legs brushed together when one of them leaned to get their drink from the coffee table. So finally, after spending half of the movie working up the courage to make some sort of move, he reached over and brushed his fingers against Ezra's.

Ezra glanced over and smiled. He turned his palm to meet Oliver's, and they laced their fingers together. Then, like a switch flipped, whatever anxious energy or hesitation Oliver had dissipated and settled into a giddy anticipation that was much easier to manage. By the time they started the second movie, Ezra had wrapped his arm around Oliver's shoulder while they shared a blanket. Then, by the end of the third movie, some weird indie movie with Anna Kendrick, they'd put in an order for Chinese takeout and were both half lying on the couch with Fiona curled up in the space behind Oliver's knees.

The credits rolled, and Oliver swung his feet back to the floor and stretched, wincing at the stiffness in his back.

Ezra rested a gentle hand on his back. "Alright?"

Oliver angled himself toward him. "Yeah, I'm getting a little stiff, but I'll be okay."

"Can I do anything to help?"

Oliver gave him a small smile and shook his head. "I'll be alright. I'll let you know, though."

"Okay."

They shared a look. Oliver wasn't sure who started first, but they were slowly leaning toward each other. Their faces were only inches away when the intercom buzzed, breaking the moment.

Ezra leaned back. "I'll get that," he said before standing and heading to the door.

"Do you want me to get plates, or do you want to eat out of the containers?" Oliver asked.

"Containers are fine with me," Ezra said. "Do you want to pull *Psych* up, though? We can watch an episode while we eat."

Oliver switched streaming platforms, and once they'd sorted their food, he hit play. They ate in relative silence until Ezra reached over and attempted to steal one of Oliver's dumplings.

"Hey!" Oliver protested. He held the carton out of reach. "I offered you some, and you said no."

"Yes, but it's a proven fact that food tastes better when stolen from another person's plate," Ezra said.

"Oh, is it?" Oliver raised an eyebrow.

"Yes." Ezra playfully leaned over and succeeded in stealing a bite this time. He smiled triumphantly as he shoved the entire dumpling into his mouth.

Oliver smirked, then reached over and stole a piece of Ezra's orange chicken and popped it into his mouth. "Okay, you may be onto something," he admitted once he finished chewing.

"Told you," Ezra said.

They smiled at each other again. Then, after a long moment, Oliver decided to fuck it and just leaned in. It was barely a kiss. A peck—over just as quickly as it started—and when Oliver pulled back, he bit his lip and looked away. "Sorry, I, uh—I couldn't help it."

Ezra chuckled, and Oliver looked back at him to see him softly gazing at him. He tossed his fork into his carton and gently took Oliver's carton in his other hand. He set both on the table, then reached up and cupped Oliver's cheek as he leaned in to kiss him, this time more properly. Their lips brushed together, soft and hesitant, for a few long moments before they parted again.

"Sorry, couldn't help it," Ezra murmured, and they both let out a breathy laugh. Ezra quickly pressed another brief kiss on his lips, then pulled away and went back to his food.

When they finished eating, Ezra said that he should head home before it got too late. Oliver didn't want him to leave, but he also didn't want to seem too forward by suggesting that Ezra stay, so he stood and walked with Ezra to the door. He stood and waited for Ezra to slip his shoes back on.

"I had a great time," Ezra said, taking a step toward Oliver.

"Me, too." Oliver smiled, then stared down at his feet and shuffled them nervously. "I'd like to see you again if that's alright."

Ezra smiled and closed the distance between them. "I'd like that," he said, wrapping his arms around Oliver's shoulders.

Oliver pressed his hand to the small of Ezra's back while his other hand went to cradle his head. Ezra buried his face into Oliver's neck, and when Oliver's breath hitched, he pulled away and stared up into Oliver's eyes. Oliver leaned in to bring their foreheads together for a moment before closing the rest of the distance.

Their mouths brushed together, still soft and hesitant like before, before pulling apart again. But then Oliver felt Ezra's hand move to cradle the back of his neck, giving him more confidence. He tangled his fingers in Ezra's impossibly soft curls and deepened the kiss, letting his lips part ever so slightly in an invitation, one that Ezra readily took. Oliver stood, reveling in the soft caress of Ezra's mouth against his, until they both reluctantly pulled away to catch their breath, eyes closed, with their foreheads pressed together.

"So, I'll let you know when I get home?" Ezra whispered.

Oliver nodded, his forehead still pressed to Ezra's, then stepped back and crossed his arms. Otherwise, he might be tempted to pull Ezra back.

"Goodnight, Olls."

Oliver smiled. "Goodnight."

Ezra smiled, then opened the door and stepped through.

18

Ezra

Saturday Night, September 12, 2020

The door shut, and Ezra walked down the hall a few steps before resting against the wall and letting out a sigh. He really did have a great time. It was one of the best first dates he'd ever had, to be honest, so he was beyond happy. But he was also disappointed. He didn't want to leave. He would have been content to spend the rest of the night watching movies with Oliver in his arms, especially since he wasn't really sure when he'd get to do it again. With anyone else, he probably wouldn't have even hesitated to turn the date into a sleepover, but Oliver was different. He really wanted things to go well, so he didn't want to push things too quickly. But Oliver had sounded almost as disappointed as he was when he'd said he should probably leave, so maybe…

Ezra reached into his pocket and grabbed his phone.

Josie Miller
September 12, 2020, 9:03 PM

Ezra Beaumont
Do you need the car tomorrow?

Josie Miller
Nope. Date went that well, huh?

Ezra Beaumont
I'm about to find out.

Josie Miller
Don't do anything I wouldn't do.

He rolled his eyes and slid his phone back into his pocket, then went back to Oliver's door. He ran his hands through his hair, pulling on it slightly, and let out a slow, controlled breath. Then, before he could talk himself out of it, he lifted his hand and knocked on the door twice. The door wrenched open so fast that Ezra's fist still hung in the air, poised to knock, revealing a smiling and flushed Oliver.

Ezra half smiled and dropped his hand. "What if I didn't go yet?"

"Oh, thank fuck," Oliver huffed in relief, and he closed the distance between them in the doorway. He cradled both sides of his face, and Ezra let out a small, relieved laugh, which Oliver muffled with a kiss. They stumbled back into the apartment, and Ezra kicked the door behind him before wrapping his arms around Oliver's waist, pulling them flush together. Oliver melted into him, walking him into the door with a soft thump as he threaded his fingers through his hair to angle his head back to further deepen the kiss.

Oliver's lips disappeared from his. "I wasn't ready for you to leave yet, but I wasn't sure how to ask you to stay without being too…"

"Me neither." Ezra chased his mouth, not ready to part yet, and continued in between quick kisses. "I'm not expecting anything, though. For the record."

Oliver nodded and broke the kiss across Ezra's cheek. "I'm not either," he murmured as he pressed a few soft kisses along Ezra's jaw.

Ezra gasped and brought a hand up to the back of Oliver's head to drag his mouth back to his. He let out a sound somewhere between a moan and a whine as Oliver pulled at his bottom lip with his teeth. God, he sounded so needy, and part of him felt like he should be embarrassed. But based on the way Oliver's breath hitched and his hands fisted the back of his shirt, he wasn't the only one desperate for the contact, so he couldn't be bothered. After a few minutes, they both broke apart, their ragged breaths mixing as they attempted to compose themselves.

"*C'était…autre chose*," he said, once his breathing had regulated at least a little.

Oliver groaned. "Ezra, English, please."

Ezra let out a soft chuckle. "Sorry, *mon chou*."

"You're doing that on purpose, aren't you?"

"Maybe just a little," he admitted.

"You're the worst," Oliver said, rolling his eyes before kissing him softly to show he didn't mean it in the slightest. "Also, monshoo?"

Ezra smiled at the butchered French pronunciation. "Close. *Mon chou*," he repeated, enunciating each word more carefully.

"Mon chou?" he tried again, and Ezra nodded. "What does it mean?"

"It's just a term of endearment. It doesn't really have an exact translation to an English equivalent," he explained.

"Oh." Oliver's cheeks flushed a slight pink.

"Too much?"

He shook his head. "I like it," he murmured.

Ezra smiled and leaned back in for a soft, slow kiss.

"So, do you want to stay?" Oliver asked once they parted again.

"I really, really do," Ezra said with a breathy chuckle. "Although, maybe not against this door because I kind of have a doorknob digging into my lower back."

Oliver smiled sheepishly as he stepped back. "Sorry, I—"

Ezra shook his head and pushed off the door to cut him off with a searing kiss. "Don't you dare apologize for kissing me like that." He kissed him again. "*C'était tellement chaud.*"

Oliver groaned and shoved at him. "If you insist on torturing me, can you at least fucking translate? I swear, I'm downloading Duolingo tomorrow."

He laughed and kissed him. "It was hot."

"Oh," Oliver said, his cheeks flushing even more.

Ezra grinned. "*Tu es si mignon,*" he said, and when Oliver frowned, he laughed and kissed his cheek. "So cute."

Oliver smiled. "So, it's not that late. Would you want to watch another movie? Or keep watching *Psych*?"

"If that's code for cuddling and making out, then yes," Ezra teased.

"It most definitely was," Oliver said, smirking. "Although—and this isn't a come-on because I'm still not expecting anything—but would it be okay if we sat on my bed instead of the couch? I have my TV set up so you can see it through the door, and it's more comfortable, and my hips—"

"Olls," Ezra said, cradling his cheek to cut him off. "That's fine. If it'll be more comfortable for you, then I want that." He brought their mouths together for a gentle kiss. "Besides, if I'm staying the night, I'm going to end up in your bed, anyway."

Oliver laughed self-consciously. "You make a good point. I just wanted to make sure."

He hummed and brought their lips together again. "I appreciate that. Consent is sexy."

Oliver kissed him. "Agreed."

"Do you want my help cleaning up first?"

"No, I'll get it if you want to pick what we're watching."

"Can do." Ezra kissed him one last time before pulling away.

"Oh, also, do you want a pair of pajama bottoms before we get settled? That way, we won't have to get up again."

"That sounds like an excellent idea. Peak lazy efficiency," Ezra teased.

"Listen, I have comfort down to a science, okay?" Oliver said, teasing right back as he walked over to the TV stand and opened a drawer.

"I've gathered by the sheer volume of pillows and blankets."

Oliver whipped a pair of flannel pajamas at him, and Ezra couldn't help laughing. "Just go change and pick something to watch," he said, rolling his eyes as he picked up takeaway containers, then added under his breath, "menace."

Ezra laughed again and swiped the remote off the couch, then headed into the bedroom. Since it wasn't an official room, there were no overhead lights for him to turn on, but there was a wall-mounted lamp, so he flicked that on. He glanced out and saw that Oliver was in the kitchen, so he didn't bother closing the door to change out of his skinny jeans and into the pajama bottoms. Not that he cared if Oliver saw him in his boxers, but that might contradict the "no expectations" mentality they seemed to have adopted if he did.

He'd just settled on top of the covers and against the

pillows and had selected something to watch when Oliver came back out of the kitchen. He went to the dresser again and pulled out another pair of pajamas, then headed toward the front door, presumably to make sure he locked it and to shut off lights, but when he came back into view, he'd also changed pants and taken his cardigan off, which meant that the watercolor tattoo on his left forearm was completely visible.

"No covers?" He skirted around the bed and smiled.

"Wasn't sure if you wanted them yet," Ezra said with a shrug.

"I mean, almost always, but maybe not yet." Oliver climbed onto the bed and, without hesitation, scooted close to curl into Ezra's side. "What are we not watching?"

"*Parks and Rec.* You've seen it, right?"

"Of course I've seen it."

"Then it's perfect." Ezra pressed play, then took Oliver's left hand and pulled on his arm to get a better view of the tattoo in person. It was of an open book in black and white with a vibrant watercolor smoke pattern rising out of it. "Wow, it's even more gorgeous in person," he said. "Where did you get it? Because I might need the artist's info next time I get work done."

Oliver lifted his head to look at him. "Next time? Eight tattoos aren't enough for you?"

Ezra smirked and turned on his side so they were chest to chest. "I thought you thought my tattoos were hot," he said, resting a hand lightly on Oliver's hip.

"I do," Oliver said, trailing his hand up Ezra's shoulder to tangle his hand in the hair at the nape of his neck. "But I also find them distracting. To answer your question, though, my friend Mary's girlfriend did it. She's home in Portland. That's how they met. Mary went with me to my appointment."

"Aren't you also how Ryan and Anna met?" Ezra slid

his hand to the small of Oliver's back.

He nodded. Their faces were only inches apart.

"You're a very good wingman, then."

Oliver nodded again. "Hey, Ezra?"

"Yeah?"

"Kiss me."

And so he did.

The sun woke Ezra the next morning, streaming in brightly through the window above Oliver's bed. He squeezed his eyes shut to block out the light. It was much too early for how late he'd ended up getting to sleep last night, but he still felt like he'd slept better than he had in months. He shifted to bury his face in the pillow, hoping it would block more light than his eyelids did. But when a pair of warm arms tightened around him, he realized he was not resting on a pillow, but on Oliver's chest. His eyes fluttered open again, and he lifted his head to look at him—still asleep, based on his breathing. Oliver was beautiful in the morning, with his mussed hair and his kiss-swollen lips, a smile playing at the corners. Ezra allowed himself to smile as he rested his head back on Oliver's shoulder and nuzzled his face into his neck.

"Morning," Oliver mumbled sleepily.

"Sorry, I didn't mean to wake you," Ezra whispered, lips brushing against skin as he spoke.

"It's alright." Oliver turned his head and pressed a kiss to Ezra's forehead. "Did you sleep alright?"

Ezra pressed a kiss to Oliver's neck. "Beautifully. Your bed is like a fluffy cocoon of blankets and pillows. I love it."

Oliver laughed. "So, do you have plans for today?"

"Not really, but I'm sure you'll want to get on with your day so I can head out after I catch a quick shower, if that's alright," Ezra said, propping himself up to look at him.

"Oh, I didn't mean—" Oliver reached up to tuck a wild strand of hair behind Ezra's ear. "I was just wondering if you had somewhere to be. Otherwise, I was going to make breakfast."

"Oh." Ezra's face split into a grin. "Breakfast sounds lovely."

Oliver smiled in response and leaned in for a quick kiss but stopped short. "Sorry, I bet I have morning breath, you—"

Ezra chuckled. "I probably do, too. But I don't care if you don't."

Oliver shook his head, and Ezra closed the distance, kissing him soundly. Ezra's hands skimmed along the hem of his T-shirt as he turned onto his back and pulled Oliver on top of him. Oliver smiled into the kiss and let his hands travel up into Ezra's hair, tangling the strands between his fingers.

"So how do you take your eggs?" he asked once they pulled apart.

"Scrambled?" Ezra suggested

Oliver kissed him again. "Done." Another kiss. "You can grab a shower while I cook, and I think there's an extra toothbrush in the medicine cabinet from the last time I went to the dentist."

"You're amazing," Ezra murmured, pulling him in for another kiss.

Ezra closed the front door behind him and kicked his shoes off, setting them on the mat by the door. The living room was empty, so Ezra made his way to the kitchen to wash his hands and see if Josie was studying at the kitchen table as she usually did on Sunday afternoons.

"Ah, there he is. You're a little later than I thought you'd be," Josie said as soon as he rounded the corner. Then she grinned. "I take it the date went well, then?"

"It did," he said, suppressing a grin, then strolled over to the kitchen sink to wash his hands. "Thank you again for lending me the car."

He looked up to see her wave a hand. "Like I was using it. Okay, but seriously, sit. Spill. Because you look positively chuffed. I made tea."

Ezra laughed. "Chuffed?" he repeated. He sat, took the empty mug presumably set out for him, and started fixing his tea.

"Pleased, thrilled, delighted," Josie elaborated. "Also, don't think I haven't noticed that you're wearing a different shirt than the one you left in."

Ezra paused, adding sugar to his cup and looked down at the T-shirt he stole from Oliver, then smiled to himself.

"Oh, my God. You're so smitten, aren't you?"

Ezra brought the mug to his lips to hide his grin. "Maybe," he mumbled. "Okay, completely. It just—he feels almost too good to be true."

Josie grinned. "I'm so happy for you, Arch. You deserve to be happy."

"Thanks," he said, looking down at his mug and smiling.

"Although," she started, then switched to French, "putting out on the first date?"

Ezra snapped his head up. "We didn't," he replied in French.

"That hickey tells another story," Josie said.

He brought a hand up to cover it. It had been years since he'd had a hickey, and it wasn't big, so it would probably fade by the next morning. But surprisingly, he liked it. It was like a little reminder that the night before actually happened. Also, the look on Oliver's face when he realized how carried away he'd gotten was adorable and priceless. "That's as far as it got," he admitted.

"So you quite literally only slept with him."

"We weren't in a rush," Ezra said with a shrug. "I like him a lot, so I want to make sure I do this right."

"That's sweet," Josie said, smiling.

"Don't make fun," Ezra said, frowning.

"I'm not," she insisted. "I remember I felt the same way when I first met Ted."

"Didn't he knock you up within two weeks of meeting him?" Ezra asked, eyebrow raised.

"I didn't say I succeeded," she said, suppressing a smirk.

He laughed, then his phone buzzed in his pocket, and he pulled it out.

"That him?" Josie asked, this time in English. "You get the same look on your face every time he texts," she added in explanation.

He nodded, then swiped his phone open.

Oliver Wheeler 🖥

September 13, 2020, 3:42 PM

Oliver Wheeler 🖥

I know this is probably poor dating etiquette to text this soon, but I just wanted to say again that I had an amazing time last night. And this morning.

Ezra Beaumont

I had an amazing time, too.

Also, screw dating etiquette.

Oliver Wheeler 🖥

Well, in the spirit of that... What would

you say if I asked to see you again next weekend?

I'll cook this time.

> Ezra Beaumont
>
> I would say that I would love that, and only 15% because you're offering to cook.

Oliver Wheeler 🖥

What about the other 85%?

> Ezra Beaumont
>
> Fiona, obviously.

Oliver Wheeler 🖥

Oh, I get it. You're using me for my cooking and my cat.

> Ezra Beaumont
>
> I'm kidding.
>
> It's more like 80% you, 15% your cooking (which is really just a more specific aspect of you), and 5% Fiona.

Oliver Wheeler 🖥

I'm content with that ratio.

So, would you stay the night again?

> Ezra Beaumont
>
> If that's an invitation, then yes, absolutely.

Oliver Wheeler 🖥

It was.

> Ezra Beaumont
>
> Then I'll make sure I bring an overnight bag 😊
>
> And I'll wash and bring back the t-shirt I stole.

Oliver Wheeler 📇

No rush

So, Friday or Saturday?

Ezra Beaumont

Friday.

7?

Oliver Wheeler 📇

Sounds perfect 😊

19

Ezra

Friday Night, September 18, 2020

The five days leading up to Ezra's second date with Oliver had flown by. It was a strict contrast to the two weeks leading up to their first date that had gone by achingly slow, which had probably been because of nerves. This time, though, there was nothing but excitement—well, 90% excitement and 10% nervous anticipation. This was their second official date, and they'd planned for him to spend the night, which had some implications. Ezra still had zero expectations, but he would have been lying if he said he didn't hope something would happen. He'd been thinking about it all week—the way Oliver pushed him against the door, Oliver's lips and teeth on his neck, the soft sighs Oliver made as Ezra roved his hands over his clothed body— he needed to stop thinking about it. He shook his head to clear it and lifted his hand to knock on Oliver's door.

A slightly frazzled-looking but smiling Oliver greeted him a minute later. "Hi."

Ezra smiled, but the mask he still wore hid it. "Hi."

"Come in," he said, stepping aside. He started backing toward the kitchen. "Sorry, I have a cheese sauce on, and if I don't keep stirring—"

Ezra laughed. "Go. I'm going to wash my hands."

Oliver smiled again, then disappeared into the kitchen. Ezra smiled fondly and kicked off his shoes before heading to the bathroom, dropping his bag by the door to the bedroom on the way. He washed his hands, took off his mask, and went back to his bag to shove the mask, his wallet, and keys into an outside pocket.

He followed the delicious smell to the kitchen to find Oliver standing over the stove, stirring a cream sauce with a battered wooden spoon. "Smells good in here," he said, leaning against the doorway. He wanted to go in and hug him, but the kitchen was tiny, and he didn't want to be underfoot.

Oliver looked up and grinned. "Hi," he said again. He abandoned the pot, took the three steps across the kitchen it took to close the distance, and settled his hands on Ezra's waist.

Ezra rested his hands on Oliver's biceps and smiled as Oliver leaned in, stopping just short of kissing him.

"Can I?" he asked.

"I thought you had to keep stirring," Ezra said, slightly teasing.

"It'll be fine for a few seconds."

"Then by all means…" The rest of his sentence was muffled by Oliver's lips pressing softly against his. Ezra wrapped his arms around Oliver's neck to bring them closer, and Oliver's forearm pressed into his lower back. After a few seconds, they parted, smiling, and Ezra pushed at his chest. "Okay, go stir."

Oliver laughed and went back to the stove. He reached up, grabbed a spice shaker, added a dash, and stirred a few times, then brought the spoon up to taste.

"Come taste this, and tell me what you think."

Ezra took a few steps and leaned to try whatever sauce was on the spoon Oliver was holding out for him. The moment the sauce touched his tongue, he almost moaned. "Fuck, that's really good. What is that?"

"Truffle bacon-gouda mac and cheese," Oliver said. "Or, well, it will be when I add the noodles. And chocolate mousse pie with a meringue crust for dessert. I also made another loaf of sourdough, but that's for breakfast tomorrow."

"Jesus Christ, Oliver. Are you trying to win me over with food?"

Oliver looked back at the pot and stirred in an attempt to hide his smile. "No comment."

Ezra leaned over and kissed his cheek. "Can I do anything to help?"

"I just have to add the noodles, and it will be ready. But if you want wine, it's in the fridge. The glasses are in that cabinet"—he pointed behind him—"and the bottle opener is in the drawer over there, as well."

"And now you're plying me with alcohol," Ezra teased, pulling the bottle out of the fridge. He got two glasses down. "If you're trying to seduce me, I should tell you that it's unnecessary. I'm already thoroughly charmed."

"Again, no comment," Oliver said over his shoulder as he poured spiral pasta into the pot. "But good to know."

Ezra grinned to himself and uncorked the wine. He poured himself a glass, then paused, holding the bottle over Oliver's glass. "Small, medium, or large—pour?"

"Small, please," Oliver said, and Ezra poured the glass and re-corked the bottle. "If I drink too much, it can set off a flare, so I don't, which means I have the tolerance of a high schooler at their first party."

He laughed and picked up both glasses, then turned

to lean against the counter. "Well, we don't want that—as much fun as I'd probably have witnessing drunk Oliver."

"You'll probably see him eventually," Oliver said, turning with a bowl in each hand. He gestured for Ezra to go out to the living room. "Although, from what Juliet and Ryan say, high Oliver is much more fun."

"Is that something that happens often?"

"Well, I have a medical card to help manage my joint pain, so yeah."

"I'm a little jealous," Ezra said, sitting on the couch. "I think the last time I got high was in Amsterdam, which feels like forever ago."

Oliver set the bowls down and sat with his legs crossed under him, and Ezra couldn't help smiling. "I don't mind sharing."

"Do you ever sit with your feet on the ground?" Ezra asked as he handed Oliver the smaller glass of wine.

"Nope. And before you ask, no, it's not good for my joints, but I gave up that battle a long time ago because if I try to not sit like a goblin, I get restless."

"Fair enough." Ezra laughed and held up his glass. "Cheers."

Oliver smirked. "What are we toasting to?"

"Good company?"

"I'll agree with that," he said and clinked his glass against Ezra's.

As they took a sip, Fiona hopped up on the couch between them, sniffing the air.

"Oh, well, hello, Your Highness," Ezra said with a laugh. She chirped and purred as he scratched her head.

"Ignore her; she just smells the bacon," Oliver said, setting down his glass. He scooped Fiona up and set her on the ground.

Ezra laughed at the indignant meow Fiona let out. Then they settled in to eat, opting for conversation over background television.

After seconds and pouring themselves a second glass of wine, Ezra was pleasantly full and just venturing into tipsy territory. He leaned back onto the couch while Oliver insisted on dealing with the leftovers and at least soaking the pot.

Oliver poked his head out of the kitchen. "Do you want dessert now or later?"

"Later. Too full. Now get back out here," he said, stretching his arm along the back of the couch.

Oliver smiled and flipped the kitchen light off before making his way back to the couch. He sat with his legs propped up on the coffee table and leaned into Ezra's side. "Hi."

"Hi," Ezra said as he wrapped his arm around Oliver's shoulder. He smiled at him, taking in his flushed face. Oliver was right about his tolerance. He wasn't drunk by any means, but he was definitely a little tipsy. It was endearing.

"Dinner was amazing."

"Yeah?"

Ezra nodded and cupped his cheek with his free hand. "I feel very spoiled," he said before leaning in for a kiss.

Oliver sighed into it, then pulled away after a few moments. "Do you want to watch a movie while we wait for food to digest enough for dessert?"

"That sounds perfect."

They put on a random comedy, but after about twenty minutes, it ended up serving just as background noise. Ezra wasn't sure which one of them initiated the kiss. But one moment, Oliver was curled under his arm, and the next he was in Ezra's lap with his hands cradling Ezra's face and angling it up into the kiss. Ezra's whole body relaxed into the kiss. His arms wrapped tightly around Oliver's back, pulling him closer. Oliver made a small sound in the back of his throat, then his hands were in Ezra's hair, fighting against the messy bun at the nape of his neck.

"Can I take this out?" Oliver asked, his hand going to the elastic.

Ezra nodded and brought their lips back together while Oliver pulled his hair free. He sat back and took Ezra's hand so he could slide the elastic around his wrist, then combed his fingers through his now free curls.

"You have a thing for my hair, don't you?" Ezra asked with a smirk. He pulled Oliver closer so he could mouth at his collarbone.

Oliver hummed and nodded. "A little." He wound the strands around his fingers and pulled a little to angle Ezra's face into a passionate kiss. Time became even more of a blur as their hands and lips roved wherever they could reach. And Ezra was content to stay like that for hours, but when he felt Oliver rock his hips forward and a hard bulge pressed into his abdomen, he pulled away with a low moan.

Oliver looked down at him with pupils so blown that Ezra could hardly see the green of his irises. "Do you want to—"

Ezra nodded before he could finish the question. "Bedroom."

A nervous, electric energy hung in the air between them as Oliver nodded and scooted backward off his lap, pulling Ezra with him by the front of his shirt. Ezra gripped his hips and brushed their lips back together while he walked him backward.

Oliver's hands slid under his T-shirt, soft fingertips exploring flushed skin, but then he pulled back. "Wait, for clarity's sake, we're having sex, right?"

Ezra couldn't help but laugh a little. Oliver was a paradox sometimes. Wildly confident, but with these flashes of shyness, and it was completely endearing. "Yes."

"Okay, good. We're on the same page."

They both wanted this. And although the confirmation didn't wash away the nervousness they were both feeling, it made it so they didn't care. So they simply adjusted course when they bumped into half of the furniture on the way across the tiny living room. When Ezra's T-shirt got stuck on his head as it came off and Oliver's button-down got stuck on his wrists because he hadn't stopped to unbutton them first, they laughed into the kiss they didn't want to break and kept walking backward.

The back of Oliver's knees hit the bed, and they broke apart. He brought his hands to the button of Ezra's jeans and paused. "Okay?"

Ezra nodded. "You, too?"

He nodded, too, and they brought their lips back together for a kiss. But it was brief because Oliver broke away with a scoff. "Button fly? Really?"

"They're my lucky jeans," Ezra said with a smirk. "They make my ass look fantastic."

Oliver rolled his eyes and shoved Ezra back a step. "Alright, well, turn around then."

Ezra laughed, and he obliged, turning and giving his ass a little shake. He heard Oliver's sharp intake of breath and looked over his shoulder.

"I haven't seen this one yet," Oliver said, his voice a little raspy. He reached a hand out and traced his fingers over the branches of the Tree of Life that spanned most of his upper back.

"Oh, yeah," Ezra said, suppressing a shiver at Oliver's featherlight touch. "I sometimes forget about that one since I don't see it often."

"It's gorgeous. Also, I have to say that the jeans do make your ass look great." Oliver's hand trailed down to his lower back, then hooked in one of his belt loops, which he used to spin him back around.

Ezra laughed and braced himself on Oliver's chest so they wouldn't crash together and fall over. "Nice move."

"Thanks." He bent to kiss his jaw. "You didn't need the lucky jeans, though." His lips moved to the sensitive spot behind his ear where there was a magnolia inked into his skin. "I'm pretty sure you could have come over in neon orange parachute pants and I'd still want you to fuck me."

Ezra gasped and surged forward, claiming Oliver's lips with his, effectively stopping their conversation. Things got a little more frantic from there as they shed the rest of their clothes and fell into bed.

Ezra hovered over Oliver, his hands gripping Oliver's thighs as tightly as they were wrapped around his waist. He gasped as Oliver sucked at a spot on his collarbone.

"Do you want what you said?"

"What?" Oliver asked, pulling back to look at him. But before Ezra could repeat himself, he continued. "Yeah, I do, if that's alright with you."

"That is very alright with me." Ezra leaned down and kissed him hard. "Where's—?"

"Pocket on the side of the bed."

Ezra kissed him again, then leaned over to grab lube and a condom from the small pocket. Oliver pulled him down for another languid kiss, and Ezra was about to bring his hand between Oliver's legs when he heard a soft chirp and felt a shift on the bed behind him. Oliver broke the kiss and looked down at the foot of the bed where Fiona had jumped up.

His face went scarlet, and he grabbed a pillow to throw at her. "You freaky little voyeur, get out of here."

Ezra stifled a laugh and sat back on his heels. "I'll get

the door." He made sure Fiona was out of the room and closed the French doors, then settled on the bed over Oliver again, burying his face in his neck.

"I'm so sorry," Oliver said with a groan.

"It's fine, Olls," Ezra said, chuckling against his neck.

"Are you laughing?" Oliver asked, indignant.

"A little." He lifted his head and grinned. "Now, where were we?"

Their lips met for a kiss while Ezra's fingers worked Oliver open. When Oliver moaned softly, he broke away, intent on watching Oliver's face. He was beautiful—the way his cheeks flushed and his kiss-swollen lips parted in a gasp when Ezra crooked his fingers.

When Oliver was finally ready, he let out a low moan which Ezra couldn't help wanting to absorb with a kiss. Ezra pulled away to roll on a condom, then positioned himself at Oliver's entrance and pressed inside. He stayed still for a moment, showering Oliver's neck and chest with open-mouthed kisses as he allowed him to adjust, then rocked his hips. They found an easy rhythm, moving together as they clutched each other and traded kisses that ended up being more a sharing of breath than anything else.

Oliver's nails dug into his back, and Ezra felt himself barrel closer to his peak. "Ezra, I'm—"

Ezra crashed their mouths together and brought a hand between them to help bring Oliver over the edge. He let out a soft cry and bit down on Ezra's lower lip as he tumbled over the edge, his body clenching around Ezra as he spilled over Ezra's hand. Ezra rocked his hips forward again, his pace becoming more erratic while he chased his own release. A wave of pleasure washed over him as he came. Oliver's legs locked tighter around his hips, and he surged up to swallow Ezra's moan in a messy kiss.

They stayed like that, wrapped around each other for several minutes while their breath returned to them. When he felt his heart rate had slowed enough, Ezra lifted off of Oliver and rolled to the side.

Oliver sighed happily and nestled into the crook of Ezra's arm. "I know we should get up, but I don't want to yet."

Ezra pressed a kiss to his hairline, earning a pleased hum. "Neither do I." He'd get up to clean himself up and dispose of the condom in a minute, but he wasn't ready to let Oliver out of his arms yet.

20

Oliver

Sunday Evening, September 20, 2020

Ezra ended up staying for the weekend.

It had barely even been a question. When they'd woken up wrapped up in each other late Saturday morning, it wasn't unlike after the first night they'd spent together. Except this time, they were naked. They'd made breakfast together—or Oliver had made them breakfast while Ezra had hugged him from behind and watched with his chin hooked over Oliver's shoulder. But after, instead of Ezra going home like he had that first time, he stayed.

They kept finding excuses for him to delay leaving. First, it was showering, which involved more fucking against the cold tile than the actual cleaning of their bodies, and finishing the movie that had gotten interrupted the night before. They'd made lunch, and, of course, watched an episode of *Psych* while they ate, which turned into another, and another, which somehow turned into them fooling around on the couch. At that point, it was dinner, which turned into more *Psych* until it was dark. It only made sense for Ezra to stay the night again.

Sunday morning and afternoon were much of the same. Cooking together, spending another lazy, clothing-optional afternoon wrapped up in blankets and each other on the couch. Except, this time, Ezra did actually have to go home because they had work in the morning.

So, they stood by the front door, dressed, with Ezra's arms wrapped around Oliver's waist, and Oliver's hands threaded into Ezra's hair while they kissed good-bye.

"I'll text you when I'm home," Ezra said, pulling away the barest amount.

"Okay," Oliver said before bringing their lips together again, then asked between kisses, "Can I see you again next weekend?"

Ezra groaned. "I can't. I'm sorry. Willow's birthday is Saturday, and I promised—"

Oliver's heart melted just the littlest bit. "Don't apologize. I can't even tell you how completely endearing it is that you two are so close."

"Yeah?"

Oliver smiled and nodded. "Definitely." He kissed him, then released his grip on Ezra's hair, letting his hands smooth down his back. "So, the following weekend, then?"

"Yes. Unless…well, what about Thursday? I could bring dinner, then head back Friday afternoon—assuming you want me to spend the night, that is."

"I think it's safe to say that I always want you to stay the night," Oliver said. "Thursday sounds perfect."

"It's a date then." Ezra grinned and brought their mouths together one last time. "Okay, I really should go now."

Oliver nodded, and they reluctantly released each

other. "Drive safe," Oliver said as he opened the door for Ezra.

"I will. Bye, *mon chou*." Ezra smiled, then looped his mask around his ears before stepping through the doorway. Then he doubled back, lowered his mask, and pressed a quick kiss to Oliver's cheek. "Okay, for real, this time," he said, then disappeared down the hall.

Oliver laughed and shut the door, flicking the locks into place. He went back to the couch and collapsed onto it, not even caring that he had a stupid grin on his face because who would see it? Although, even if someone were there to see it, he still wouldn't care. His phone buzzed on the coffee table, so he picked it up to find several notifications from a group thread that he did not remember creating.

Anna, Juliet & Mary
Sep 20, 2020, 5:42 PM

Juliet Ríos

Hello ladies! I created a group chat because I knew we'd all want to know how Oliver's sex weekend went and also knew he'd only want to talk about it once

Mary Wen

Brilliant thinking

Anna Coleman

Hi!

Also, sex weekend? Really Jules?

Juliet Ríos

What? You think they spent the entire weekend together and didn't at least fool around?

As Ezra would say (probably)...not bloody likely.

Mary Wen

Oh, they definitely hooked up.

Anna Coleman

Maybe we shouldn't speculate and talk about him like he can't totally read all of this, and just wait until he answers

Mary Wen

Well, he's taking his sweet ass time

Juliet Ríos

Wait, do you think he's still there? He being Ezra.

Oliver Wheeler

Okay, 1) Ezra just left;

2) I'm with Anna. Sex weekend? Really, Jules?

Juliet Ríos

You're telling me you spent 48 hours straight with him and DIDN'T have sex with him?

Oliver Wheeler

That's not what I'm saying at all. I'm simply objecting to calling it a sex weekend.

Mary Wen

Well, that's an Oliver confirmation if I've ever heard one.

Juliet Ríos

Ah ha! So you two did fuck!

Oliver Wheeler

If I say yes, will you leave it alone?

Mary Wen

Ollie, I think you know that isn't likely.

Juliet Rios

Come on, just give us something

Oliver Wheeler

Anna? A little help?

Anna Coleman

Sorry, hun, I'm with them.

Oliver Wheeler

You, too?

Anna Coleman

Seeing as Ryan is on the phone getting his own debrief right now but won't tell me anything, yes.

Oliver Wheeler

Wait, really?

Ezra called him?

Anna Coleman

Pretend I didn't say that

At least tell us how the weekend was

Oliver Wheeler

It was honestly amazing. We didn't even do anything special, really. We just watched movies or TV, cooked together, cuddled with Fiona...kinda just coexisted.

And fine, we also had sex, but it was just one aspect of an overall amazing weekend.

Juliet Rios

And how was it?

Like on a scale from 1 to 10.

Oliver Wheeler

I don't like the idea of putting a person's sexual capabilities on a rating scale, so I'm only answering this because I don't think you're going to let it go otherwise...but like, 12.

Mary Wen

REALLY?

Oliver Wheeler

Honestly, I think it may have ruined me for all potential future first times.

Juliet Ríos

Okay, yeah, I'm gonna need more details because there's no way it was that good. First times are never that good.

Oliver Wheeler

It was, though.

I mean, yeah, there was some awkwardness, but even with the fumbling—Jesus fuck. We kinda just laughed it off. And after that we just stayed in bed and talked for hours about nothing. I don't know; it was just...I didn't really want to make a big deal out of it lest I jinx the whole fucking thing, but I'm not even kidding. I think it was the best sex of my life.

Anna Coleman

That sounds really sweet, actually.

Juliet Ríos

Best sex ever?

Oliver Wheeler

Ever. Like I said, I think I'm ruined.

Juliet Ríos

Well then.

Anna Coleman

So when are you seeing him again?

Oliver Wheeler

Thursday. Willow (his little cousin)'s birthday is Saturday, and he promised that he'd be home for it.

Mary Wen

Cute

Oliver Wheeler

You have no idea.

Mary Wen

Here's the important question though: What does fickle Queen Fiona think of him?

Juliet Ríos

Oh, yes. Because the best I've ever gotten out of that cat is mild indifference.

Anna Coleman

That's better than Ryan, who gets active distaste.

Juliet Ríos

Yeah, but Ryan hates cats. I love cats and cats love me

Oliver Wheeler

She adores him. She even let him rub her belly, which she hardly lets me do on any given day.

Juliet Ríos

Alright, what's his secret?

Oliver Wheeler

Apparently Jackson Galaxy YouTube videos.

Anna Coleman

He looked up videos on how to impress
cats?

Oliver Wheeler

Yup

Mary Wen

Okay, keep him please? I know it's early,
but you have to keep him.

Oliver Wheeler

I plan on it 😊

21

Ezra

Thursday, November 5, 2020

"Morning, Josie," Ezra said as he walked into the kitchen mid-morning.

"Well, you're awfully chipper this morning?" Josie said.

"Am I?" Ezra asked. "Also, coffee?"

"Just made a fresh pot," she said. "And yes, you are. Would your chipper mood have anything to do with you getting to see a certain curly-haired copyeditor again tomorrow?"

"Can't I just be in a good mood without it being about a man?" He reached into a cabinet to grab a mug.

"You can, but you're not."

She was right; he wasn't. His good mood was at least ninety percent related to Oliver. They'd been dating for a month and a half now, and he wasn't even being hyperbolic or dramatic when he thought it had been the best month and a half of his life.

Josie's phone pinged, and she picked it up to read. "Oh, God, what now?"

"What?" Ezra poured his coffee, then leaned against the counter.

"It's my news alert set up for Beaumont and Carmichael."

"Why on Earth do you have an alert set up for BCH?"

"Curiosity mostly," she said as she swiped her phone open.

There was a pause as she read, then he watched the color drain from Josie's face. "What is it?"

"It's—shit." Josie got up without another word and bolted into the living room.

Ezra set his coffee down and followed. "Josie, what the hell happened?" he barked, switching to French. Willow was upstairs in her room on a Zoom call for class, but he couldn't be too careful.

Josie silently flipped on the TV and tuned to the mid-morning local news.

"What—"

"Shh," Josie hissed.

Ezra snapped his mouth shut and stared at the TV, where his mother's headshot was plastered on the screen in a frame floating next to the newscaster's head. "…Caroline Beaumont, Chief Executive Officer of Beaumont and Carmichael Holding Group, and well-known philanthropist, was found in her Manhattan penthouse earlier this morning by her brother and CFO of Beaumont and Carmichael, Edward Carmichael. Early reports suspect the cause of death to be cardiac arrest, and there is no suspicion of foul play at this time. Let's jump over to our field reporter, Bethany Chase, who is coming to us live from the Beaumont and Carmichael headquarters…"

Whatever came after that, Ezra couldn't hear past the ringing in his ears. No, it couldn't be. His chest tightened, and his vision constricted. The room began to move around him. Or maybe he was moving. His back hit the doorframe that separated the living room and the kitchen/dining room. So, he was moving.

"Archie, I'm so sorry."

He was vaguely aware that Josie was standing directly in front of him, murmuring in low French, which he somehow still had the ability to translate. But she also seemed a million feet away.

"Take a deep breath," she said, this time in English.

That's when he realized he was hyperventilating. He tried to take a deep breath, but it lodged in his airway. He shook his head. "Can't—"

"What do you need?" Josie asked, reaching a hand out to touch his shoulder.

He flinched and side-stepped her. "Arrête." *Don't.*

"I'm sorry," she said, yanking her hand back.

He stumbled toward the front door. He needed air—needed space. The room was closing in on him, and he couldn't breathe. He needed to get out of there.

"Where are you going?" Josie called after him.

He just shook his head. He tried to catch another breath, but he still couldn't. He shoved his feet into his shoes and somehow remembered to grab his mask and keys off the hook.

"Ezra, maybe you should take a minute—" Josie started, but he was already out the door.

Hours later, Ezra found himself standing in front of Oliver's apartment building in the pouring rain, staring up at it. He wasn't even sure how he'd gotten there, or how long he'd been walking around. His phone had died hours ago, and his mind had shut off.

It was a bad idea to be here. He knew it was. They'd only been dating for a month. It was too soon to be pushing his baggage on Oliver. They should still be in that honeymoon phase—when things were easy and they couldn't keep their hands off each other. But it was like his feet carried him there without him knowing it. Like his subconscious knew he needed him. Maybe if he saw that crooked smile and those kind eyes, everything would be okay. He pressed the intercom button, and Oliver's voice rang through the speaker after a few moments.

"Who is it?"

"Ollie…" Ezra croaked, and that was all he could manage, but it didn't matter because the door buzzed and clicked open, allowing him entry.

Oliver's door was already open, and he was standing there with a towel in his hands by the time Ezra made it up the stairs. "Fuck, you're soaking wet. Come here. I've been out of my mind." He made a move toward him, but Ezra shook his head.

"I shouldn't. I've been outside for hours and—" He broke off and ran a hand through his dripping-wet hair. "I don't want to risk you getting sick. I just had to see you. This was a bad idea, I'm sorry."

"And I don't want you catching anything from being out in the rain for several hours."

"You can't catch colds from the rain. That's a myth," Ezra said feebly as he stared at his feet.

"Hypothermia isn't, though," Oliver countered. "It's November, you aren't even wearing a coat, and you're shaking. Now, come here."

He hadn't realized he was shaking until Oliver pointed it out, but now that he had, it was all he could focus on. He was freezing. Reluctantly, he nodded, his head still hung, and stepped close enough for Oliver to wrap the towel around his shoulders.

Oliver wrapped the towel tight around him, then guided him into the warm apartment. "I've been so worried. Josie called Ryan, who called me, and I've been trying to call you for hours."

"My phone died," Ezra mumbled. "Forgot to charge it last night."

"Did you walk all the way here?"

Ezra nodded. "I don't remember it, though."

"Oh, Ezra." Oliver rubbed his arms over the towel. "Take your shoes off and stay here, okay, sweetheart?"

He nodded again and did as he was told, while Oliver walked over to the dresser. By the time he was done with his shoes and had looked up, Oliver was gone. Ezra heard the shower turn on, then Oliver reappeared.

"I set out some fresh clothes for you on the counter, and the shower is heating up for you," Oliver told him. "I'll call Ryan and let him know you're alright. And if you give me your phone, I'll charge it for you, alright?"

"Okay," Ezra croaked.

He moved on autopilot as he padded to the bathroom, stripped off his soaking-wet clothes, showered, and slipped into the new clothes Oliver had set aside for him: the same pair of plaid pajama bottoms he wore the last time he was here, a clean pair of boxers, a T-shirt, and a stretched-out mustard jumper, which he noticed smelled like Oliver as he pulled it over his head. When he shuffled out of the bathroom, he heard Oliver in the kitchen talking on the phone in hushed tones.

"Yeah, his phone died— Ryan, I wasn't going to turn him away. Don't be ridiculous."

Ezra stopped in the doorway, hugging his arms around his own waist, and Oliver looked up from the mugs he was pouring hot water into.

Oliver offered him a small smile. "I've got to go; he just got out of the shower— No, I'll have him call you later because he doesn't need you to yell at him right now," he snapped into the phone. His face softened. "Yeah, I'll tell him. And can you call Josie? Okay, thanks. Bye, Ryan."

"I'm so sor—" Ezra started.

"No, it's okay," Oliver said, closing the distance between them. He went to wrap his arms around him, but Ezra shook his head. Oliver let his arms drop back to his sides. "You're still shaking. Do you want some tea?"

Ezra nodded, so Oliver turned to grab their mugs and extended one to him. He took it between his hands and held it up to his mouth but didn't drink it.

"Do you want to talk about it?" Oliver asked.

Ezra shook his head.

"That's okay. I'm here for you. Whatever you need."

He looked up from his mug into Oliver's eyes, which were focused on him so softly, with so much care. It was too much. He turned to face the counter and set his mug down with shaky hands. He let out a shuttered exhale, and his knees shook so hard that he had to grip the counter just to keep himself from sinking to the floor. He felt Oliver come up behind him, but he didn't touch him again.

Ezra gasped. "She's gone."

"Shhh, I know, sweetheart." His ears were ringing, but somehow Oliver's calming voice broke past the fog.

"And I found out on the fucking news," he said in between more gasps for breath.

"I know. I'm so sorry. Just try to breathe, okay?"

"Can't—" He gasped again as his chest got tighter—not that it had ever fully loosened since watching the newscast.

"You can. I know it's hard. You're having an anxiety attack, but it will pass if you breathe, okay?"

Ezra tried to take a deep breath, but he couldn't. An anxiety attack. He'd never considered that was what these were, but it made sense.

"Can I touch you?"

Usually when he felt like this—in the midst of an anxiety attack—the last thing he wanted was to be touched, but he nodded. Oliver wrapped one arm around his waist as he pressed himself along Ezra's back, and it was like a grounding weight. He clutched at the arm pressed against his stomach.

"You're okay. I'm right here," Oliver whispered. He squeezed him tight. Ezra squeezed his eyes shut and sagged into Oliver's hold, his legs unable to continue supporting his own weight. "I've got you."

Ezra nodded and gasped again as he tried to catch another breath.

"Can you feel me breathing?" Oliver asked before deeply inhaling. Ezra nodded again, feeling Oliver's chest rise and fall. "Okay, just breathe when I do. Can you do that?"

Ezra nodded one more time, then focused on Oliver's breathing, trying to inhale and exhale in time with him. They stood like that for a long time, until finally, the tightness in Ezra's chest loosened and the ringing in his ears quieted. He sniffed loudly and let out a slow, shuddering exhale.

"Thank you for being here," he whispered shakily.

"Shhh, you don't have to thank me," Oliver murmured into Ezra's damp hair. He pressed a kiss to his head. "I care about you. Of course, I would be here for you."

Ezra let out a soft, broken sound and turned in Oliver's arms to face him. He wrapped his arms around his neck and pressed their foreheads together. "I don't know what I did to deserve you," he admitted in a whisper.

Oliver leaned back and slid his hands up to wipe away the handful of tears streaking Ezra's face. "I could say the same about you," he said before cradling Ezra's neck and tilting his head to press a kiss on his forehead. "Now, why don't you go crawl into bed while I reheat our tea?"

Ezra nodded and pulled Oliver in for a brief hug, then stepped back and shuffled out of the kitchen toward the bedroom. As he walked past the couch, Fiona hopped down and started weaving herself between his legs. Ezra sniffed, then bent to pick her up.

"Hello, beautiful creature," he mumbled, cradling her to his chest. She went limp in his arms and purred as he pressed his face into her fur. "I love you, too."

After a long moment, he continued on to the bedroom, then set her on the end of the bed so he could crawl under the covers. Once he settled in, Fiona made her way onto his lap and curled up.

A minute later, Oliver came into view, walking through the living room carrying two mugs. He stopped in the doorway. "Well, it looks like you're in good paws," he said, smiling fondly.

Ezra nodded, smiling half-heartedly. Oliver scooted around the bed to his side and set one mug down before handing Ezra his.

"Thank you," Ezra said, taking a sip. "Ollie, did you put whiskey in this?"

"Seemed like you could use it," he said as he carefully climbed under the covers.

"It's three PM," Ezra said.

"We're in the middle of a pandemic. Time has no meaning," he said light-heartedly.

Ezra attempted another smile, but he didn't even need to see his own face to know it didn't reach his eyes.

Oliver sighed and set down his tea, then extended his arms out for him. "Come here." Ezra nodded and nudged Fiona off his lap in favor of scooting to curl into Oliver's side. Oliver kissed his forehead, then combed his fingers through Ezra's wet and tangled curls.

"I couldn't find a comb," Ezra mumbled into the

crook of Oliver's shoulder.

"I don't have one," he said apologetically. "But if you sit up, I can try to finger-comb it for you. It would be better than nothing."

Ezra nodded. "Okay." He scooted away, then sat up with his back to Oliver, his legs crisscrossed underneath him. Oliver sat up behind him, then there were careful hands running through his hair. Ezra shut his eyes and let his head tilt back.

"You know, Willow keeps telling me that this is how I should detangle my hair anyway," Ezra said, forcing a conversational tone into his voice. Maybe if he pretended he was alright, he would be. "She says she has a friend with hair like mine, and *she*—being the friend—says that combs are bad for the curls. She also says I should do something called the 'Curly Girl Method', but I have no idea what that is, and it sounds like way too much—"

"Ezra," Oliver said, gently interrupting him. "You don't have to pretend to be okay. Nothing about this is okay. Your mother died, and you don't have to talk about it if you don't want to, but you also don't have to force yourself to act as if everything is business as usual."

"I just—I don't know what I would even say if I wanted to talk about it. I hated her, Ollie," Ezra said, his voice breaking. "Honestly, she's dead, and I still hate her."

Oliver stopped combing through his hair for a moment and wrapped his arms around his neck from behind. "That's understandable. She disowned you."

"It wasn't just that. She made me miserable my entire life—which only got worse after my dad died. He wasn't great either, but he paid more attention, at least, and once he even said he was proud of me, but it was always conditional. But my mother…" he trailed off, and Oliver gave him a reassuring squeeze. "She constantly ignored me. She never gave me an ounce of attention unless I did something wrong. Then it was—well, it was never good. Once at school, when Ryan and I got caught smoking weed, she was so livid that, I swear, if Ryan hadn't refused to leave my side, she might have actually hit me."

"For smoking weed?"

"They were threatening to expel me—and before you ask, no, not just for the weed. I'd been acting out. Skipping class, mouthing off to teachers, drinking, continually setting off the fire alarms by smoking cigarettes in the stairwells. You know, the typical cry-for-help behavior," he said. "But no one saw it as that except for Ryan and his parents. All everyone else saw was a bored rich kid acting out."

Oliver's arms tightened around him more, and Ezra knew he was thinking about his first assessment of him, which was exactly that. He turned to look at him. "Hey, I thought we'd agreed you wouldn't feel bad about that anymore."

"I'm trying," Oliver said, frowning. "But the more I hear about your childhood, the more I realize how wrong I was, and it makes me wish I could go back in time and hug teenage you all that much more."

"Keep hugging me now, and I'll be okay."

"I was planning on it."

Ezra gave him a small but genuine smile, then turned back and settled against his chest. "I didn't end up getting expelled—my mother threw a bunch of money at the problem, and the school let it slide—but she did basically write me off after that. I would never be good enough to head the company one day, so she started in on Elizabeth. Grooming her, putting way too many expectations on her, manipulating—"

"Sorry, but who's Elizabeth?"

Ezra froze. He hadn't meant to bring her up. He hadn't spoken about her since the accident. But in talking about his mother, she was bound to come up. The familiar tightness in his chest started again, but he took a deep breath to stave off the coming panic.

"My sister," he said finally.

"I didn't know you have a sister," Oliver whispered.

"We didn't really get along. She was three years younger and clearly the favorite child. We had little in common other than shitty parents, but we had that at least." Ezra sighed and stared at his lap. "She was the only one in my family that knew I'm bi. I was seeing this guy for a while when I was at Trinity, and Liz found out about it. She was the only one who knew besides friends, and she never told our family. Mind you, she wasn't the most enthusiastic supporter of it, but I think that was mostly because she was worried about our mother's reaction."

"When did she die?" Oliver asked. When Ezra didn't answer right away, he added, "You kept using the past tense."

"Three years ago. The magnolia on my neck is for her. It was her favorite flower," Ezra said, his voice shaking. "The official story was that there was an accident, and she drowned. But there were rumors that alcohol and drugs had been involved, which didn't sound like her at all. She was kind and good—like 'volunteering at soup kitchens every weekend' kind of good. But—" His voice cracked.

"It's okay, sweetheart," Oliver whispered.

"I think the pressure got to her. I was in Ireland, and we didn't talk much. She had my mother's full, horrible attention, and I think, to cope, she had gotten mixed in with a dangerous crowd."

"I'm sorry."

Ezra sniffed. "Anyway, that's why I skipped town

and bounced around Europe for so long. She died right before my graduation ceremony from Trinity, and I was trying to process the whole thing because it felt like my fault."

"It wasn't," Oliver said.

"I know. At least, now I do. If it's anyone's fault, it's my mother's. But now she's dead, too, so…"

Oliver clutched him tighter, and they both fell silent. After a minute or two, Oliver pulled away and continued to finger-comb through his hair. Ezra let his eyes drift shut again, and after another few minutes, Oliver tapped him on the shoulder.

"Hmm?"

"Do you have a hair tie?"

Wordlessly, he held up his arm, and Oliver pulled the band off of his wrist. "Did you braid my hair?"

"I did," Oliver said, sounding a little proud of himself.

For the first time since he'd heard the news, Ezra felt a real grin creep onto his face. He turned to face Oliver. "You know how to braid hair?"

Oliver grinned back. "I do."

"When did you learn to braid hair, and how did I not know about this until now?" Oliver's smile slipped, and Ezra furrowed his brow. "What is it?"

"I—I used to braid my mother's hair for her"—he sighed and looked at his lap—"after she got sick."

"Oh," Ezra said, unsure of what else to say.

"When she got sick, her doctors put her on a drug combination that didn't involve chemo, which great because that meant she didn't lose her hair, and she loved her hair. But she still had a lot of low energy days because of the toll they took—to where she could barely brush her hair."

He sighed again. "It got so bad that it started to mat up in the back, and she threatened to just cut it so it wasn't a problem. But like I said, she loved her hair, and I didn't want her to have to cut it. So, I had Mary teach me how to French braid. That way, it would help prevent the matting."

Ezra still wasn't sure what to say, but after a long pause, he asked, "Can I ask—just, you hardly talk about her so—"

Oliver nodded and laid back against the pillows again, holding his arm out for Ezra. He followed, draping himself half over Oliver's body and tucking his head in the crook of his neck.

"What do you want to know?"

"What was she like?"

"She was…It's hard to describe. Being around her felt like being near the sun. She was warm and kind but also…"

"Also?"

"Fiercely loyal. She did not give a flying fuck when it came to telling someone off. Like, when I got the RA diagnosis in high school, she had absolutely no problem calling my school out on their ableist bullshit. And if you think I have a foul mouth, she was worse by a mile."

Ezra laughed. "She sounds like someone else I know." He pressed a kiss to his neck.

"You think?"

"Warm, kind, loyal, foul mouth…" He ticked them off on his fingers. "Sounds like the exact description Ryan gave of you."

"Well, if I have to be one of my parents, I'm glad it's her. Not that I don't love my dad," Oliver said. "We get along fine, and I know he loves me, but I don't know. I had more in common with my mom. We'd read together, and she taught me how to bake. She's also the only one of my parents I ever came out to."

Ezra lifted his head to look at him. "You're not out

to your dad?"

Oliver shook his head.

"Is there a reason you aren't?" Oliver sighed, so Ezra quickly added, "You don't have to answer that."

"No, it's okay. I don't know, really. There's this distance between us. Ever since I got the RA diagnosis, he's been so overprotective. I guess I'm just afraid of giving him another reason to worry. Things are hard enough for a disabled person, much less a queer one. I didn't even really mean to come out to my mom. I was still figuring it all out, but she was going downhill so fast, and—"

He shook his head again. "Sorry, I don't mean to make things about me and my parents, especially since your—"

"You aren't," Ezra blurted. "I asked. Just because my mother was a piece of work, doesn't mean I don't want to hear about yours."

Oliver gave him a half-smile. "I think she would've liked you."

Ezra couldn't help smiling. "Yeah?"

"Yeah. I think my dad would, too, if I could ever work up the courage to tell him."

"You don't have to until you're ready."

"I know. But I think I want to, eventually. I never had a reason before because I've never seriously dated a guy since Nick, so it was easier to keep chickening out."

Ezra's stomach fluttered. The "now things are different" at the end of Oliver's statement went unsaid, but it still hung in the air between them. They stared at each other for a long moment, then Ezra dropped his head back to Oliver's shoulder and tucked his face into his neck.

22

Ezra

Thursday, November 5, 2020

An hour later, Oliver got up to refill their tea. When he returned with another two steaming mugs of tea, Ezra sat up and accepted one. "You're limping," he said with a frown.

Oliver sighed and set his mug down to climb back into bed. "My hips are just a little inflamed today. I think it's just the rain, so I'll be okay. Come back?" He motioned for Ezra to come closer.

Ezra scooted close, rested his head on Oliver's shoulder, and laced their fingers together so they could still drink their tea. "Is there anything I can do to help?"

Oliver took a small sip of his tea and set the mug down again. "I took some meds and put some anti-inflammatory gel on earlier. It should start working soon. Mostly, it's just my back now, which seizes up when my hips flare up."

Ezra lifted his head and stretched to put his mug down. "I could give you a massage."

"You don't have to; I'll be fine."

"I know I don't have to, but I want to, *mon chou*," he said before lifting a hand to cup his cheek and kissing him. "Now, let me help."

"I'm supposed to be helping you right now," Oliver protested.

"You're already helping." Ezra sighed. "Please? I just need something else to focus on. Something to do."

"Okay, but I'm going to do you first, okay?"

"Oliver—"

"Nope, no arguing. You're still radiating tension, and you need to relax your muscles or else you won't be able to move tomorrow—trust me."

"Fine."

Oliver smiled. "Shirt off, please."

"That's the real reason, isn't it? You just want me shirtless," Ezra teased, but even to his own ears it fell a little flat.

Oliver played along, though. "I can have two reasons," he said.

Ezra complied and lay on his stomach with his arms at his sides. Oliver straddled his hips and ran his fingers along his back, tracing the branches of his Tree of Life tattoo.

"God, I love this tattoo," he mumbled under his breath before leaning down to press a kiss to the base of his neck where the tree extended to. Then he pressed a kiss to his shoulder where the wing of the phoenix wrapped around. "And this one."

Ezra smiled into the pillow. "Are you massaging me or admiring my tattoos for the umpteenth time?"

"Yes," Oliver said. Then he dug his thumbs into the muscles at the base of Ezra's neck.

He didn't have any knots in his muscles for Oliver to work out. It was more of an all-over clenching left over from his body's anxiety and panic response and walking close to eight miles in the cold rain. So Oliver didn't have to apply too much pressure to loosen the tension in his back, which was probably better for his wrists, anyway. After a few minutes, Oliver moved onto his arms, then the backs of his legs, squeezing the muscles to prompt him to relax.

When he was done, he straddled Ezra's hips again and leaned down to press a few light kisses on his neck and cheek. "Good?"

Ezra nodded against the pillow then, without opening his eyes, and turned his head more to catch Oliver's lips for a quick kiss. "Your turn. Shirt off."

Ezra felt Oliver smile against his skin, then another kiss to his cheek, before Oliver's warm weight disappeared. He gave himself a few seconds before opening his eyes and sitting up.

Oliver stripped off his sweater, then lay on his stomach, bringing his arms up and folding them under his head to create a pillow. Ezra straddled his hips, then rubbed his hands along the planes of his back. "Anywhere in particular?"

"Lower back," Oliver said, his voice muffled by his pillow.

"Okay, I'll end there," he said. He leaned down and brushed a kiss to the base of Oliver's neck, then sat back up and gently worked out his sore muscles.

"You're great at this," Oliver said after a few minutes.

"I spent some time in Sweden," Ezra joked, earning a quiet chuckle. He scooted back to sit on Oliver's thighs so he could focus on his lower back.

"Funny," Oliver deadpanned.

"You laughed, didn't you?" Ezra smiled and brushed his thumbs over the dimples on Oliver's lower back. "Have I told you how much I love these?"

"You may have mentioned it—fuck," Oliver broke off with a soft moan as Ezra dug his thumbs into the dimples and rotated out.

"Okay?"

He nodded against the pillow and groaned as Ezra pressed the heel of his hands into the muscles above his hip bones. "That's good—fantastic. I knew you were good with your hands, but Jesus."

Ezra laughed and continued working out the tense muscles in Oliver's back, pulling soft moans from him, which was beginning to be a problem. He shifted uncomfortably, and after another few minutes, he stilled his hands. "Better?"

Oliver hummed happily, then rolled over, still caged between Ezra's knees, and smiled up at him. "Thank you," he said, resting his hands on the tops of Ezra's knees.

"You're welcome. I'm glad I could help," he said, shifting forward to lean on his hands, further caging Oliver in as he leaned down to kiss him. Then he added, "And, I'm always happy to see you shirtless, so it's a win-win."

Oliver laughed and slid his hand up Ezra's bare arm to cup his cheek. "The feeling is mutual," he said with a smirk. He lifted his head off the pillow to meet Ezra's lips for a gentle kiss. When he started to pull away, Ezra chased after him, shifting to slot a leg between Oliver's thighs.

Oliver pulled away as he undoubtedly felt Ezra's growing arousal press against his hip. "Oh," he said, mildly amused.

"Don't act surprised after all of those obscene little noises you were making," Ezra teased.

Oliver smirked. "I couldn't help it."

"Sure, I totally believe that." He grinned, then brought their lips together for a deep kiss. Oliver hummed into it, then gasped as Ezra nipped at his bottom lip with his teeth. His hands flew up to tangle in

Ezra's braided hair. Their mouths moved together desperately, a little too much tongue and teeth, until Oliver pulled away sharply,

"Wait," he said, panting for breath. "We don't have to—"

Ezra cut him off with a kiss just to the right of his mouth. "I want to. *Je te veux. Toujours. Tellement de*," he whispered between kisses that he trailed across Oliver's cheek and down his neck.

Oliver sighed and tilted his head back. "I want you, too."

Ezra quickly lifted his head and stared down at Oliver with a questioning smirk.

"I told you I was going to start learning French," he teased. Then his face softened. "Are you sure, though? You've had a long, emotional day. We can just curl up and watch movies for the rest of the day. Whatever you need, it's okay."

Ezra nodded. "I want—" He shook his head, then rested his forehead against Oliver's. "I want to feel something good. I need to feel like the world doesn't exist outside of you and this bed."

Oliver gently cupped his cheek and brought their lips together for an impossibly delicate kiss, and when he pulled away, Ezra let out a shaky exhale.

"Okay." Oliver kissed him again. "What do you need?"

"You. I don't care how. I just need you."

Oliver nodded and pushed at his shoulder to guide him onto his back so he could straddle his hips. He slid his palms from Ezra's stomach up to his chest, then into his hair as he leaned down to bring them chest to chest. "*Tu as moi*," he whispered, before bringing their mouths together for a gentle kiss. *You have me.*

Ezra pulled away and looked at him with both amusement and fondness.

"What? Did I say it wrong?" Oliver sat up self-con-sciously. "My accent is probably terrible."

"No," Ezra said, chuckling. "Your accent actually isn't bad. Also, I see what you mean now. It's sexy when you speak French. It would be 'tu m'as' though, not 'tu as moi'," he explained. Then he gave a genuine smile and ran his hands up Oliver's back to bring him back into his arms.

"What's the diff—?" Oliver started to ask, but Ezra cut him off with a kiss.

"Do you really want me to explain French grammar to you right now?" he teased.

Oliver smirked. "No, I suppose not." He kissed his cheek, then trailed soft kisses down to his neck, pausing near his ear. "I want you to let me take care of you." He punctuated the statement with a kiss to the sensitive spot just behind his ear.

Oliver continued his path down Ezra's body, but took his time, alternating between soft, teasing kisses and light bites until Ezra was squirming. "Olls," he gasped, although he wasn't sure whether it was for en-couragement or as a complaint that he was teasing him for too long.

Oliver rested his chin on Ezra's stomach and looked up at him. "Patience, love," he said. "We can take our time. It's just you and me."

"You and me," Ezra repeated.

Oliver sat back on his heels and hooked his fingers in the waistband of Ezra's pants and boxers. When he paused for confirmation, Ezra let out a sharp exhale and nodded. Oliver smiled and leaned forward to kiss him slowly. When Oliver dropped his pants to the floor, Ezra sat up and teased the waistband of Oliver's pajamas.

"You, too." He leaned up for a kiss.

"We're focusing on you first," Oliver whispered.

Ezra hummed and brought their lips together again. "I want to see you. All of you."

Oliver nodded and climbed off the bed to strip out of his own pants. Then he straddled Ezra's hips again, and it was just them—nothing between them. Oliver kissed him softly on the lips as he pushed him to lie back, and Ezra sighed into it. Oliver was everywhere, mouth and hands exploring. He kissed his way down Ezra's chest and settled between his thighs. He pressed a gentle kiss to his hip bone, then to the crease of his thigh, and Ezra tightened his grip on the sheets as Oliver took him in his mouth. Oliver's hand slid to Ezra's, fisted in the sheets and laced their fingers together, forcing Ezra to open his eyes and look down at him. Oliver lifted his head and sent Ezra a smile that made his breath catch in his throat.

God, he'd never felt so…safe. Cared for. Anchored. Oliver was a tether back to reality. It was as if Oliver could read his mind, giving him everything until any thoughts left in Ezra's head were gone, replaced with incoherent feelings of pleasure and warmth, which was as overwhelming as it was exactly what he wanted. But he also wanted more. He needed Oliver to take as much as he was giving.

He squeezed Oliver's hand. "Olls, wait," he breathed.

Oliver lifted his head again and used his free hand to rub a soothing circle on his hip. "Everything okay?"

Ezra looked down at him, open-mouthed, and nodded before tugging on Oliver's hand to pull him back toward the head of the bed. Their lips met in a deep, passionate kiss, and Ezra locked his legs around Oliver's waist to bring him closer to where he wanted him.

Ezra rarely wanted that. For him, it required a vulnerability he rarely allowed himself outside a long-term relationship. And he hadn't had one of those since before leaving Ireland right before graduation, so it had been years since he'd wanted to be the one being fucked rather than the one doing the fucking. But this wasn't a hookup or a fling. This was Oliver, and in that moment, all he wanted was to feel that closeness. The connection. That feeling of being so full of another person, it was almost impossible to tell where one person ended and the other began.

Oliver broke the kiss and pulled back enough to look at him, silently asking him the question, and Ezra nodded. "If you're okay with that."

Oliver nodded, then brought their mouths back together. They kissed tenderly until Oliver finally broke away to get the lube and a condom out of the pouch hanging on the side of his bed. He returned and settled back over him. "It's been a little while since I've done this on someone else, so you'll have to tell me what you like," Oliver whispered.

Ezra nodded, then surged up to kiss Oliver, muffling the moan that escaped him as Oliver brought his hand between Ezra's legs. Oliver carefully worked him open, only breaking their kiss to ask Ezra what he needed or to murmur a quiet assurance in his ear, until Ezra could no longer stand it.

"Olls," he said with a gasp.

Oliver nodded in understanding and pulled away only long enough to roll on a condom. Then he was back, gripping the back of one of Ezra's thighs as he pressed into him, letting out a shuddered breath as he did. Ezra clutched at Oliver's back and buried his face into his neck as he bit back a cry.

Oliver stilled. "Okay?" he whispered in his ear, and Ezra nodded against his neck. Oliver threaded his fingers through Ezra's hair to pull his head back enough so it forced him to look him in the eye.

Ezra's breath caught, and the back of his eyes stung

with tears at the pure adoration and patience written all over Oliver's face. "Move, please," he whispered.

Oliver nodded and leaned down to kiss him as he started to rock his hips.

The rest of the world fell away again as they picked up a rhythm, their irregular breath and the slight creak of Oliver's bed frame the only sounds in the room, the soft, worn sheets and the warmth of skin against skin the only feelings. Ezra felt the familiar pressure building in his lower belly like a stretched rubber band ready to snap. He locked his legs around Oliver's hips again.

"I've got you," Oliver mumbled against Ezra's lips as he snaked a hand between them.

The pressure built more until it snapped, and Ezra let out a soft moan as he tumbled over the edge. Oliver muffled it with a kiss and stayed with him through the shockwaves. When his senses returned to him, he heard Oliver's breath hitch. Ezra tightened his legs around Oliver and broke the kiss to trail his lips to Oliver's neck, sucking at a spot he knew was sensitive. Oliver shuddered and let out a soft curse as his hips stilled and he found his own release.

They stayed in their embrace for a few minutes. Finally, their heart rates slowed, and a wave of exhaustion hit Ezra like a ton of bricks. Oliver dropped a kiss to Ezra's shoulder on top of the phoenix there, then lifted off Ezra and rolled to the side to climb out of bed.

"I'll be right back with a washcloth," he said.

Ezra nodded but didn't open his eyes. Oliver was back only a minute later, warm washcloth in hand. Ezra's eyes fluttered open as he felt the bed dip beside him and warmth on his stomach. He opened his mouth to protest, saying that he could clean himself up, but he couldn't bring himself to do it. It felt nice to let someone take care of him for once. "Thank you," he said instead.

"*De rien, mon amour*," Oliver replied, a soft smile playing on his lips.

Ezra hummed contentedly. "Would you mind handing me my clothes?"

Oliver nodded and handed him his pajamas, then dropped the washcloth in the corner where a pile of dirty clothes sat before putting his own pajamas back on. When they were dressed, Oliver climbed back into bed and gestured for Ezra to come over and rest his head on his chest. He complied, and the last thing he remembered after that was Oliver stroking his hair.

23

Oliver

Friday Morning, November 6, 2020

The next morning, Oliver woke before his alarm to a text from Ryan telling him to take the day off. Usually, he would have protested, but then he glanced over his shoulder at Ezra, still sleeping beside him, and decided not to question it. It wasn't like he could get any work done, anyway. He had gotten no work done yesterday either, too worried about Ezra wandering around Queens, not answering his phone. And while Ezra was safe now, Oliver still worried.

Carefully, Oliver turned over to face Ezra, who still had the covers pulled tightly around his shoulders and his hands tucked under his chin, almost defensively. It was almost unnerving. Oliver was the one who curled in on himself, who sat with his legs pulled into his chest and buried his face in his hands. Oliver didn't like to take up space. But Ezra did. He'd spread out across the bed or prop his feet up on the coffee table and stretch his arm across the couch when they watched TV together. Seeing him like this made Oliver want to do something, anything, to help.

Ezra's hair was covering most of his face, so Oliver gently brushed it back and behind his ear to press a kiss to his forehead. Then he climbed out of bed and crept quietly out of the room. Since there was no chance of him getting back to sleep, he might as well make breakfast.

Fiona leapt off the bed and padded after him, chirping and weaving herself between his legs as he made his way to the kitchen.

"Ma'am, if you trip me, I won't be able to feed you," Oliver said to her, although, as always, it was useless. When it was time for Fiona's breakfast, she always pretended that she couldn't understand English.

After dumping a can of wet food into a bowl for his demanding cat, he opened the kitchen window so the small room wouldn't overheat when he turned the oven on. Then he set about making sourdough biscuits.

Between the soothing sound of the rain outside and the repetitive motion of rolling and folding the dough, Oliver fell into an almost meditative state—or at least as close to one as his constantly buzzing brain could get. So when Ezra wrapped his arms around Oliver's waist from behind and nosed the base of his neck, he jumped and dropped the spatula he was using to make the scrambled eggs.

"It's only me," Ezra mumbled into his shoulder.

Oliver rested a hand on Ezra's arm where it pressed into his stomach. "I know. I didn't hear you coming, is all. What are you doing up?"

"The bed was empty," Ezra said. "And I smelled bacon."

"I was planning on bringing you breakfast in bed. It'll be ready soon if you want to get back in bed," Oliver said.

Ezra shook his head against Oliver's shoulder. "I

enjoy watching you cook."

Oliver squeezed his arm, then picked up the dropped spatula to continue stirring the pot of eggs. "How are you feeling?"

"Cold, body achy, and headachy," Ezra groaned.

"Well, walking around in the rain for several hours, then drinking a bunch of whiskey will do that," Oliver teased gently.

"How are you not at least a little hungover?"

"I didn't drink as much as you did," Oliver said. He reached for the salt, pepper, and garlic powder to season the eggs. "But the good news is that once we get some breakfast in you, we can spend the rest of the day in bed doing nothing."

"I should probably call Josie and get a ride home, though. I don't have any clothes here or anything."

Oliver frowned to himself. "Is it selfish of me to say that I want you to stay?"

"No more selfish than me wanting the same thing." Ezra pressed his lips into Oliver's skin.

"Having you here…it makes me feel less like I want to crawl out of my skin. I haven't felt this comfortable since this whole thing started. I just—" He sighed. "You make me feel good."

"What if—" Ezra paused for a long moment. "What if I stayed?"

The eggs were done, so Oliver turned the burner off and moved the pot off of the heat. "I'd love that, but as you said, you don't have any of your stuff here."

"No, I mean, what if I quarantine here with you for a little while?"

Oliver turned in Ezra's arms to look at him.

"I know it might seem a little fast to commit to spending that much uninterrupted time together, but— I don't know, I think it'd be nice. And I could always leave if you get sick of me," Ezra explained in a rush.

"You're serious," Oliver said in disbelief. "You'd honestly want to stay here with me?"

"I would." Ezra smiled nervously, then added in a smaller voice, "If you'll have me, anyway."

Oliver blinked at him for a few moments before letting himself smile. "Okay."

"Okay?" Ezra repeated hopefully.

"Yeah. I want you here," Oliver said.

Ezra's face lit up. "I'll see if Josie would mind me keeping her car for a while, then."

The oven beeped, letting Oliver know that the bacon was ready.

"Should you get that?" Ezra asked.

"Probably," Oliver said, but he made no move to extract himself from their embrace. Instead, he cradled Ezra's face with both hands.

Ezra hummed and leaned in so their lips were almost touching. "I like my bacon extra crispy, anyway."

Oliver laughed, then brought their lips together.

After breakfast, which was eaten in bed, Ezra grabbed his phone and powered it on. He winced as it buzzed incessantly in his hand, alerting him to the likely dozens of missed calls and text messages. "You called me, like, twenty times," he said, frowning.

"I told you I was worried out of my mind. But it's alright," Oliver said, not wanting him to feel guilty.

"No, it's not. You weren't the only one. Ryan called me fifteen times, Josie...Jesus. She called me over thirty times from both her cell phone and the house phone. And I have about a dozen texts." He set down the phone and looked at Oliver. "I'm so sorry. I was stupid and—"

"Shh." Oliver pressed a palm to his cheek. "You don't need to apologize to me. I'm just glad you're okay."

"I should call Josie, though."

"Yeah," Oliver said, pulling his hand away. "Ryan said he would call her to let her know you were alive, but you should still call her."

Ezra nodded and bit his lip as he stared at the phone.

"Do you want me to give you some privacy?" Oliver asked.

He shook his head and shot a hand out to grab Oliver's arm. "Please, stay."

Oliver nodded and laced his fingers with Ezra's while he dialed his cousin.

"Hey, Jose, I'm so—" Ezra barely got a few words out before Josie started yelling in what sounded like French on the other line.

Oliver had been picking French up surprisingly fast over the past month, but between the garbled phone speaker and the speed at which Josie was speaking, he couldn't make out anything concrete.

Ezra winced and pulled the phone away from his ear for a moment. "Look, I know I royally fucked up, but can you please stop yelling? I have a massive headache."

Josie's voice on the line grew quieter, and Ezra put his phone back to his ear.

"I know, I shouldn't have run off like that, but I couldn't—I just needed to get away. Oliver said I was having a panic attack, which sounds about right." He was silent for a moment, then frowned at whatever Josie must have said. "You're right. It was reckless, and I'm sorry. I'm also sorry that I waited until now to call you."

Oliver squeezed Ezra's hand, earning a grateful smile.

"I'm guessing Willow is in the room? Can you tell her I'm sorry, too?" Ezra asked, then he let out a relieved sigh. "Thank you. You, uh, haven't heard any information about a funeral, have you?" He was silent for a few moments then nodded. "Yeah, I figured as much. Yes, I'll text you when I'm ready for you to come get me. Thank you. I love you, too. Okay, bye."

He hung up and dropped his phone in his lap before leaning his head on Oliver's shoulder.

Oliver pressed a kiss to his hair. "Everything okay?"

Ezra nodded against his shoulder. "I think so. I scared Willow, too, though, so I may spend a night or two there before coming back here to make it up to her, if that's alright."

"Of course," Oliver said. "What did she say about a funeral?"

"She doesn't know. There was no information from any of the news outlets, and she hasn't heard from her father since she married Ted, so she didn't even know he was in town. But she said she would try talking to her mother. Apparently, Aunt Annabelle isn't as strict on the whole disowning thing as Uncle Edward," Ezra said.

Oliver nodded and kissed Ezra's hair again. "Now, what do you need?"

"I think I need tea, a cat, a bad romcom, and cuddles," he said as he snuggled closer into Oliver's side.

"Well, that sounds like my ideal day off, so I can do that," Oliver said with a smile.

Ezra craned his neck to look up at him. "Thank you."

Oliver closed the distance between them and kissed him. "You're welcome, sweetheart."

Sunday Afternoon, November 15, 2020

"Oh, there is absolutely no way I am getting my body into that shape," Oliver said, looking at the paused yoga video on his television. He wasn't quite sure how Ezra had managed to convince him to get onto a thin rubber mat in the middle of his living room and attempt to contort his uncooperative-at-best body into various shapes, but here he was.

They'd been quarantining together for the past week. After the day Ezra had shown up on his doorstep soaking wet and mid-panic attack, he'd gone back home to spend a few days with Willow to make up for scaring her and to see if Josie had learned anything about the funeral. But then, he'd come back with a duffel bag and his guitar.

They'd already fallen into a pretty nice rhythm. They'd sit in comfortable silence on the couch during the day while they worked. Then, at night, they would cuddle and watch movies or read, which usually led to them having increasingly amazing sex. One night, Oliver had even convinced Ezra to serenade him with his guitar. It was like heaven. He'd never been this content with another person before. Which, thinking about it, was likely how he ended up trying yoga. He was so content and happy being surrounded by everything that was Ezra that he couldn't help wanting to indulge him.

"You can modify the shape to your needs, you know," Ezra pointed out as he seamlessly switched from the tabletop position into a downward-facing dog. "The point of yoga is to build strength, awareness and harmony in both the mind and body, not to hit the pose correctly every time. See, look, my heels don't reach the ground either."

"Can't we just go back to child's pose?" Oliver asked. "I liked that one."

Ezra shifted into a plank, then into an upward-facing dog. "You just liked that one because it's basically curling into a ball, which is how you spend most of your day," he teased.

"Okay, fair," Oliver conceded, "but it also opened my hips up and stretched out my back, which was nice."

"Well, the downward-facing dog also stretches the back, and it opens up the back of the legs," Ezra said before shifting out of the pose and into a seated position. "Come on, just try it. I'll even adjust your posture for you."

"I see what this is now," Oliver said with a smirk. "You're only trying to get me to do yoga because you want an excuse to put your hands all over me."

"No, I'm trying to get you to do yoga because I think it will help with your joint pain. Also"—he crawled forward and leaned in close—"do I need an excuse to put my hands all over you?"

"You do not." Oliver smirked, then threaded a hand in Ezra's hair to pull him in for a kiss.

Ezra hummed into it, then pulled back. "This doesn't get you out of trying yoga."

"Of course not."

They fell back against the mat, the yoga video forgotten as their lips moved together, unhurried and exploratory. But just as Oliver was about to slip his hands beneath Ezra's workout tank, his phone rang. Ezra sat up, ignoring Oliver's protest, and grabbed the phone off the coffee table.

"Who is it?" Oliver asked, begrudgingly sitting up, as well.

"Mary."

"Give it here," Oliver said with a heavy sigh.

Ezra laughed and handed him the phone, then kissed his cheek and whispered, "We'll pick this up later," in his ear just as Oliver answered the FaceTime call.

"Hello, hello—oh, did I interrupt something?" Mary waggled her eyebrows.

"We were doing yoga," Oliver explained, but in the

small window in the corner showing his own video, he saw his blush betray him.

"You? Yoga? Come on, Oliver, at least make the lie believable."

"We were actually doing yoga," Ezra said, squishing his face next to Oliver's to fit into the frame. "Also, hi, I'm Ezra. Ollie talks about you all the time."

"Oh, I know who you are. I stalked your Instagram a few months ago because Ollie wouldn't stop talking about you," Mary said with a smirk.

"Mary!" Oliver whined.

"It's alright, *mon chou*. I wouldn't stop talking about you, either. Ryan was sick of me," Ezra said before kissing Oliver's cheek.

Oliver looked at him and smiled.

"Okay, well, while this is completely adorable, I did call for a reason," Mary interrupted.

"Sorry," Oliver said. "What's up?"

"Well, do you remember how I started ring shopping before all of this pandemic shit started, so I had to put those plans on hold?" Mary asked.

"Yeah. Hang on, did you propose?" Oliver exclaimed. "Did you propose and not tell me beforehand?! Mary!"

Mary laughed. "I didn't propose! Robin beat me to it."

"Wait, really?!" Oliver beamed at the phone. "You're affianced?"

She grinned back. "I'm affianced. Or 'engaged', as normal people would say."

"Oh, Mar, I'm so happy for you."

"Thanks, Ollie," she chirped.

"So, I'm not just calling with good news. I have a question for you."

"What?"

"Would you do me the honor of being my person of

honor?"

"Me?" he asked in disbelief. "But you have a sister for that."

"A sister that is still in high school," Mary pointed out. "She'll still be a bridesmaid, but I can't imagine having anyone else be my best person."

Oliver felt a surge of warmth through him as he looked at his best friend in the entire world. "Does this mean I have to throw you a bridal shower?"

"And a bachelorette party," she added. "I expect strippers."

"Male strippers or female strippers?" Ezra asked.

"Well, if it were just for me, obviously female strippers, but—"

"It is just for you," Oliver interrupted. "It's your bachelorette party."

"True, but I also want to make sure all of my friends have a good time, and since not all of them are raging lesbians, I should probably include some variety," Mary said. "But we can go into the details later. We haven't even set a date yet."

"Well, whatever you and Robin need, you just need to call me. I know I'm halfway across the country, but I want to be as involved as I can be," Oliver said.

Mary smiled, then looked off-screen. "I'll be right there, love," she said, before turning her attention back to Oliver. "Thanks, Ollie. I've got to go. Robin and I are getting on a Zoom call with the parents to break the news."

"You called me before you called your parents?"

"Well, yeah," she said as if it were obvious. "Alright, I love you, you cranky old man."

"Love you, too, you crazy lady," Oliver said with a smile. "Give Robin my love."

"I will," Mary said. "And Ezra, it was nice to meet you."

"You, too," Ezra said.

Oliver hung up, then settled back into Ezra's arm with a massive grin. "I can't believe my best friend is engaged."

"I have no frame of reference, but she seemed thrilled," Ezra commented.

"Oh, she was positively beaming. I haven't seen her that happy since the time she called me in the middle of the night after her and Robin's first date."

"That's cute," Ezra said. "And also familiar."

"Right, Ryan did the same thing to you, right?"

"Yup. I can't fault him, though, seeing how it turned out."

"Yeah, I guess when you know someone's it, you have to call your best friend in the middle of the night about it." Oliver meant it as a joke, but once the words were out of his mouth, he realized that sentiment also applied to him. Because if Ezra hadn't knocked on his door again immediately after the end of their first date, he would have called Mary to debrief the entire thing. But it was too early in his and Ezra's relationship to start on that thought train. It was just the engagement fever making his brain go fuzzy.

He craned his neck to look at Ezra. "Now, I believe we were in the middle of something?"

"Our yoga video?" Ezra supplied innocently.

Oliver narrowed his eyes, and Ezra broke out into a grin before kissing him soundly.

24

Oliver

Saturday Night, November 21, 2020

"The call is starting," Ezra called out from the living room.

"Start without me," Oliver called back. He scooped more icing out of the mixing bowl and spread it on top of the cake.

"Ollie," Ezra whined.

"I'm almost done." Oliver set down his icing knife and went to poke his head out of the kitchen. "You guys start without— Hey, what are you doing? I told you to stay out of here."

"You've been in here for hours," Ezra said from the doorway. "It's my birthday."

"I know, which is why I've been in here making you a birthday cake," Oliver teased.

"Which I appreciate, and it looks amazing," Ezra said as he closed the distance between them and wrapped his arms around Oliver's waist. "But now, I would appreciate it if my boyfriend would come out and join the birthday party he planned for me."

Oliver tucked a few strands of hair behind his ear. "Boyfriend, huh?"

"I would have thought that'd be obvious by now. But yes"—he leaned up to brush their lips together—"you're my boyfriend."

"I'll be out in a minute, I promise," Oliver said, earning a heavy sigh from Ezra. "I'm just getting candles and plates."

"You get your ass out into the living room with that cake," Ezra said, already turning out of Oliver's arms and toward the cabinet. "I'll get plates."

Oliver laughed and picked up the cake stand. "We also need drinks."

"I'll also grab those, then. Now go dial into the call. We're late."

"We wouldn't be late if you'd just started without me," Oliver called over his shoulder as he left the kitchen.

"Shut up," Ezra called back.

Oliver laughed again, then set up the cake on the coffee table next to his laptop. Ezra had set up an external webcam on the television so it would be easier to see everyone, so all Oliver needed to do was join the Zoom call link. He logged in, and soon the television screen filled with three camera feeds. When Oliver suggested a Zoom birthday party, he'd envisioned a small thing with just Ryan and Anna, but Ezra insisted on inviting Juliet, Mary, and Robin, too. He'd said something about wanting Oliver's friends to be his friends. Of course, after he'd added Juliet and Mary to the planning chat, the initially quiet evening had morphed into as exciting a party as they could have via Zoom. Which is how, after off-key singing and cake-eating, they ended up playing *Never Have I Ever*.

Although he hated most drinking games since they weren't as fun when he substituted water for alcohol, he loved his friends, and Ezra was having a great time. Ezra had also looked up recipes for mocktails beforehand, which was a sweet gesture, so he didn't mind all that much.

"Never have I ever," Juliet drawled as if she needed time to think of something. Then she grinned and said, "Never have I ever gotten caught having sex by my parents."

"Oh, come on. That's not fair," Ryan complained.

"Yeah, that's not fair. You targeted us," Anna echoed, but both of them lifted their cups up to drink.

"What? No one said targeting another player was against the rules," Juliet said innocently.

"Yeah, and you two were asking to get caught. Who has sex at their parents' house in the middle of the day?" Ezra asked.

"We didn't think they were home!" Anna exclaimed.

Everyone laughed, then Oliver looked at the window on the screen where Mary and Robin sat. "Mary, it's your turn," he said, trying to keep the game moving.

"Oh, God, alright," Mary said. She hummed as she thought, then she glanced at Robin.

"Never have I ever hooked up with someone in my friend group."

"Okay, rude," Robin said, shoving at her fiancée before taking a drink.

Oliver froze, then trained his gaze on Juliet's frame, trying to gauge whether she was going to let the cat out of the bag, so to speak. She toasted the screen, then took a long drink from her beer.

"Wait, who? We don't have that many other friends," Anna said.

Oliver took a deep breath, then lifted his mocktail to his lips. He felt Ezra look at him, and he bit his lip before turning to see his reaction. Ezra gave him a quizzical look.

"You two— When? How—?" Anna stammered.

"Do you really want to know the how of the situation?" Juliet asked with a smirk.

"How did neither of you tell me this?!" Anna looked at Ryan. "Did you know about this?"

Ryan shook his head. "Scout's honor."

"You weren't in the Scouts, mate," Ezra said.

"It was only a few times," Oliver said, more to Ezra than to Anna.

"It was more than once?" Anna asked, indignant.

"And it meant nothing," Oliver continued.

Ezra smiled and linked their fingers together. "Don't worry. It doesn't bother me."

Oliver let out a relieved breath.

"Yeah, we were just bored and horny—and drunk," Juliet said. "Well, at least for the first time. I don't know how you didn't just figure it out. Usually, you're pretty observant, Anna. We weren't sneaky about it, and I was not subtle at all in my indignation that Oliver here claimed Ezra was the best sex of his life—"

"Jules!" Oliver exclaimed, whipping his head toward the camera. He could see in the window that reflected his own picture that his face was bright red.

Ryan laughed, and Mary buried her face in Robin's shoulder to hide hers.

"You said that, huh?" Ezra teased.

Oliver pulled his hand out of Ezra's so he could bury his face in both hands. "I hate this game."

Ezra pried his hands away from his face, then tilted his chin to look at him. He held a hand in front of the webcam before pulling Oliver into a deep kiss.

Oliver melted into it, humming against Ezra's lips as he felt the embarrassment leave his body.

"We can still see you," Oliver heard Ryan call out.

Oliver opened his eyes and pulled away enough to see Ezra flip off the camera. He laughed, which Ezra then cut off with another kiss. His hands came up to cradle Oliver's face as the kiss turned soft. After a few seconds, they parted, and Ezra pulled him under his arm, where Oliver was content to stay until they got off the call.

Close to midnight, everyone decided it was time to go to bed. Once the call ended, Oliver shut the laptop and turned to face Ezra, who immediately pulled him in for a kiss.

"Thank you for planning this, *mon chou*. It was great."

"You're welcome, sweetheart," Oliver said in between kisses. Then he pulled away before he got too swept up. "But I want to talk to you about the Juliet thing. I'm sorry I didn't tell you before—"

"Olls," Ezra said, cutting him off with a hand on the cheek. "You don't have to apologize. It's not like we've done a full diagnostic of every one of our exes."

"I know, but—"

"There are no lingering feelings, right?"

"Definitely not," Oliver said. "I mean, she's one of my best friends, and I love her, but not that way. It was just sex."

"Then it's fine," he said with a shrug. "Besides, how can I be mad when I know that I'm the best sex of your life?"

"I'm going to murder Jules," Oliver said with a groan. He tried to get up, but Ezra laughed and pulled Oliver into his lap.

"See, and I was thinking of sending her a fruit basket for letting that bit of information out."

"Careful or it'll end up being a double murder." Oliver's breath hitched on the last syllable as Ezra placed an open-mouth kiss just below his ear.

He felt Ezra smirk against his neck. "Hey, you have to be nice to me. It's my birthday."

Oliver sighed dramatically and pulled back to look at

him. "So it is," he said. Then, in contrast to his teasing, he leaned in to press a series of slow, dirty kisses to his lips.

Ezra hummed into his mouth, then broke away to suck at his neck, earning another gasp. "Although, just for the record…"

"What?"

"Same."

Oliver furrowed his brow.

"And I'm not just saying that to make you feel better," Ezra added. Oliver continued to stare at him, and Ezra cocked his head. "You don't believe me?"

"I—"

Oliver opened his mouth to say something, but then Ezra's lips were on his, and his hands were on his ass. "Guess I have to prove it, then."

Ezra stood, and Oliver let out a surprised sound before wrapping his legs around Ezra's waist.

He laughed as Ezra walked to the bedroom. "I can walk, you know."

"I know," Ezra said. His lips met Oliver's again, and after that, Oliver couldn't bother trying to form coherent sentences.

Ezra

Thursday, November 26, 2020

"Are you sure you want me to go?" Ezra wrapped his arms around Oliver's waist from behind and hooked his chin over his shoulder to watch him slice carrots.

"For the third time, yes. I'm sure," Oliver said. "You should be with your family. You haven't had a proper

Thanksgiving in what? Seven years?"

"Longer than that," he mumbled. "Thanksgiving was never a joyous occasion in the Beaumont household."

"So you should go."

"I just hate leaving you to be all by yourself," he said, pressing his lips to Oliver's neck.

"I'll be fine. The turkey is in the oven, and I have a Zoom call with Dad and Mary." Oliver set the knife down and turned in Ezra's arms. "Besides, you have to bring the pie we made."

"I'll be back tomorrow," Ezra promised. "Likely with leftovers."

Oliver smiled and kissed him. "And I'll be here with different leftovers."

Ezra sighed and kissed him again. "Text me Dog Show updates since I'll miss some of it while driving?"

"As long as you promise to wait to read them after you get there."

"I promise."

"Good." Oliver kissed him, then playfully pushed him away. "Now go. So far, your cousins seem to like me, and I don't want that to change because you're late for dinner."

"Fine, I'm going," Ezra said begrudgingly. He grabbed the foil-covered pie off of the counter, then headed out into the living room to put on his coat and shoes.

The drive to Astoria was mostly uneventful, although there was a surprising amount of traffic given that people weren't supposed to be gathering. After about an hour, Ezra pulled up to Josie's house. Ted's car was missing from the driveway, which seemed odd, but he parked on the street anyway, to leave the space for him. After grabbing the pie and his overnight bag, he walked up the short sidewalk and used his key to let himself into the house.

"I come bearing pie," he called out as he shut the door behind him. The dog show was playing on the television, but otherwise, the living room was empty.

"Archie!"

The shriek came from the kitchen, and he barely had time to prepare himself before Willow came running out.

"Willow, let him get his coat off and wash his hands before you tackle him," Josie yelled after her.

Willow stopped short and frowned.

"Hey, kid, why don't you take this pie into the kitchen for me, and I'll be right there, okay?" Ezra said.

She took the dish in both hands, cradling it carefully. "Did Oliver make this, or did you?"

"He did, but I helped."

"Good, because you're a terrible baker."

"Oi"—he ruffled her hair—"I'm not the one covered in flour."

"You were last time," she said with a grin before skipping off to the kitchen again.

He rolled his eyes as he hung his coat, then went upstairs to drop off his bag and wash his hands. As he went into the kitchen, Willow bounded toward him again and threw herself at his waist. He stooped to catch her and swung her around, earning a high-pitched giggle.

"Happy Thanksgiving, Archie," Josie said over her shoulder while she continued to stir something on the stove.

"Happy Thanksgiving. Where's Ted?" Ezra asked as he set Willow down. "Also, do you need any help?"

"No, I've got it," she said. "Ted's at the store. We forgot cranberry sauce."

"Canned or fresh?"

"Canned, obviously," Josie said. "He should be back

any minute, though, so would you help Willow set the table?"

"Sure," he said.

Dinner was delicious and joyful, a direct contrast to all the Thanksgiving dinners Ezra remembered from his childhood. Thanksgiving at the Beaumont-Carmichael household was always formal. The table was never covered in dishes that had way too much butter to be healthy. They never went around the table to say what they were thankful for. If this was what Thanksgiving was supposed to be like, Ezra could understand the appeal.

After the plates had been cleared, Ezra took over doing the dishes.

"I can help," Josie protested as Ezra shoved a glass of wine into her hand and told her to go out into the living room with Ted and Willow, who were already in a turkey coma on the couch.

"You did all the cooking," Ezra said. "I can clean up."

"Well, thank you," she said. "I'll keep you company at least, though." She hopped up onto the counter across from the sink. "Knowing Ted and Willow, they've already started watching Elf."

"What's wrong with Elf?" Ezra asked as he scraped leftovers into various Tupperware.

"Nothing," she said, taking a sip of wine. "I just can't abide watching Christmas movies before December first."

"Well, then you'll be horrified to know that Ollie and I started in on the Christmas romcoms last week."

"You're a monster."

"Blame Ollie," he retorted.

"Then Oliver is a monster, and you're simply too in love to care," she teased.

"I'm not in love," Ezra protested. "I'm just deeply in like."

"That's not a thing," she said.

He rolled his eyes and began loading dishes into the dishwasher. His phone buzzed, and he wiped his hands off before fishing it out of his pocket. He swiped open the text notification to see a picture of Fiona woofing down a plate of turkey scraps.

This is her favorite holiday, Oliver's message said under the picture.

Ezra smiled, then looked up to see Josie giving him a knowing look. "What?"

"Oliver?"

"Yes?" he answered hesitantly.

"You should go back," she said. "You clearly miss him because you've been checking your phone every five minutes since you got here."

"He was just texting me dog-show commentary," he said defensively.

"I understand. It's new, and you're still in the honeymoon phase. Plus, it's a holiday, and he's alone in his apartment." She set her wineglass down and hopped off the counter to take the dish towel out of his hands. "Go."

"But—"

"It's okay," she interrupted. "I'm not all that fussed about Thanksgiving. I'm British."

"But, Willow—"

"Will be passed out for the rest of the evening," she finished. "She will also understand."

Ezra sighed. "Are you sure?"

"Yes," Josie said.

"Thank you," he said. "I'm at least going to finish the dishes before I go, though."

"No complaints here," she said, tossing the towel back at him.

An hour later, Ezra walked through the apartment door. "Hey, I'm ba—" He looked up after setting the bag of leftovers down to take his coat off and saw Oliver looking at him with wide eyes, shaking his head. He was sitting on the couch with his laptop, covering the camera with his hand.

Ezra stopped and cocked his head, then understanding dawned on him. Oliver was still on the call with his dad—his dad who did not know that Ezra was staying there. Ezra winced as Oliver turned his attention back to his laptop.

"Sorry, Dad, I have to go. Fiona is getting into the leftovers. I love you." After a few seconds, Oliver shut his laptop and pulled out his earbuds.

"I'm so sorry," Ezra blurted.

Oliver was silent for a long moment before mumbling, "It's okay."

Ezra swore under his breath and shrugged off his coat. "No, I was thoughtless." He rushed over, knelt in front of Oliver, and rested his hands on his knees. "I didn't think you'd still be on your call. I'm so sorry."

Oliver let out a sigh, then took Ezra's hands in his. "It's okay. I don't think he suspected anything."

Ezra frowned. "Are you sure?"

Oliver offered a tight smile and nodded. "Yeah, it'll be fine. If he asks about it later, I'll figure it out. I might just tell him the truth."

"Really?"

His smile became a little more relaxed. "Yeah, I've been thinking about it recently. But more importantly, what are you doing here? Why aren't you at Josie's?"

Ezra smiled faintly. "Josie's British. She's not all that fussed about Thanksgiving."

Oliver laughed and pulled him up and into his lap. "So it's not at all because you might have missed me?"

"That may or may not have contributed to it," Ezra admitted.

Oliver laughed again and leaned in for a kiss. "I may or may not have missed you, too."

25

Ezra

Friday Evening, November 27, 2020

"*Allons-y, mon chou,*" Ezra said, nudging Oliver's shoulder. He did his best to crouch down in the narrow space between the bed and the wall so they would be at face level.

"Ezra, not now. I'm in a lot of pain." Oliver groaned as he turned to face him.

Ezra brushed a stray curl away from his face, then brushed a kiss on his forehead. He'd seen Oliver amid a flare in the past few months since they'd been seeing each other in person, but never this bad and usually with some sort of warning or catalyst. He'd have a slow buildup of inflammation, or if it came on suddenly, he'd overdone it kneading a loaf of sourdough or by going on a bit too long of a late-night walk without using his cane. But this one came out of nowhere, which, from Ezra's research, seemed to be the worst kind of flare.

Ezra wasn't sure what to do, but he'd read that slight movement and heat could help, so he thought he would try that. "I know, love, but getting up and moving a bit will help, I promise."

"Ezra, just leave me alone," Oliver said in warning.

"I ran an Epsom salt bath for you. The warm water should help so you can get to sleep."

Oliver's eyes opened, and his face softened—not enough to cover the grimace, but enough. "You did?"

Ezra smiled and nodded. "Just a short walk to the bathroom."

Oliver groaned and threw the covers off.

"I could try to carry you?" Ezra suggested.

"No, I can walk," Oliver grumbled, swinging his legs over the edge of the bed with a wince.

Ezra stood up as quickly as he could in the cramped space and held out his hands. "Here, at least let me help you up." Oliver reluctantly took his hands, and he guided him to a standing position.

"Fuck, I hate this."

"I know," Ezra said. He guided Oliver around the bed, his hands on his waist for stability, then when they cleared the door and there was more room, he took Oliver's arm and draped it over his shoulder. He pressed a soft kiss to the hinge of Oliver's jaw, earning a soft hum.

"Come on, love." He helped Oliver into the bathroom and plucked at the hem of his sweater. "Arms up if you can."

Oliver raised his arms with another wince. Once his sweater was off, he looked around the bathroom. "You lit candles," he said.

"I wanted to make it relaxing for you," Ezra said. "Now, come on, pants, too."

"You do it. I like it better when you undress me," Oliver said, his voice still strained despite the attempt at a joke.

"Cheeky," Ezra teased. He pressed a quick kiss to Oliver's cheek before pulling at his pajama bottoms and letting them fall in a puddle on the floor. "Come on, let's get you settled," he said once Oliver had stepped out of his pants.

Oliver sighed as he sank into the warm water, closing his eyes for a moment in relief.

Ezra smiled and pressed a kiss to his temple. "Just shout if you need me." He turned to leave, but Oliver made a soft sound of protest that made him turn around.

"Ezra? Stay?"

"If you want me to."

Oliver nodded, reaching his hand out as if asking for Ezra's. "I'm sorry. I've been grumpy all day."

Ezra smiled, crouched by the tub ledge, and laced their fingers together, giving his hand a squeeze. "It's alright, *mon chou*. I understand."

"Join me?" Oliver asked.

"I don't think we'd both fit very well," Ezra said with a laugh.

"We could squeeze?" Oliver looked at him hopefully. "I like when you hold me."

He leaned forward and kissed him slowly. "You need to let your body relax, and it won't do that if I'm in there, taking up all the space."

Oliver sighed, so Ezra tilted his chin to bring their lips together again. "Another time, I promise, because I do very much like the idea of having you nestled between my legs in a bubble sea."

That made him smile. "Will you still keep me company?"

"That I can do." Ezra pressed one last quick kiss to the corner of Oliver's mouth before standing up. "I'll be right back, though."

He watched Oliver nod and lean his head against the shower wall with his eyes closed before slipping through the door and making his way to the kitchen.

After grabbing the cranberries from Oliver's freezer, he went back to the bathroom. He grabbed an extra towel from the shelf above the hamper and shut off the bathroom light, leaving them in the soft candlelight, then folded the towel into a cushion and sat on it cross-legged next to the tub near Oliver's head.

Oliver's eyes fluttered open and looked at Ezra softly. "Chocolate and candlelight? How romantic," he said.

"Don't make fun, or I'll put the chocolate back," Ezra teased, resting his arm on the tub ledge.

"I'm not making fun. I love it," Oliver promised. He lifted his hand out of the water to rest it on top of Ezra's. "And I'm not just saying that so you don't take the chocolate away."

Ezra leaned down to press a kiss to the back of Oliver's wet wrist, which was warm, either because of the bathwater or the inflammation. He couldn't tell which. Then they sat in silence, casually eating chocolate-covered cranberries until the bag was empty.

"So, is the bath helping at all?" Ezra asked after a while.

"It is. Thank you—not just for the bath itself but for all of this." Oliver went to gesture around the room with his free arm but winced and dropped it back into the water. "No one has ever done something like this for me. It's very—"

"Very?" Ezra leaned more onto the tub ledge and let their entwined hands slide off the edge back into the water.

"Intimate," Oliver finished, shifting to rest his head on Ezra's bicep.

Ezra's breath caught. He lowered his head to rest on top of Oliver's, nuzzling his curls. "This is probably the most intimate thing I've ever done," he admitted, his voice so quiet, he wasn't sure if Oliver would actually hear him.

"Me, too," Oliver whispered. He squeezed Ezra's hand, then lifted it to kiss the back of his hand. "Can we go back to bed?"

"Sure, *mon choupinou*. Do you need help to get up?"

"No, I think I can do it. Can you just get my towel for me?"

"I can do that." Ezra kissed the top of his head and stood up. He grabbed the towel hanging from the rod on the back of the door and turned around, waiting for Oliver to pull himself up before wrapping the towel around his shoulders.

"I'll take care of cleaning up. You just climb back into bed, okay?" Ezra leaned up to press a kiss on Oliver's cheek, but Oliver caught his lips for a sleepy kiss.

"Thank you," Oliver whispered, gazing up at him fondly, almost lovingly.

Ezra's heart fluttered, and he felt a rush of an emotion that it was way too early to be feeling. "You're welcome," he whispered, his throat dry.

Oliver smiled and rested his hands on Ezra's shoulders to brace himself to step over the tub ledge. "Don't take too long," he said before shuffling out of the bathroom.

Ezra let out a breath he hadn't realized he'd been holding and leaned down to drain the tub. He dried his hand on the hand towel and picked up the towel he'd used as a cushion and Oliver's discarded clothes and threw them in the hamper, then blew out the candles. He went around the rest of the apartment, shutting off lights before heading back to the bedroom, where he found Oliver already in bed, his eyes closed and the covers pulled up to his chin. Ezra smiled to himself. He was so cute. And then he realized, not for the first time, that he had it so bad for this man, and fuck if that wasn't terrifying. He shook his head and told himself not to dwell on it and shut off the lights so he could climb into bed.

"You were right," Oliver mumbled.

"About what?" Ezra asked, rolling to his side to face him.

Oliver rolled to face him, too, and laced their hands together between them. "About the bath helping me be able to get to sleep. I'm exhausted."

Ezra chuckled and brushed his lips against Oliver's knuckles. "It's okay. Go to sleep."

Oliver hummed and scooted closer. "*Bonne nuit, mon amour.*"

Ezra smiled and tucked their clasped hands under his chin. "*Bonne nuit.*"

It didn't take long for Ezra to feel Oliver's breathing even out, letting him know he was most likely asleep. Ezra was close to falling asleep, too, but something was keeping him awake.

"Hey, Olls?" he whispered and waited for a response. Nothing. He took a deep breath and opened his eyes to peek at Oliver's face, so soft while he was sleeping. "Je pense que je tombe amoureux de toi." *I think I'm falling for you.*

Oliver

Middle of the Night, November 28, 2020

Although he'd fallen asleep quickly, Oliver didn't stay that way. He woke suddenly, discomfort pulling him from the dream he'd been having. He and Ezra had been in Paris, lying in bed with the sun streaming in.

Ezra was muttering something in French to him, soothing even though he wasn't sure what he was saying.

But now Oliver was back in his bedroom, a sharp pain low in his sternum, making it hard to breathe. He knew what it likely was—he'd felt this pain before. The first time it had happened was in college, and Ryan ended up taking him to the ER. They'd done an x-ray and an ECG and came back with the conclusion that it was pericarditis, an inflammation of the tissue surrounding the heart brought on by his RA. They'd sent him home with some prescription-strength ibuprofen and told him to rest.

He'd experienced it a few times after that, each time getting progressively worse to where he needed corticosteroids to treat it. So even though he was sure what it was, it would make sense to get it checked out, which meant he had to wake Ezra. He didn't want to. He didn't want to rely on him so early for something like this. It was bad enough that Ezra had seen him in one of his worst flares in a while. But emergency room visits? He didn't sign on for that. But Ezra had taken his flare in stride, drawing him a bath to help with the inflammation, so maybe it wouldn't be so bad.

A wave of sharp pain hit, and Oliver suppressed a whimper. He needed to sit up; lying down always made the pain worse. He tried to sit up, but his entire body still radiated pain, and this time, he couldn't hold back his whimper.

Ezra stirred next to him and turned over to face him. "*Mon chou*, are you alright?" He shifted closer and reached out to rub his hand along Oliver's bicep.

Oliver let out a controlled breath through his nose as another stab of pain hit him. "Ezra, I don't want you to freak out, but I think I need to go to the emergency room."

Even in the dark, Oliver could see the look of panic

on Ezra's face. He bolted up and flipped on the string lights used to light the bedroom instead of a lamp.

Oliver winced at the sudden brightness, but Ezra didn't seem to notice as he barreled through a series of questions. "What? Are you alright? Sorry, dumb question. If you were alright, you wouldn't need to go to the emergency room. What is it? What's wrong?"

"Ezra, please," Oliver said wearily, "I need you to stay calm. I've got some chest pain. I've felt something like it before, so I'm pretty sure I know what it is, but I should still go to the doctor just to make sure."

He heard Ezra take a deep breath, hold it, then let it out as if to calm himself, but his voice was still laced with anxiety when he spoke. "Okay, yeah, okay. We can go." He reached out to touch Oliver's face but must have changed his mind because he jerked his hand back and almost fell out of bed in his haste to get up. "I'll go get the car and then we can go."

He was halfway to the front door before realizing that he was still in his pajamas. "Fuck, clothes."

Ezra came back into the bedroom and searched the floor for his pants. "I'll get you a pair of pants," he said while hopping into his skinny jeans.

"I can get up," Oliver said. He tried to take a deep breath but winced.

"Just give me a minute. I'll help you get dressed. Just—give me a minute, alright, Oliver?"

Oliver. Ezra never called him that anymore. He was always Ollie or Olls.

Ezra all but ran into the living room and began riffling through the dresser for a pair of real pants for him to wear. When he returned, he sat on the edge of the bed and touched Oliver's back. "Oliver? Do you think you can sit up?"

He rolled over, and despite the radiating pain in his wrists, pushed himself into a seated position. "Ezra, can you please stop looking at me like that? I'll be fine."

Ezra shook his head and tried to put on a neutral expression. "I got you some pants."

"Thank you." As Oliver moved to climb out of bed to get changed, Ezra backed away. "I'll bring the car around, alright?"

Oliver nodded, and Ezra hesitated for a moment before pressing a quick kiss to his forehead and leaving the bedroom.

The drive to NewYork-Presbyterian Hospital only took ten minutes since it wasn't all that far from Oliver's apartment, but it felt like an eternity. All Oliver had wanted was a few minutes of silence before the guaranteed overstimulation he was about to experience in the emergency room. And to Ezra's credit, once he helped Oliver into the passenger seat, he took Oliver's lead and didn't speak. He also didn't protest when Oliver turned off the radio even though Oliver knew he hated driving without some sort of music. However, he spent the first quarter mile of the drive drumming his fingers against the steering wheel, which was almost worse.

Oliver squeezed his eyes shut and tried to block it out and focus on the sounds of the city surrounding him instead, but the street was quiet for once. All he could hear was the tapping, and it was grating on his last nerve. Maybe they were almost there. When he opened his eyes to see they were pulling to a stop at a stoplight not even halfway to the hospital, he couldn't take it anymore.

"Ezra, can you stop with the drumming? You're driving me fucking insane," he snapped.

Ezra stopped and gripped the steering wheel in a vise. "Sorry," he said through clenched teeth.

Oliver sighed and closed his eyes again as the traffic light turned green. He knew he should feel bad for snapping, but he'd told Ezra that he would be fine. This was Oliver's life: week-long flares, days he couldn't even walk from his bedroom to the bathroom without using a cane, doctor's appointments, medical procedures, trips to the ER. None of this would change. He would deal with this for the rest of his life, and based on Ezra's current state, he wasn't sure Ezra could handle it. He was clearly anxious and probably on the verge of a panic attack based on his breathing. Oliver needed someone with a level head for moments like these. But even more so, he didn't want to be the reason for Ezra's distress.

When they made it to the hospital, Ezra threw the car in park and left it running while he ran around the front to help Oliver out. Oliver opened the door and climbed out of the car before Ezra could get to him.

"Here, Oliver, let me help—"

"I've got it," Oliver said, his voice clipped.

"Okay, well if you want to head in, I guess I'll go park the car and meet you," Ezra said, although it sounded more like a question.

"It's fine. You don't have to stay."

"Shouldn't someone be here with you?"

"I mean, you being here won't make any difference, and they won't let you in because of Covid, anyway."

"Oh, right," Ezra said, staring at the pavement. "Well, if you need me to, I could just hang in the car or something—"

"Ezra, just go, okay?" Oliver said, then winced at how harsh it sounded. "I'll be fine."

"Do you at least want me to call someone for you? Your dad—"

Oliver pinched the bridge of his nose. Shit, he should call his dad just to keep him in the loop, but he didn't feel like calling him from the ER. His dad still didn't know who Ezra was other than a work friend, but he couldn't think about that right now. And the last time this happened, Ryan was the person to call his dad, so it probably wasn't that weird.

"Fine." He sighed as he got his phone out to forward the contact. "Call my dad and tell him I'm here since I won't be able to. But otherwise, please just—"

"Yeah, I'll go. Keep me posted, I guess," Ezra said, shoving his hands into his pockets.

Oliver nodded noncommittally, then looped a mask around his ears before heading through the sliding hospital doors into the sterile, bright emergency room.

26

Ezra

Saturday Morning, November 28, 2020

Ezra decided to wait until he got back to Oliver's apartment to call his dad. He hoped maybe the drive back would help him calm down, that the tightness in his chest might loosen and he could breathe again. But it didn't. He spent the entire drive white-knuckling the steering wheel so he wouldn't drum his fingers against it, even though Oliver wasn't even in the car with him anymore. And when he pulled up to the curb and parked again—in the same spot since he hadn't been gone all that long—he found that he could barely remember the drive. His ears rang, and his vision narrowed, so he threw the car door open and stumbled out into the cold air. He'd forgotten to grab a jacket on the way out, so the cold, almost-December air hit him like a wall of ice, but it actually helped shock his system. So he leaned against the cool metal of the car and took a few deep breaths until the panic subsided, then he shakily made his way inside.

Fiona was at his feet the moment he unlocked the

door. Fiona was clearly worried about her owner not being there—either that or she was hungry. Normally, when she weaved her way back and forth between his legs, Ezra would scoop her up into his arms and scratch her chest when she would go limp in his arms. But right now, all he could do was stare at the keys in his hand. The first time Ezra had left the apartment after starting to stay at his place full-time, Oliver had told him to take the set of spare keys since Oliver's own keys were more keychains and fidget toys than actual keys. And at the time, he'd clipped the keys to his car key, not thinking anything of it. But then they just sort of stayed there, and it wasn't until he'd opened the door a few seconds ago that he realized he'd started to think of them as his keys, not Oliver's spare keys.

When he looked around Oliver's apartment, he saw bits of himself scattered around—his laptop on the coffee table, the yoga mat he'd convinced Oliver to order, his guitar in the corner, his camera gear sitting on the bookshelf. He knew if he opened the bottom two drawers in the dresser, they'd be filled with his clothes, and that if he walked into the bathroom, his plain manual toothbrush would be right next to Oliver's electric one. Without realizing it, he'd moved his entire life into Oliver's apartment. He'd made himself at home here.

How had this happened? He'd only known Oliver for, what, nine months? They'd only been dating for two and a half months. How had he let himself get so invested so fast that he moved in with his boyfriend of two months?

It was too much, too fast. Things were getting too serious, and Ezra didn't do serious. He'd proved in the past that he wasn't capable of it. He thought he'd finally started to process some of these feelings but apparently not. All of his inadequacies, all of his fears and failures, that desperate need to escape—it just came rushing back. He couldn't think straight. He felt like he was underwater.

His phone buzzed in his pocket, so he pulled it out with numbing fingers. It was Oliver.

They're keeping me for observation. Can you remember to feed Fiona?

Ezra unlocked his phone and typed out a quick reply, **Yeah, will you need me to pick you up?** It wasn't the right thing to say. He knew it wasn't the right thing to say. But when Oliver's reply came through and said, **No, I'll just call Ryan and Anna,** he realized it didn't matter. He wanted an out, and Oliver gave it to him.

Ezra didn't bother taking off his shoes. Instead, he went to the entryway closet where he'd shoved his empty duffel bag. He pulled it out and went over to the dresser. As he dropped to the ground, he found Oliver's dad's contact and dialed. He held the phone to his ear with his shoulder to free up his hands, then yanked open the drawers and started shoving clothes into the duffel bag.

The phone rang for a while, and Ezra realized that was because it was barely 06:30 in the morning on a Saturday. But Oliver's dad would probably rather be woken up with the news that his son was in an emergency room than receive that news several hours later at a more reasonable hour.

Finally, his dad picked up. "Martin Wheeler speaking," he said groggily, the Oregon accent sounding much thicker than Oliver's.

"Mr. Wheeler, hi," Ezra croaked. He cleared his throat and stopped shoving clothes into the bag in favor of holding the phone to his ear more properly. "My name is Ezra. I'm Oliver's…friend. He wanted me to call you because—"

"What happened?" Mr. Wheeler's voice went suddenly hard. "Is Oliver okay?"

"He's fine, sir," Ezra said quickly. He wasn't so sure of that, but Oliver had said he was fine, so that's what he was going with. Then he took a moment before continuing. He had to be careful. Oliver's dad didn't know about their relationship, so he had to make it sound like Oliver had called him in the middle of the night, not woken him up whimpering in pain. "Ollie woke up with some chest pain, but he said that he was pretty sure he knew what it was because he's had it before. I took him to the emergency room, but because of Covid protocols, he had to go into the waiting room alone, so I'm not sure what's going on right now," Ezra explained in a rush.

"Was he in the middle of a flare?"

"Yeah, it seemed—from what he said, it sounded like a worse flare than normal. He'll call you himself when he's able, but he seemed pretty exhausted."

"I'll bet he was. Well, thank you for keeping me in the loop—Ezra, was it?" Mr. Wheeler asked.

"Yes, sir."

"You're the new editorial assistant—Ryan's friend. Ollie told me about you," Mr. Wheeler said.

"He did?" Ezra asked, unable to keep the surprise out of his voice.

"When you first started," Mr. Wheeler explained. "I'm glad to hear that you two ended up on the right foot despite starting on the wrong one. I know my son can be a little…headstrong at first, but you already know that, I'm sure. You must be good friends now if Oliver trusted you enough to wake you up to take him to the emergency room."

"Yeah, Olls has been a pretty great friend. But I also live a lot closer to him than Ryan does." It was a lie, but it seemed like Mr. Wheeler was catching on, and the last thing Ezra needed to do at that moment was out Oliver to his father. "Well, I know you're about an hour behind us, so I'll let you go. Sorry to have woken you."

"No worries, son. Thank you for calling and for taking such good care of my boy."

"It was nothing." Ezra swallowed hard past the tightness forming in his throat. "Goodbye, Mr. Wheeler."

He didn't even bother waiting for Oliver's dad to say goodbye before hanging up. He let his phone drop to the floor and shoved his hands into his hair, pulling slightly to ground himself. His chest was tight, and he couldn't think. He needed to get out of there.

He shoved the last of his clothes into the bag, then went to the bedroom to grab his phone charger and e-reader. Next, into the bag went his toothbrush and laptop, which barely fit since he was packing so haphazardly. He left the bag on the floor and went to the kitchen to feed Fiona, then grabbed it again on the way to the bookshelf to get his camera. Last was his guitar, which was already in its case. He made his way to the door and was again impeded by Fiona getting underfoot. Usually, once she was fed, she would sit and consume every last bit of kibble. Almost nothing could distract her. But there she was, loudly purring as she weaved between his legs. She was telling him not to leave. That was the only explanation for her not immediately scarfing down all of her food.

He looked down at the cat. "I'm sorry, Fi, but I can't—" His breath caught, and he swallowed around it. He shook his head and unclipped Oliver's spare keys from his own and dropped them in the bowl. Then he opened the door, locked the handle, and made sure Fiona didn't make a break for it before shutting the door behind him.

Ezra shut and locked the door behind him, then kicked his shoes off. Since he'd just come from a hospital, he'd left his mask on. He hadn't gotten past the double doors, but he still didn't want to take any chances. He hoped no one would be up since it was still early, but when he heard a clatter from the kitchen, he realized he would never be that lucky.

"Ted, did you forget some—" Josie stopped short when she rounded the corner from the kitchen. "Archie, what are you doing here?"

"Uh, I live here?"

"I mean, why aren't you at Oliver's?" Josie asked.

"I had to take him to the ER. They're keeping him for observation," Ezra said, walking past her.

"Hospital? Hang on." She jogged around him and blocked his path. "What do you mean, hospital?"

"His RA flared up pretty bad, and it led to some chest pain, so I dropped him off at the emergency room."

"You just dropped him off? You didn't stay?"

"Well, they didn't let me into the emergency room with him seeing as there's a plague, remember?" Ezra snapped. "I'm going to go to my room." He sidestepped Josie, careful to keep his distance, and went up the stairs to his room.

"Right, but why aren't you at least waiting at his apartment?" Josie continued following him.

Ezra stepped into the bathroom and closed the door behind him so he could wash his hands. When he came back out, Josie was still there, clearly not ready to let this go.

"Who's going to pick him up from the hospital?" she asked, switching to French since Willow's room was within hearing distance.

"Josie," he warned, continuing to his bedroom.

"He's your boyfriend, right? You're supposed to be

taking care of—"

"He doesn't need me, okay?" he snapped, switching to French, as well.

"Did he say that or did you assume that so that you could run away like you tend to—"

"Yes! He said exactly that, Josie!" he shouted. "I asked him when he needed me to pick him up from the hospital, and he told me not to worry about it and that he would call Ryan. It was clear he didn't want me around, so I left."

"Archie?"

Ezra froze when he heard Willows's voice from the doorway. He hadn't meant to scream like that. He was just so tired. Tired, scared, and hurt. He hadn't slept, and getting out of Oliver's apartment hadn't helped ease his anxiety at all. He still felt like he couldn't breathe. He hadn't been able to take a full breath since he woke up to the sound of Oliver whimpering in pain next to him. And then there was the look on Oliver's face when he told him to go after helping him through the emergency room doors—that look of cold detachment.

"Is everything alright?" Willow asked, looking between Ezra and her mom.

"Everything is fine," Ezra said, forcing a smile.

"Archie's just having a bad day, sweetheart," Josie said.

"Why are you guys shouting?" Willow continued, not buying his lie. "L'hôpital?" She looked frantically at her mom. "That's 'hospital,' right? Why was Archie in a hospital? Is he okay? He was with Oliver. Is Oliver okay?"

Ezra shoved his hands through his hair. "Josie, please get her out of here," he begged in French.

Josie looked at him sympathetically before taking Willow by the hand. "Come on, sweetheart. Archie and

Oliver are both alright, don't worry. But Archie needs to be alone for a few days, so we're all safe, okay? Like he did when he first came back from Italy."

Josie shut the door behind her. And then he was alone.

27

Oliver

Sunday Morning, November 29, 2020

As the nurse walked Oliver out of the hospital doors, he found Anna and Ryan both standing on the curb, masks on. Anna rushed forward to meet them, extending her arm for him to take as the nurse passed him off. He turned to the nurse and thanked them, then let Anna help him to the car.

"You both didn't need to come," he said as Ryan opened the back door for him.

"If I said we both needed the excuse to get out of the apartment, would you believe me?" Ryan asked.

"No," Oliver said. He climbed into the car and immediately leaned his head back against the headrest and closed his eyes. Despite being asleep the majority of his time in the hospital, he was exhausted. The front doors opened and slammed, then the car moved. Anna and Ryan were silent for a minute, and Oliver thought maybe he could get away with not talking about what happened with Ezra and him, but then Ryan broke the silence when the car came to a stop at a red light.

"So, are we going to talk about why Ezra isn't the one picking you up?" Ryan asked.

"Ryan—" Oliver started, opening his eyes.

"Did he leave you?" Anna asked. "Because I swear to God, if he did— Ryan, I know he's your best friend, but if he left Oliver at the hospital, I will absolutely destroy—"

"He didn't leave me." Oliver raised his voice to cut off her tirade, and it nearly took all of his energy. "I told him to go. They wouldn't let him into the waiting room with me, so I didn't see any sense in him hanging around."

"Okay," Ryan began patiently, "but I think what my wife is trying to get at is, did he say he couldn't pick you up?"

"No, I told him I didn't need him to," Oliver said.

"What happened? Did you get into a fight?" Anna asked.

Oliver sighed and pinched the bridge of his nose. "Can we not talk about this now? I haven't slept more than a few hours in a row in two days, and I'm in desperate need of a shower."

He saw Ryan look at him through the rearview mirror. "Sure, Ollie."

The rest of the drive was silent. When they pulled up in front of his building, Anna jumped out of the car to open Oliver's door for him. She extended a hand to help him out.

"Do you want one of us to stay with you?" she asked once they'd gotten to his apartment door.

"No, I'll be alright," he said. "I kind of want to be alone."

"Okay, if you're sure." She stared at him for a moment, then wrapped her arms around his waist. "We were already in a car together; a few-seconds hug doesn't change much," she mumbled into his chest.

He sighed, then let himself relax into her hug. "Thank you."

"Love you. Get some rest," she told him as she pulled away.

"Love you, too," he said. He spent a second watching her leave, then unlocked the deadbolt and tried to open the door. The doorknob didn't move, and his heart sank. He never locked the doorknob, so if Ezra did, he had a sneaking suspicion of why he would. When he got the door open, his suspicion was confirmed.

Ezra had left. He should have expected it. He told Ezra to leave him at the hospital, then said he wouldn't need him to pick him up once the hospital discharged him. Why would Ezra stay when Oliver had done everything to make it clear he didn't want him without saying those words? But Oliver's heart hurt anyway.

There were empty spots around the apartment where he'd gotten used to seeing Ezra's stuff. His laptop was missing from the coffee table. His guitar was no longer in the corner. The camera bag was gone from the bookshelf. The bottom two dresser drawers were half open, so he could see that they were empty. He didn't bother going into the bathroom, but he knew Ezra's toothbrush would be missing. Ezra had clearly packed in a rush. Oliver's eyes snagged on the yoga mat still propped up against the dresser, and tears started welling in his eyes. He'd left it. Oliver hadn't even wanted the damned thing—he hadn't even wanted to try yoga in the first place—but Ezra had convinced him. Then he just left it behind, which was somehow worse than if he'd taken it. The empty spaces were a reminder of what was once there, but he could fill them again and it wouldn't be as noticeable. The yoga mat, though… Every time he looked at it, it would remind him of Ezra. He could get rid of it, obviously, but somehow the thought of that hurt worse than keeping it. Honestly, the thought of filling the spaces Ezra had left behind hurt, too.

But he was too tired to process any of that at the moment. He dropped his keys into the bowl, noticing that the spare keys he'd, at some point, just assumed were officially Ezra's keys, were in there, too. Then he stripped off his coat and hung it on the hook. As he turned toward the bedroom, Fiona made her presence known by jumping on the back of the couch and meowing at him. He reached out to pet her, but she swatted at him and jumped down. She was mad at him, and since there was still food in her bowl, he could only assume it was because her new favorite person was gone.

And he had been the one to chase him away.

Tuesday Afternoon, December 1, 2020

Oliver rolled over and checked the time. Three PM. He'd only meant to go back to sleep for another hour after texting Anna that he was feeling better, but that hour had turned into seven. He had several texts from her and Mary, and a missed call from his dad. He could ignore the texts, but he knew he should call his dad back; otherwise, he would worry about him. So Oliver sat up with a groan and propped himself up on his pillows.

The phone didn't ring long before his dad's voice rang through the phone. "Hey, kiddo."

"Hey, Dad," Oliver said, forcing a cheerful tone into his voice.

"How are you feeling?" Martin asked as if he could see straight through Oliver's facade.

Oliver sighed. "Tired, but better. I took the week off,

so I've got the rest of the weekend to recover before I have to work on Monday."

"Good. Make sure you're taking it easy, alright? And make sure you don't forget to go get a Covid test in a few days—"

"I know, Dad. I've got it under control," Oliver said irritably.

"Sorry, sorry. I know you do. I just worry. It's my job, you know," Martin said.

"I know. Sorry, I'm just tired," Oliver apologized.

There was a silent pause, then Martin spoke again. "So, is your friend with you? The one that called from the hospital."

"Ezra," Oliver supplied.

"Yes, Ezra. Did he stay to keep an eye on you?" Martin asked.

"Uhhh, no, he went home once he dropped me off at the hospital," Oliver faltered. "I had Anna and Ryan pick me up to take me home.

"You haven't mentioned Ezra since he started working with you. I'm glad to hear you two became friends."

"Yeah, we got off on the wrong foot, but we figured it out," Oliver explained, keeping details as vague as possible.

"Ah, well, I like him. He seems like a very close friend, waking up and driving to take you to the hospital in the middle of the night like he did," Martin mused.

Oliver dry-swallowed. "Uh, yeah, he's a good friend." He took a deep breath to control the shaking in his voice.

"He seemed like a nice young man from the brief conversation we had on the phone. It sounds like he cares about you." There was something in his tone that Oliver didn't quite recognize, but it almost sounded as if he was hinting at something.

Oliver murmured something unintelligible in agreement. He felt his heart beating hard against his chest, and he couldn't tell if it was from the nerves or the inflammation.

"Ollie, son—it's alright. I know," Martin said.

"Dad?" he croaked.

"Your mother, before she died," Martin started tentatively, "she didn't mean to let it slip what you told her. You have to know that. She would never have knowingly betrayed your trust, but she was on a lot of medication, and she wasn't always— Well, you remember; she wasn't always the most present of mind toward the end."

Oliver squeezed his eyes shut and pulled his knees into his chest. His dad knew. He thought back to all the times that he and his dad had ever talked about his love life. All the times that he'd been so careful to stay ambiguous about pronouns when he'd been seeing a guy; his dad had been ambiguous, too, anytime he'd asked. It had always been, 'Are you seeing any new people?' or 'When can I expect you to bring someone back for Christmas?' He'd known the whole time but said nothing.

"I'm sorry, Dad. I didn't mean to lie, I just—" Oliver's breath hitched.

"It's okay, kiddo. You weren't ready, and I know you and your mother had a different relationship than you and I do. It's alright. You don't need to apologize," Martin assured him.

"No, I—I wasn't even ready to tell Mom. I was barely figuring it out, but I didn't want—" Oliver let out another choked sob. "I didn't want her to go without telling her. Then things got so difficult, and I couldn't find the right time to tell you—"

"Shhh, it's alright. I understand. You would tell me when you were ready. I thought that maybe—" Martin took a shaky breath that had Oliver wondering if he was crying, too. "I thought that maybe having Ezra call was your way of telling me. Ezra is more than just a friend, I'm assuming?"

Oliver wiped at his eyes with the sleeve of his sweater. "Yeah, he is. Although, I'm not so sure about that anymore," he admitted with a sniff.

Martin hummed. "Do you want to tell me what happened?"

"He was here when I started having chest pain. I told him I needed to go to the hospital, and he looked so panicked. I told him he didn't need to worry, but he had no poker face, and I could read him like a book. Then, when we got to the hospital, I knew they wouldn't let him in with me for obvious reasons, so I told him to go home. Then I told him he didn't need to pick me up—that I'd just have Anna and Ryan do it—and when I got home, he was gone."

"Oliver…"

"I was so tired, and I'd been in a flare all day, and he just kept—and then I—" Oliver let out a frustrated groan. "I snapped. He was suffocating me, Dad. Yes, I'm sick, but that doesn't mean I can't take care of myself. I don't need people treating me like I'm made of glass."

"You pushed him away," Martin said.

"I didn't—I just don't need someone freaking out every time something happens. I can't—I couldn't stand Ezra looking at me the way he was. The entire drive, he just kept looking at me with such pity and worry, and I couldn't handle it. I hate it when people look at me like that. Like I'm something broken that needs to be fixed."

"Well, of course, he was worried about you, Ollie. The boy cares a great deal about you," Martin countered.

"How would you know that?"

"I heard it in his voice when he called. Call it an old man's intuition, but I know what someone in love sounds like," Martin said wisely.

"You aren't that old, Dad," Oliver said, choosing to gloss over the 'love' idea.

"Fine, then dad's intuition. Either way, that boy loves you."

"How could he? We haven't even known each other for that long. We've only been dating for a couple of months. Sure, we haven't gone a day without talking since April, and we spent a lot of time together—I mean he was kind of quarantining with me here for the past two weeks—" He stopped short and realized he'd said a little too much.

"You were quarantining together?" Martin asked.

"He got a Covid test and tested negative before he ever stepped into my apartment. Don't worry," Oliver said.

"Well, I'm glad to hear that, but that's not why I'm surprised. I'm surprised because that sounds pretty serious for 'not even knowing each other for that long,'" he quoted.

"I know. It was probably way too fast, but I couldn't help it. I just wanted to spend more time with him, and with the pandemic that was going to be hard and—" Oliver shook his head. "He was the first one to suggest it, but that doesn't mean he loves me. I mean, if he hadn't, I was going to at some point—and it's only been a few months."

"You asked how he could love you after only a few months… It's pretty clear from hearing you talk that you feel that way about him, so it's not a stretch that he feels the same way," Martin said matter-of-factly. "So the question is, why did you push him away?"

"You didn't see the look on his face, Dad. When he

woke up, and I told him I needed to go to the emergency room, he looked so…scared. I can't put him through that. He can't want someone in his life that will put him through that again." Oliver took a deep breath and let it out shakily.

"Oliver, you can choose who you want in your life, but if Ezra wants you in his life, that's his choice. You can't decide that for other people. Even if you think it's protecting them, it's not fair to them." Martin paused for a moment to let his words sink in before continuing. "I understand that it's scary to let someone in, and you don't have to let someone in just because they want to be a part of your life. But with the right person, it's also rewarding. And worth it."

"I just—I don't know."

"I'll just say this last thing, and then I'll drop it. You deserve to be happy."

"Thanks, Dad," Oliver mumbled.

"I love you, kiddo."

"I love you, too." He bit his lip nervously. "And, Dad?"

"Yes?"

"Thank you for being supportive about me—well, you know."

"It makes no difference to me who you love. Or don't love—that'd be okay, too. All I want is for you to be happy. I'd support you no matter what," Martin said. "Now go get some more rest. You sound exhausted."

"I will, and I'll talk to you soon."

"I'm holding you to that. You don't call me enough," he teased.

Oliver chuckled. "Bye, Dad."

28

Ezra

Sunday Morning, December 6, 2020

A week had passed since Ezra had left Oliver's apartment. Although he hadn't stepped foot in the hospital with Oliver, he still used needing to quarantine as a reason to stay holed up in his bedroom. But he'd just gotten a call with his negative Covid test results, so he didn't have it as an excuse anymore. Plus, it was Sunday, which meant it was Ted and Willow's father-daughter day, so Josie was likely the only one in the house. If there was a good time to face her after what had happened the day he got back from Oliver's, it was now.

He made his way downstairs and into the kitchen. As he predicted, Josie was alone at the kitchen table, surrounded by law textbooks and a pot of tea. He lingered in the doorway until she looked up.

"Test came back negative?" she asked.

He nodded and shifted his weight. "Do you want silence to study, or—"

"Oh, just get in here and have some tea," she said,

shutting her textbooks and shoving them aside.

Ezra sighed in relief and went to grab a mug from the cabinet before taking the seat opposite her. They were both silent as he prepared his tea, Josie clearly wanting to give him time to start the conversation. He stared into the mug, then broke the silence.

"I'm sorry." Josie fixed her eyes on him as she waited for him to continue. "I shouldn't have yelled at you when I came back from Oliver's," he said. "I was exhausted and terrified, and I lashed out at you. And scared Willow. Then I hid in my room for a week, which was pretty shitty. So yeah, I'm sorry."

"It's okay, Archie. But now that you're not…"

"Acting like a total ass?" he supplied.

"Yeah, that. Are you ready to talk about what happened?"

Ezra absentmindedly swirled the spoon in his tea. "I'm not sure there's much to talk about. I ran. Things got hard, and I ran, just like I always do."

"Yeah, I'm going to need more than that," Josie said.

"I don't really know, okay?" he admitted, exasperated. "I freaked the hell out. He was in the middle of a bad flare, so I was worrying about him most of the day. I tried to be nice and run him a bath, and it actually seemed to help, so I thought everything was fine. But then I woke up in the middle of the night to him whimpering in pain, and he just looked so… And I didn't know what to do. I was freaking out, on the verge of another panic attack, and all I wanted to do was run. But I couldn't because I had to take him to the emergency room.

"So we got in the car, and I was not handling the situation well. I knew I wasn't handling it well, too, because he snapped at me in the car. Then he told me he didn't need me to stay with him—seeing as they wouldn't have let me in the waiting room with him, anyway."

"That makes sense," Josie said. "So then, did you run away, or did he tell you to leave? Because it sounds like the latter."

"It was probably a little of both, but even if he hadn't told me to go, I would have anyway," Ezra admitted. "I panicked the entire way back to his apartment, and once I got there, I saw my stuff spread out throughout his apartment. It hit me how serious things had gotten. I had basically moved in with him."

"Yeah, you did," she drawled as if it were obvious. "Did you not realize that when you packed to go over there?"

"Not really. I mean, we've only been dating—or we had only been dating for two months. I thought of it as just an extended sleepover." Once the words were out of his mouth, Ezra realized how stupid it sounded.

"You brought all of your worldly belongings with you," Josie said, confirming his stupidity.

"Well, in my defense, I don't have a lot of belongings. I embraced the nomadic lifestyle those three years I traveled after graduation," Ezra said with a sigh. "I think I was just so swept up in the relationship's newness that I didn't let myself think about it. Because, once I thought about it, I knew deep down that I would run. It's what I always do. You said it yourself the day after my mother died: I run instead of facing my problems like a coward."

"I should apologize for that. It wasn't fair of me to yell at you the way I did," she admitted.

"You were right, though," he insisted. "I always run. I don't even know why I do it, but I do. I get this feeling like if I don't escape, I'm going to…I don't know."

"It's a fight-or-flight response."

"And my response is always to take flight. I ran off

to Ireland for college to get away from my parents. After Elizabeth died, I ran and hid in Europe for three years. I ran out when you told me that my mother had died—"

"Except that time you ran to Oliver," she emphasized. "So that's something. You weren't running just to escape. You were leaving in search of comfort and support—which I would have given you, but I don't fault you for wanting to find comfort in the arms of your boyfriend."

"Except it didn't mean much because I ran away from him when things got tough. I was so worried that I was going to lose him, but then I ran and ended up losing him, anyway." Ezra took a sip of his now lukewarm tea. "It's like Liam all over again."

"Liam?" Josie asked.

"My college boyfriend. The first person I ever—or the first person I thought I ever loved," he amended. "I'm not sure if I actually did because when I heard about Elizabeth, I ghosted him. It was during finals, so he thought it was just the stress of that, but then he found the obituary. He went to my apartment to find me and try to be there for me, but I wasn't there. I'd already packed up the essentials in my duffle and sent anything else back to the States to Ryan."

"You didn't tell him you were leaving?"

Ezra shook his head and stared at the table. "No, I didn't. He found me at the train station before I left and—well, it was a shit show. And I regret it, I do, but now I'm doing the same thing with Oliver. How can I expect someone to love me back when I keep running away?" His voice broke, and he took another sip of his tea to cover it.

"Do you love Oliver?" Josie asked

"I think maybe I do. Is that crazy?"

"No, I don't think it is. I knew I loved Ted after only

knowing him for a few weeks, and you've known Oliver for months."

"But I also thought I loved Liam," Ezra said, his voice cracking again. "We were together for almost a year, and I just packed up and tried to leave him. How could I have actually loved him if I did something so shitty? I can't shake the feeling that maybe I'm too broken to be capable of love."

"Oh, love," Josie said sympathetically. "You aren't broken. That is 100 percent the trauma from our shitty family talking. I would know since I've thought the same thing."

"But you and Ted have been together for eight years," Ezra said.

"I've also been in and out of therapy for about seven of those years. I almost walked away from him, though. When I first found out I was pregnant, I freaked out and ghosted him for days. Then when I finally told him, he proposed on the spot, which made me freak out even more, so I turned him down. It took about a month without him for me to realize I was making a mistake by pushing him away. Ted, though, the stubborn romantic, refused to give up. He'd given me space, but he had been looking for flats and jobs in London the entire time." She smiled fondly. "So when I got the sense to call him, he was still in London."

"Did he propose again?" Ezra asked, now fully invested in the story.

"Yeah, about five—no, six more times—once a week until my parents disowned me. I didn't say yes until after that. I figured that any man who was still willing to marry me and raise a child with me after seeing what kind of family I come from was the real deal."

"Wow."

"Yeah, he's a keeper, and I think Oliver is for you, too. He makes you happy, and I think he's good for you. When I picked you up from the airport back in February, you seemed lost. But now, you're a lot more self-assured. I don't think that's solely because of him—I think not being under our family's thumb has helped with that, too—"

"But I think he's a big part of it," Ezra admitted. "I like who I am around him. I'm scared, though. I don't want to build a life only for things to change later and leave me with a giant Oliver-shaped hole."

"Yeah, taking a risk can be terrifying, but it can be worth it. You just have to decide if Oliver's worth it."

"I don't know." Ezra blinked as tears welled in his eyes. "But I miss him."

"Then I think you have your answer," Josie said.

"Yeah, I think I do," he said. "Can I—"

"Yes, you can borrow the car. But when you move back in with him, I'm going to need it back this time."

Ezra laughed wetly. "That's assuming he takes me back."

She smiled. "He will."

Oliver

Sunday Morning, December 6, 2020

Mary Wen
December 6, 2020, 11:23 AM

Mary Wen

Hey, it's been a few days and I've tried to give you space, but I need you to answer your phone now.

I have something I need to talk to you about.

Oliver Wheeler

Is everything okay?

Mary Wen

HE ANSWERS.

Yes, everything is fine. I just figured that you might answer if I made it sound severely important.

Oliver Wheeler

Rude. You worried me for a moment there.

Mary Wen

Yeah, well now you know how I feel. You tell me you were in the hospital, then check out for nearly a week.

You know Anna has been texting me and she's super worried about you? Ryan and Juliet, too.

And can you PLEASE tell me what the hell happened between you and Ezra? You guys had some sort of fight? At least that's what I got from Anna.

Oliver Wheeler

I'm sorry for checking out. It's been a rough week, not that I'm excusing it. I pushed you away, pushed everyone away, really, and I need to be better about that. It's one of the things I'm going to work on, I promise. I've been doing a lot of thinking this week, and I realize that I need to make some changes.

Mary Wen

Ok, I'm loving this self-realization thing
it seems like you've got going on, but I
think I need you to start from the beginning. I need context.

I'm calling you.

Oliver's phone rang, and he answered. "Hey," he
croaked, before clearing his throat. "Sorry, hi."

"Flare-up?" Mary asked, skipping a greeting.

"No, I just haven't spoken out loud in a few days,"
Oliver said.

"Alright, well, you're gonna talk now. Go," Mary demanded.

"Wait, you had something you wanted to talk about.
Can we do that first before we get into my mess of a
life?"

"It was just wedding stuff. It was just an excuse to
get you to answer."

"Please? I could use the distraction," Oliver begged.

"You're not trying to get out of filling me in, are
you?" she asked skeptically.

"No, I know better than that," he teased.

"Honestly, it's not that important. We set a date. October 11th next year."

"Mar, that's not 'not important.' That's a big deal!"
Oliver exclaimed.

"It's just a date. I also wanted to see what your
schedule in the spring is for dress shopping, but you
can get back to me on that. Now spill," she com-
manded.

He sighed. "Okay, well, the short version is that I
snapped at Ezra when he dropped me off at the hospital, made him leave, and haven't heard from him since.
I came out to my dad, and he gave me some classic dad

advice. And now I've spent the past week re-evaluating my life."

"Wait, you came out to Martin?" she gasped. "What do you mean you made Ezra leave? Alright, I need the long version. Start with the Ezra thing."

He took a deep breath and relayed everything that happened between the morning of his bad flare-up and the afternoon he realized Ezra had left.

"Oh, Ollie," Mary cooed. "The bath. That sounds so romantic."

"It really was." Oliver smiled softly. "I mean, it would have been more romantic if I hadn't been in an excruciating amount of pain, and he'd been in the bath with me instead of sitting on the floor outside of the tub. Still, it was so sweet." His smile fell. "Then, not even a few hours later, I snapped at him when he was just trying to help. Even worse than that, I basically told him to get out of my life."

"Oliver," Mary scolded. "I love you, but dick move, dude."

Oliver groaned. "Yeah, I know, I know. I was scared. I saw how scared he was for me when we were on our way to the hospital, and I didn't want to put him through that again. I wanted to protect him, which isn't fair to him, and I know that now, but at the moment…"

"You thought pushing him away would be easier than letting him in."

"I didn't want him to worry about me. That's what being with me would be like. Days where I can't get out of bed because I'm in too much pain, trips to the hospital. I don't know if I can put him through that constant worry."

"That's not only your decision, though," Mary countered.

"My dad said the same thing," he admitted. "He told

me I can't keep choosing for people whether or not they get to love me."

"Martin Wheeler. I love that man," Mary said. "So, how did your dad react to you coming out? How did you come out? And why now?"

"Well," Oliver said, "this is the funny thing. He already knew. He asked me about Ezra because when I went into the emergency room, I had Ezra call him to let him know because I was too tired at the time to deal with it. Anyway, my dad said that it sounded like Ezra is a close friend and cares about me a great deal—and of course, I'm panicking—"

"Of course, you were," Mary echoed.

"Then he let me off the hook and said he's known the whole time. Apparently, my mom let it slip because of all the drugs she was on." He let out a slow breath. "So, I guess he's been supportive this whole time. I just never even knew."

"That is the most Wheeler thing I have ever heard. That tracks so much," she said with a laugh. "So, what else did your dad say?"

Oliver bit his lip, unsure if he should even mention what his dad said about Ezra loving him. The idea of it was absolutely crazy. There was no way. It was too soon. But no matter how hard he tried to shake the thought, he couldn't. He'd spent the past five days turning over the words in his head, wondering, and even scarier, hoping they were true. "He said he thinks Ezra is in love with me," he whispered finally. If he could talk about how he was feeling with anyone, it was Mary.

"Really?"

"He said he could hear it in his voice."

"Well, I only got to meet Ezra twice, and once we were playing a drinking game, so I can't say for certain, but I think your dad might be right. I can, however, say with complete certainty that you're in love with him," she said.

"I—I haven't really known him all that long. What if it's not real?"

"So? Just because it's early doesn't mean it's not real. I mean, look at Robin and me. We fell into the lesbian stereotype and moved in together after only knowing each other two months, yet here we are three years later, happy as clams and planning a big, old gay wedding."

"I know you're right. I'm just…"

"Scared?" Mary finished.

"I've never felt this way before, which is just so crazy because I've been in love before, or I thought I had been. But this is different." Oliver pulled his knees into his chest. "Mary, what if I screwed up? I haven't heard from him since he left. What if he wants nothing to do with me now?"

"Ollie, I bet he's sitting at his cousin's house thinking the same thing about you. He's probably too scared to reach out."

"You think?"

"I do. But I think you need to tell Ezra how you feel regardless," Mary said.

"You may be right," Oliver said with a sigh. "I don't know what to say, though. I drafted about fifty different texts last night and ended up deleting every single—" He stopped short as his phone buzzed in his hand. "Hold on, I have a text."

He pulled the phone away from his ear to see Ezra's name flash across the top.

"Ollie?" Mary's voice was barely audible from the speaker.

Oliver quickly brought the phone back to his ear. "It's him."

"No shit, really? What are the odds?"

"I have no idea," he said. "Fuck, what do I say?"

"Start with an apology, maybe, but otherwise, you'll figure it out."

"Okay."

"I love you. Keep me posted," Mary said.

"Love you, too."

Oliver felt like his skin was vibrating as he pulled the phone away from his ear and disconnected the call. He could do this. Ezra texted first, which meant that he wanted to talk. All Oliver had to do was apologize and lay his heart out, hoping Ezra would take it.

He took a deep breath to steady himself, then opened his text messages.

29

Oliver

Sunday Morning, December 6, 2020

Oliver stared at his phone.

[Oliver], ever since I first looked upon your wonderful and incomparable beauty, I have dared to love you wildly, passionately, devotedly, hopelessly.

Earnest.

Oliver had spent most of the night drafting versions of an apology to Ezra—the latest version of which still sat in the text bar half-finished and unsent—and Ezra was quoting *The Importance of Being Earnest* at him.

It wasn't one of the most well-known quotes from the play, but Oliver had read it enough times to recognize it, even with Ezra swapping his name in to replace Cecily's—with proper grammar, too, which was strangely sweet.

He didn't ask how Oliver was feeling after his hospital stay, didn't offer an apology for running off without a word, didn't go for a simple "hi" or "I miss you." No, he opened with a quote from a farce. Arguably, he had picked one of the more romantic lines—when taken out of context, at least—but Earnest was still an entirely unromantic play.

But it was also a play that Ezra had only read because of Oliver and whose author they watched a movie about on their first date. And before they truly became friends, Ezra had always used a quote as an excuse to talk to him. So maybe that's what this quote was. It was his version of "I miss you."

Oliver didn't quite know what to say, so he went with Cecily's response to the line—or at least what he could remember of it. He deleted the drafted apology and typed, **Hopelessly doesn't seem to make much sense, does it?** hoping that Ezra would find it funny rather than a rejection of his olive branch.

The three little dots danced as Ezra typed his response.

[Oliver]!

Then: **Can I call you?**

Oliver's finger already hovered over the FaceTime icon, and he dialed before giving it a second thought. Nearly instantly, Ezra's face filled the screen. His hair was a mess, like he'd been running his hands through it, as he often did when he was nervous or frustrated, and his blue eyes sparkled as they stared into the camera, filled with nervous energy.

Oliver's heart fluttered. Shit, he'd really missed seeing his face.

They stared at each other for a moment, but then Oliver took in the surroundings around Ezra. "Are you in a car?" he asked.

"I— Yeah, I am. I'm in front of your building," Ezra admitted, and Oliver's breath hitched. "I wasn't sure if you'd want to see me, so I thought I'd be safe and text you first, but I hoped—"

"Did you get tested after getting back from the hospital?" Oliver interrupted.

"Yeah. Negative. Got the results today. Did you—?"

Oliver nodded. "Negative," he croaked. He swallowed hard to calm his nerves. "Can you— Do you want to come up?"

Ezra nodded. "Give me a minute." And with that, the call disconnected.

Oliver clamored out of bed so quickly that he nearly fell. He didn't expect to actually be seeing Ezra, or else he would have gotten ready. He was still in his pajama bottoms, but he didn't have time to change into real pants. At least he had showered and had on his favorite green sweater, the one his mom had gotten him that brought out his eyes. Unable to wait, Oliver bolted to the door, pressed the button on the intercom to let him in, and flung the door open. He stood in the doorway and watched as Ezra heaved the building's massive front door open. Oliver felt his breath hitch when he locked eyes with him, and he was hit with an overwhelming desire to fling himself into his arms. But he didn't. One, Ezra needed to wash his hands first, just to be safe, and two, Oliver needed to apologize before he did that.

"Olls," Ezra murmured as he reached the doorway.

"Come in," Oliver said quickly, stepping to the side.

Ezra toed off his shoes and shrugged out of his jacket before gesturing to the bathroom. "I'm just going to—"

"Wash your hands, yeah." He nodded and hung Ezra's coat for him. Once Ezra disappeared into the bathroom, Oliver nervously sat on the couch to wait for him.

A minute later, he came out of the bathroom, removing his mask and tucking it into his pocket. He quickly walked over to the couch and stopped in front of where Oliver was sitting.

"I'm so sorry," Oliver blurted out at the same time as Ezra said, "I missed you."

Ezra dropped to his knees in front of Oliver and stared up at him. "I'm sorry for freaking out."

"No, I'm sorry," Oliver interrupted. "I shouldn't have snapped like that. I'm so sorry—"

"Ollie, wait, no. You had every right to be upset with me. I wasn't handling the situation well at all," Ezra said in a rush. "I'm sorry. I ran away. Things got too real, and I bolted. I shouldn't have left. I should have stayed, but I was scared—"

"I pushed you away. I thought I was protecting you. But I wasn't; I was just—"

Ezra let out a strangled huff and brought his hands to rest on the tops of Oliver's knees. "We can't keep talking over each other."

Oliver exhaled sharply and took Ezra's hands in his. "I'm sorry. You go," he breathed.

Ezra squeezed his hands and stared up into his eyes. "I panicked. The entire drive to the hospital, I was terrified. I care about you so much, Oliver, and honestly, I think that terrified me more than you being in pain. I have so much baggage, and I don't exactly have the greatest track record for relationships. I could see how annoyed you were with me, and I kept thinking that you didn't need to be taking care of me and my baggage. I thought I didn't deserve someone like you, so I ran at the first opportunity you gave me. But I can't keep running from things. I can't run from you. I don't want to. I want to be with you. I want to be a person who deserves you."

Oliver squeezed his hands tighter and let out a shaky breath. "Ezra, you are—"

"I want to see you every day and meet all of your friends. To make you omelets in the morning and lie in bed while drinking tea and reading a book. I want to run you warm baths when your joints are all flared up. I want everything, and I know it probably seems like it's too fast, but I can't help it. I'm crazy about you, and I really hope I didn't screw things up by being a coward. I did not handle the situation well at all. I let my anxiety take control. I can't promise that I won't ever worry about you, but I can promise to work on understanding my anxiety so I can try to keep a more level head, at least. I want to be there for you no matter what. I realize I didn't show it very well last week, so I don't expect you to believe me. But I'll do whatever I can to prove that because I really mean it when I say I want everything."

Oliver leaned forward to rest their foreheads together. He heard Ezra let out a sharp exhale. "You didn't just run; I pushed you away. I was scared because you looked so worried, and I knew that I was the reason. I didn't want to put you through that again in the future, so I thought pushing you away would be easier. But then I talked with my dad, and he told me I can't keep deciding for other people how they want to fit into my life. He also said that sometimes worry is just part of what it means to love or be loved by someone. It's not always a bad thing. I can't control whether you worry about me or not. All I can control is how I respond to it, and it wasn't fair to you for me to snap at you and push you away the way I did. Ezra, I'm so sorry."

"It's okay," Ezra whispered. "I think I understand."

"I know we haven't known each other that long in the grand scheme of things, but I honestly keep forgetting that. Everything that you said, I want it, too," Oliver said. He closed his eyes and felt Ezra's palm against his cheek. He leaned into the contact as he continued, needing to say the thing he'd been too terrified to admit to himself before now. "Parce que je suis tombé en amour de toi." *Because I've fallen in love with you.*

Ezra pulled back, and Oliver opened his eyes to see him blinking up at him, his mouth parted slightly, a look of confusion on his face.

"Did I say it wrong?" Oliver asked self-consciously.

"Technically, it's *tombé amoureux*, not *tombé en amour*," Ezra said, looking slightly dazed. "But that doesn't matter. Do you mean it?"

Oliver smiled nervously. "I do. You don't have to say anything; I just thought you should—" His sentence was cut off by a soft pair of lips crashing against his.

Ezra slid his hand into Oliver's curls and held him close as he pressed up and moved closer to settle his torso between his legs. Then, just as quickly as his lips were on his, they were gone. "I love you, too," Ezra murmured against his lips.

Oliver held his breath. "Really?"

He chuckled and brushed their noses together. "Yes."

Oliver exhaled and wrapped his arms around Ezra's shoulders to drag their lips back together and pull him up off the floor. Ezra's hands found his waist, and they somehow maneuvered into a lying-down position on the couch, with Ezra straddling Oliver's hips without breaking the kiss. Oliver ran his hands through Ezra's hair, winding the strands around his fingers to anchor their mouths together. Teeth clashed together and tongues mingled as he felt Ezra's warm hands sliding beneath his sweater, up to his ribs. He shuddered and let out a small gasp.

Ezra worked his lips across his cheek and down his neck, stopping just below his ear. "God, I missed you," he whispered. He pressed a soft kiss to his neck. "It was only a week, but I missed you so much."

Oliver's breath hitched, and he tightened his grip on

Ezra's hair, while Ezra kept littering his neck with soft, open-mouthed kisses. "I did, too. I really fucking missed you."

Ezra kissed his way back up to look Oliver in the eyes. "You learned French for me."

"I mean, I've been learning French for you for months." Oliver smiled and slid a hand out of Ezra's hair to caress his cheek. "But you say sweet things to me in French all the time. Oh, speaking of…I looked up what 'mon chou' means. 'Cabbage'? Really?" Oliver teased.

Ezra dropped his head to Oliver's shoulder and laughed into his neck. "That's just the literal translation. But if you hate it now, I can call you something else."

Oliver shook his head with a smile. "I'm just teasing you. I like 'mon chou.'" He pressed a soft kiss to Ezra's temple.

"You said you talked to your dad. Did you come out to him?" Ezra asked tentatively.

"I didn't even need to," Oliver whispered. "He already knew. He's known this whole time."

"Well, I'm guessing he took it alright, then?"

"He did. He said he approves of you, by the way."

"But he hasn't even met me," Ezra protested.

"You called him though," Oliver pointed out. "But he said he could tell how much happier I've seemed over the past few months. So since you're the reason for that, he approves."

Ezra hummed and lifted his head to look Oliver in the eyes.

They stared at each other for a moment, then their lips were on each other again, this time softer and less hurried. Oliver smoothed his hands down Ezra's back and slipped them just under the hem of his T-shirt, reveling in the feeling of his warm skin beneath his palms. Ezra brushed his thumbs along Oliver's ribs, gently caressing his skin. With a soft exhale, Oliver sat up. Ezra got the message and dragged Oliver's sweater up and over his head. Oliver did the same and threw Ezra's shirt toward his sweater.

He looked at him as he ran his hands over Ezra's torso, tracing the tattoos on his arms and chest, before bringing his lips to his collarbone, earning a contented sigh. Oliver hummed and pushed Ezra off his lap and back onto the couch, crawling over him as he continued to nip and suck at his neck, collarbone, shoulder, and back to his neck. Ezra made a soft sound, and Oliver continued trailing his lips down his chest to his abdomen, where the tattoo of the laurel-leaf crown was inked just above his left hip bone.

Ezra arched his back up. "Fuck me," he swore under his breath.

With a smirk, Oliver smoothed a hand over the front of Ezra's jeans, his palm pressing into him where he strained against his zipper. "Is that a request, or…?"

Ezra let out a low moan and hauled Oliver back up to crash their lips together. Oliver ground himself against Ezra's lap, letting out a groan at the friction.

"Maybe later. Need you like this, first," Ezra barked between kisses. His hands flew to Oliver's ass, and without warning, he swung his legs over the edge of the couch and stood up. Oliver locked his arms around his neck and his legs around his waist to help support his weight as Ezra walked toward the bedroom.

Ezra quickly set him on the bed and pulled at his pajama pants, getting them off in one smooth motion before going for his own pants. Once his pants had joined Oliver's in a pile on the floor, he knelt on the bed and crawled toward the headboard, where Oliver leaned against the pile of pillows.

Oliver sat up and grabbed at him, already missing the feel of Ezra's skin on his. Ezra settled in between his

legs and pressed their hips together. Oliver let his head
fall back on the pillows, groaning as he ground his hips
up to meet Ezra's. He closed his eyes and let himself
focus on the feel of them, their bodies sliding together.
Ezra stilled for a moment and reached a hand up to cup
Oliver's cheek. He willed himself to open his eyes and
looked up to lock eyes with Ezra.

Oliver wrapped his arms around his back and held
him tight as Ezra thrust again, slow at first, then more
rapidly as they picked up a rhythm.

Ezra dropped his head and captured Oliver's lips in
a kiss as Oliver snaked a hand between them and
wrapped it around both of them. Ezra moaned into his
mouth, and Oliver dug his free hand into Ezra's shoulder as they both continued to buck into his hand.

"Fuck, Olls, I think I'm gonna—"

Oliver was, too. He was so close, and then Ezra went
rigid on top of him. His back arched, and he let out a
strangled moan. Oliver followed him, clutching Ezra
tightly as he circled his hips, bringing them both
through their orgasms.

They lay there, limbs entangled, as their breathing returned to normal. After a while, Ezra lifted his head off
Oliver's chest to look at him.

Oliver lifted a hand to tuck a loose strand of hair behind Ezra's ear. "Hi," he whispered.

Ezra leaned down to brush their lips together. "I really missed you."

"I missed you, too," Oliver said.

"We should probably—"

"Get cleaned up?"

Oliver nodded. "Shower?"

"Ordinarily, I'd say yes, but I'm not sure if my legs
will support me right now," Ezra said as he rolled to
the side, pulling Oliver with him.

Oliver chuckled and pressed a quick kiss to his

cheek. "I'll get us a towel."

"*Tu es incroyable*," Ezra mumbled happily.

Oliver kissed his cheek once more before rolling over and swinging his legs over the bed's edge. He stood up slowly and found that his legs were a little shaky, as well, but made it to the bathroom. He pulled a washcloth out of the basket that sat on the shelf above the toilet, wet it with some warm water, and cleaned himself up first before bringing it back to the bedroom with him. When he returned, he saw Ezra had pulled the covers back but was still lying uncovered, sprawled out in a post-sex haze. He crawled onto the bed and wiped up Ezra's abdomen and chest.

His eyes flung open, then softened as he looked at Oliver. "Oh, thank you," he whispered.

Oliver flung the washcloth into the corner, then settled back onto the bed and pulled the covers over the two of them.

Ezra turned on his side and hooked an arm over Oliver's waist. Oliver shimmied close in response, hooking his own arm over Ezra's waist, tangling their legs together, and tucking his head under his chin, not caring that his feet were close to hanging off the edge of the bed.

Ezra made a soft, happy sound and pressed his lips against Oliver's forehead, letting them linger for a while.

"Are you able to stay?" Oliver asked, hopefully.

"I was hoping I could," Ezra said. "I packed an overnight bag in case this went well, and it's in the car."

"Only an overnight bag?"

"I didn't want to push my luck," Ezra admitted. "But if you'll have me—"

"Yes."

"Yeah?"

Oliver nodded. "I want you to move back in—for

real, this time. It may be sudden, but I don't care. I want to live with you."

Ezra pulled back and tilted Oliver's face up to meet his gaze. "We're going to need a bigger apartment, though. I may not have a lot of stuff, but a studio is too small for two people to live and work in full-time."

Oliver let out a relieved breath. "You haven't even moved in, and you already need space from me?"

Ezra chuckled. "Absolutely not. I wouldn't mind my own dresser, though."

"Hmm, I guess that's fair," Oliver teased. He looked softly at Ezra, whose eyes were closing, and smiled. He pressed a light kiss to his nose.

Ezra let out another pleased hum. "I love you," he mumbled sleepily with another press of the lips to Oliver's forehead.

"I love you, too."

Oliver let his eyes close, too, and they both drifted off into a light sleep, the afternoon light streaming in through the bedroom window.

Epilogue

Ezra

Saturday, September 18, 2021

"Thanks, Jules," Ezra said, accepting the microphone from Juliet as she went back to their table. He cleared his throat and looked around the room at the sea of wedding guests before looking over at the small table Ryan and Anna were sitting at. He flashed them a smile, then turned back to the crowd.

"For those of you that don't know, Ryan has been my best friend since we were thirteen. We met at a small boarding school in upstate New York when someone decided that assigning us to be roommates was a good idea. Big mistake." He paused for laughter, then continued, "We got into so much trouble that year, and every year after, really. We were inseparable—something that didn't change even when I went to Ireland for university. Then, a few years ago, I got this call. It was the middle of the night for me because I was in Ireland at the time, and normally I would have ignored it, but it was Ryan, so I answered. And the second I answered, this kid immediately started going on about the date he had with 'the most amazing girl in existence' and how one day he was going to marry her. Let me tell you, I was still half asleep, so I didn't take him seriously, but then I met Anna, and I saw them together and realized how serious Ryan really was."

Ezra paused, then looked over at Oliver sitting at their table a few feet away, smiling fondly at him as he gave the speech he'd been stressing about giving all week. "Now, I literally had an entire extra year to figure out how to end this speech, but I didn't do that." The crowd laughed. "So, I'm going to steal from what Oliver said at their first wedding last year." Oliver smiled reassuringly. "Anyone who knows Anna and Ryan knows how different they are from each other, but they find a way to make things work despite those differences. It wasn't fate or destiny that brought them together; it was a choice, and I, for one, don't think that either of them could have made a better one. So, if everyone could join me in raising a glass." Ezra raised his champagne glass. "To Ryan and Anna."

The crowd echoed the toast, and after Ezra took a sip of his drink, he walked over to Ryan and Anna's table. They both stood and hugged him tight, Anna leaning up to kiss his cheek. The DJ came over to collect the microphone, then Ezra returned to his seat.

"Beautiful speech, love," Oliver whispered as the DJ started to announce Ryan and Anna's first dance.

"Well, half of it was you. All I did was tell some jokes and make fun of Ryan." Ezra stole a kiss before leaning back in his chair and throwing an arm on the back of Oliver's chair.

Oliver smiled and scooted closer to press into Ezra's side and rest a hand on his knee. "They look so happy." He sighed as they watched Ryan twirl Anna around the dance floor.

Ezra pressed a kiss to his cheek. "Getting sentimental, *mon chou*?"

Oliver elbowed him in the ribs and told him to shut up, then settled back into their embrace with a contented sigh. The song ended, and another long song played as the DJ announced that the dance floor was open to everyone.

Ezra stood up abruptly and extended his hand to Oliver, who looked a little put out by the sudden shift in position. "Care to dance?"

"Sure." Oliver smiled and slipped his hand into Ezra's.

Ezra led them to a spot on the corner of the dance floor and rested his arm on Oliver's shoulder while slipping his right hand into Oliver's left. Oliver pulled him close with a hand on the middle of his back.

"You know, this is the first time I've been able to just clutch and sway at a wedding," Ezra mused. "The only other weddings I've been to were all for family, and they were all very formal affairs. Waltzes and all that."

"Are you telling me you know how to waltz?" Oliver asked.

"I do, in fact," Ezra said, smiling.

"Then why am I—the uncoordinated one—leading?"

Ezra laughed. "My apologies," he teased, then stepped back to grasp both of Oliver's hands. He spun him, then pulled him back in, switching the hold so he was leading.

"Okay, very smooth," Oliver said.

"Impressed?"

Oliver simply smiled.

"I know waltz, quickstep, foxtrot, tango, some swing, and a little salsa."

"Salsa was on the list of approved ballroom dances

for the Beaumonts?" Oliver asked.

Ezra laughed. "No, I picked that up in Spain when I was crashing with a friend of a friend who was a dance instructor."

"Of course you did," Oliver said with a laugh. "God, you've lived a completely more interesting life than me. Are you sure you're content being with boring old me?"

His tone was light, so Ezra knew he wasn't serious, but he lowered his hand on Oliver's back and pulled him closer to kiss him. "Oliver Wheeler, you are a lot of things, and boring is definitely not one of them."

He smiled and hummed as he leaned in for another kiss. They settled back into their dance in silence until he broke it again. "Do you miss it?"

"Hmm?"

"All the traveling—hopping from one city to the next whenever you wanted."

Ezra stared at him for a moment. It seemed like an innocent enough question, but he could tell there was another layer to it. "I'm happy where I am now."

"So, you wouldn't want to go back?" Oliver asked.

Ezra shook his head. "Maybe for a visit, but I don't miss doing it full-time." He smiled. "And only if you came with me."

Oliver smiled back. "I've never been to Europe. I've been to Canada but never crossed an ocean."

"Maybe next year, if you wanted," he suggested, then added, "assuming things are safe."

The song faded out, and Oliver leaned in to kiss him. "Maybe France," he said before closing the distance.

The song shifted to an upbeat song, followed by a pair of squeals in the distance. Oliver pulled away with a groan. "Oh, God, no."

Ezra laughed and cocked his head. "What, you don't like Maroon 5?"

"Anna and Juliet declared this to be 'our' song in

college, so I expect they're coming to steal me away in three, two—"

Right on cue, Anna and Juliet ran up to the two of them and started tugging on Oliver's arm.

"Sorry, lover boy, we're stealing him," Juliet said.

"Well, who am I to say no to this force of nature?" Ezra teased with a gesture toward the two of them. He dropped a kiss to the hand still clasped in his. "Have fun. I'm going to go find the groom."

Oliver mouthed "help" at him as they dragged him away to dance, but there was also a hint of a smile on his lips that had Ezra smiling, as well. He made his way to the drink table where he found Ryan, standing and talking to a random Reid cousin. He sidled up next to him and threw an arm around his shoulder just as Ryan finished his 'thank you for coming' speech.

"Sorry, can I borrow the groom?" Ezra asked apologetically, and the cousin nodded and walked away.

Ryan turned to him. "Thank you."

"You looked like you needed a rescue," Ezra said.

"I did. I know that was one of Anna's cousins because I've met her at least four times, but I can never remember her name."

He laughed. "Maybe I should have made you flashcards."

Ryan laughed, too. "You've already far exceeded your duties as best man." He hesitated for a moment, then pulled Ezra into a tight hug.

Ezra squeezed him tight, then let him go. "Don't go getting all sentimental on me," he warned playfully.

Ryan rolled his eyes and turned to watch the dance floor, where Oliver was dancing with both Anna and Juliet, twirling them around.

"So, how does it feel being married for a year now?" Ezra asked as he turned his attention to their significant others and Juliet, too. He smiled as Juliet went to spin

Oliver around, sending them all into a fit of laughter.

"It's amazing. I couldn't be happier," Ryan gushed. "But it looks like you're thinking of finding out for yourself based on that dopey look on your face."

"Dopey? Look in the mirror there, mate," Ezra retorted.

"Do you think you and Oliver…?"

"We've only been dating a year," he protested even though it wasn't an actual answer, and both Ryan and he knew that.

"So? That doesn't mean you can't be thinking about it," Ryan pointed out.

The song ended, and Oliver escaped the dance floor to join them over by the drink table.

"Looked like you guys were having fun," Ezra mused, slinging his arm around Oliver's waist.

"What were you two talking about?" Oliver asked, wrapping his arm around Ezra's waist.

"Nothing important."

Oliver smiled, then gave a pointed look at Ryan. "You should go dance with your wife, so she stops trying to kill me."

Ryan laughed. "Well, we can't have that," he said and winked at the two of them but more at Ezra, before making his way to the dance floor where he pulled Anna in to dip her.

Ezra smiled. "How are your hips? Do you need to sit?"

"No, I'm okay." Oliver shifted to wrap his arms around Ezra from behind so they could both watch the dance floor.

Ezra rested his arms on top of Oliver's and laced their fingers together.

"Having fun?" Oliver asked.

Ezra nodded and tilted his head back to press a kiss to his cheek. "I love weddings."

Oliver hummed and shimmied closer. "Well, you'll have another one to look forward to soon."

Ezra knew Oliver was talking about Mary and Robin's wedding in October, but Ezra's heart skipped a beat all the same. He'd played it off with Ryan, but he would be lying if he said he hadn't been thinking about taking the next step with Oliver lately. He'd chalked it up to wedding fever, with both he and Oliver being the best people in their best friends' weddings, but maybe it wasn't just that.

He mentally shook his head to clear it. "That's true. I'm excited to see your childhood home. I can't wait to snoop around your old bedroom."

Oliver laughed. "You won't find anything interesting. I was a pretty boring kid."

"No cartons of cigarettes or Playboy magazines hidden under the bed?" Ezra teased.

"Is that what you had hidden under your bed?"

"Yup. Although, I really only put them there to piss my mother off in case she went snooping," he said proudly.

"You're a menace," Oliver said with a laugh. "My dad is excited to meet you in person."

Ezra smiled. "I can't wait to meet him. I plan on putting on the full charm to make a good impression."

"You know he already likes you, right?"

"Still, it can't hurt to solidify that opinion. Gotta make sure he knows I'm planning on sticking around."

Oliver shook his head fondly and kissed his temple. "I love you."

"*Je t'aime aussi, mon chou.*"

Bonus Epilogue

Want more of the story? Head to authordallassmith.com/qs-epilogue/ to get access to an exclusive *Queried Sick* epilogue.

For links to my Pinterest inspiration board as well as Spotify playlists inspired by the characters and plot of the book, head to my website:
authordallassmith.com/books/queried-sick

Did you like *Queried Sick?* Reviews from readers like you help indie authors get noticed, so if you liked this book, please consider leaving a review on Goodreads, The StoryGraph, Amazon, or wherever you shop for books.

Thank you.

Acknowledgements

Wow. This is really it. The end of my authorial debut. It honestly feels a little surreal to be here writing this acknowledgement. When the pandemic started, like many people, I picked up a new hobby to help cope. Some people—like my husband—started a sourdough starter. Others learned to crochet or paint. I wrote.

I'd written my first book during NaNoWriMo 2019, mostly as a test to see if I could actually do it. I'd just gotten out of a career I'd spent most of my life working toward and was feeling a little lost. Then I remembered the number of times I'd attempted to write a book as a kid and wanted to give it another shot. So I wrote that book, put it down, and forgot about it in the holidays and trying to plan my then wedding.

Then Covid hit and I needed an outlet, but the idea of trying to be an author seemed like too much of a pipe dream. So I just wrote what I wanted to read. I wrote mostly fan fiction because it felt safe. There were no stakes. But somewhere amidst the drabbles and fix-it fics, I found a spark of inspiration for the first full story I'd had since that book in 2019 (which will likely never see the light of day). And Queried Sick was born.

I'm sure every writer calls their books their babies, but it really does feel like Queried Sick is my baby. I poured so much of myself into this book—all of my pandemic worries, my grief over having to cancel my wedding just like Ryan and Anna, my uncertainty about adulthood and where I'm going with my life, my anxiety, my frustration with my immune system, and even my exploration about my own sexuality. I wrote this book because it was the story I needed to read. I learned so much through Oliver and Ezra—about writing and about myself—and now I'm sharing it with you, dear reader, in hopes that maybe you get something you needed out of it as well.

So if you're still with me, I want to start off my list of acknowledgements by thanking you. Thank you for reading Queried Sick. Thank you for going on this journey with Oliver and Ezra. I hope you loved them as much as I do.

Thank you to my support team. To my critique partner and beta readers for the valuable feedback that made this book the best it could be. To Kathy, my editor, for elevating this story to the next level. To mitxeran, my cover designer, for bringing my boys to life. To my ARC and street team for taking the time to read this book and hype me up.

Thank you to my friends and family who have supported me throughout this journey. To my husband, who read this book even though he doesn't really read romance novels (outside of our podcast) and helped me figure out html coding for my eBook formatting when I got stuck. To my parents for always believing in me and supporting my dreams.To all of my friends who went, "That's so cool!" when I said I wanted to publish a romance novel rather than "Really? A Romance novel?" A special thank you to Tatjana, Andie, and Helen for listening to me talk about this story for the past two and a half years and reading it in its many iterations, and a shout-out to Andie for helping me come up with all the query quotes in a scene that has become so dear to my heart.

Thank you to all of my Tumblr friends. If it weren't for the encouragement you all gave me on the silly, self-indulgent little fandom stories, I would have never had the courage to put my original work out into the world for people to consume. You all have helped me become a better writer, and I truly couldn't have done this without you.

Finally, I want to say thank you to all the essential workers who have been risking their health and safety over the past three years during this pandemic—hospital staff, food service workers, emergency services employees, transportation workers, and more. We could not function without your hard work.

Photo by: Owen Paterline

Dallas Smith is a queer and neurodivergent author who strives to write the type of stories she wants to read—ones with heart, humor, and meaning in which anyone can see a part of themselves represented.

To sign up for Dallas' latest news, please visit her website (www.authordallassmith.com) and subscribe! Want to connect further? Find Dallas on the following platforms:

goodreads.com/authordallassmith
amazon.com/author/authordallassmith
instagram.com/authordallassmith
tiktok.com/authordallassmith
bookbub.com/profile/dallas-smith

Printed in Great Britain
by Amazon

32190012R00205